ANCIENT
EGYPT

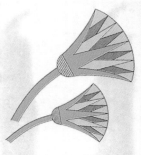

ANCIENT EGYPT

CHARLES FREEMAN

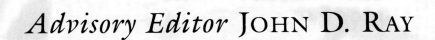

Advisory Editor JOHN D. RAY

angus

| PROJECT EDITOR | Peter Furtado |
| ART EDITOR | Ayala Kingsley |

EDITOR	Lauren Bourque
PICTURE RESEARCH	Jenny Speller
CARTOGRAPHY	Richard Watts
DESIGN	Martin Anderson, Krystyna Hewitt
ARTISTS	Roger Hutchins, Robert & Rhoda Burns, Roger Stewart
PICTURE MANAGEMENT	Claire Turner
PROOFREADING	Lynne Elson
EDITORIAL ASSISTANCE	Marian Dreier
PRODUCTION	Clive Sparling
INDEX	Ann Barrett

Published by Angus Books Ltd
12 Ravensbury Terrace
London
SW18 2RL

The edition design copyright 2005
Angus Books Limited

Planned and produced by
THE BROWN REFERENCE GROUP PLC
8 Chapel Place
Rivington Street
London, EC2A 3DQ

© Andromeda International
(part of The Brown Reference Group plc)
2005

ISBN 1-904594-70-0

Printed in Singapore

Contents

HALF TITLE Carved wooden portrait of Meritamun, 18th Dynasty *(left)*
Vivien Leigh in the 1945 film *Caesar and Cleopatra (right)*

TITLE PAGE An Egyptian Feast by Edwin Long (1829–71) *(main picture)*
1920s Art Deco design with Egyptian harpist *(below left)*
Tomb painting of musicians, 15th century BC *(right)*

LEFT The Louvre pyramid, Paris *(main picture)*
Khephren's pyramid, Giza *(below)*

INTRODUCTION

SOME NAMES FROM THE PAST are so powerful that they instantly command our deepest respect. "Great Pyramid." "Sphinx." "Pharaoh." "Mummy." The awe we feel on hearing those words is the result of more than 2,500 years of admiration of ancient Egyptian culture by outsiders. The reputation of ancient Egypt is itself a legacy handed from the Greeks and the Romans to Renaissance Europe and on to the modern world.

The ancient Egyptians themselves knew that their country was special. They loved it passionately – not in the modern political sense, but physically and emotionally – and apparently never went abroad willingly. Even as long ago as 2900 BC, Egypt's wealth was famous throughout the early city-states of the Middle East and Africa. Egypt was a mighty prize to be taken by ambitious neighbors, though few were powerful enough to overcome its natural barriers and its formidable army. Egypt itself had little appetite for conquest. The kings' motives for expansion were the search for raw materials and to secure the border with Asia. Peace and prosperity was the Egyptian ideal. For most of their long history, ancient Egyptians enjoyed both,

to a degree unequaled by any other state. This enabled them to build a civilization whose greatest achievement may have been to continue to fascinate the world long after the civilization itself disappeared. Since then, each time the door to the past has opened wider, allowing a better view, the fascination has grown.

Egypt was more than 2,000 years old when the Greeks – the first Westerners – began to arrive. They marveled at the already ancient pyramids, at the wealth, and at the massive temples where Egyptian priests were willing to share their knowledge with outsiders. From the Greeks, the Egyptians acquired a reputation as the guardians of superior wisdom. Later, Rome came to Egypt as a conqueror in the aftermath of one of the greatest love stories of history, that of Mark Antony and Cleopatra. The Romans, unlike the Greeks, did not have unqualified admiration for their new province. They professed to despise some of its more exotic traditions, even while they copied the art and architecture, and borrowed the glory of the pharaohs. Not long after Rome fell, Egypt was taken over by Muslim Arabs, and a veil of silence fell between it and the Christian West.

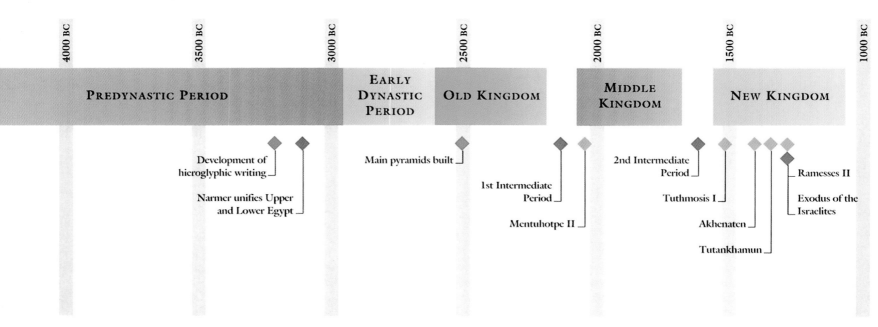

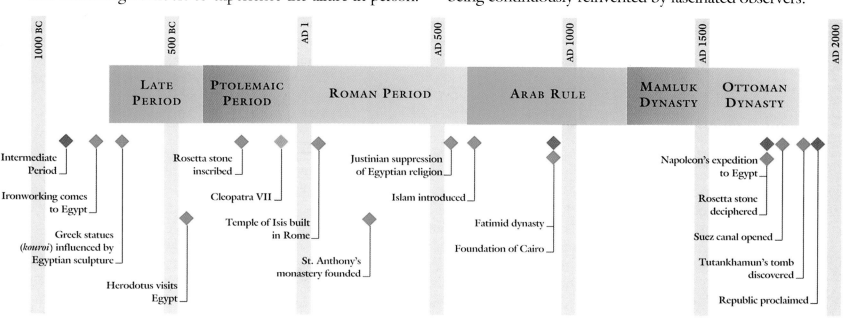

Revived interest in Rome by European Renaissance scholars soon resulted in Egypt's glory being once again taken down from the shelf and dusted off. But much of this knowledge was second-hand, filtered through Rome; and it was the arrival of Napoleon's invading army in 1798, accompanied by a smaller army of scholars intent on studying the country's ancient past, that finally opened Egypt once again to the West. Like the Greeks and Romans before them, Europeans were stunned by the overwhelming scale of the buildings and the exotic aspects of the culture. Much of the true history of Egypt remained hidden behind the ancient dead language, written in hieroglyphs – a script which no one had been able to read for over 1,500 years. This added to the sense of mystery and allure, which persisted even after hieroglyphs were deciphered in 1824. By then, Egypt's reputation had accumulated 500 years' worth of some of the wilder fancies of the West.

Since 1869, when the first commercial guided tour of Egypt was offered, tourists have flocked to the country in ever increasing numbers to experience the allure in person.

THE WINGED GODDESS as expressed in a carving of Isis (LEFT) from the tomb of Ramesses III and a 1923 ballet (ABOVE) entitled "The Mystery of Nut".

Visitors are still awed by the pyramids and other colossal monuments. And at the same time as they carry out work to preserve Egypt's priceless heritage, archeologists continue to uncover the rich secrets of its past, buried under hot sand and time.

This book is the first to combine the story of ancient Egypt – its people and its kings, its monuments and gods – with the legacy of its achievements as seen through the eyes of the cultures that followed. From its long reputation for scholarship and wisdom, to the legend of Cleopatra, to the much-debated purpose of the pyramids, to the Biblical role of Egypt as the persecutor of the Hebrews, and the clever adoption of Egyptian religious myths by early Christianity – all these themes are explored in this groundbreaking book. From its beginnings in the Nile valley, the story ranges to the temples of classical Greece and Rome; from the salons of the French Empire to the cities of the twentieth century and the Hollywood film industry. Throughout these pages, Egypt gradually unfolds – both the real Egypt and the legendary one that is still being continuously reinvented by fascinated observers.

1000 BC	500 BC	AD 1	AD 500	AD 1000	AD 1500	AD 2000

LATE PERIOD	PTOLEMAIC PERIOD	ROMAN PERIOD	ARAB RULE	MAMLUK DYNASTY	OTTOMAN DYNASTY

Intermediate Period

Ironworking comes to Egypt

Greek statues (*kouroi*) influenced by Egyptian sculpture

Herodotus visits Egypt

Rosetta stone inscribed

Cleopatra VII

Temple of Isis built in Rome

Justinian suppression of Egyptian religion

Islam introduced

St. Anthony's monastery founded

Fatimid dynasty

Foundation of Cairo

Napoleon's expedition to Egypt

Rosetta stone deciphered

Suez canal opened

Tutankhamun's tomb discovered

Republic proclaimed

THE ETERNAL KINGDOM

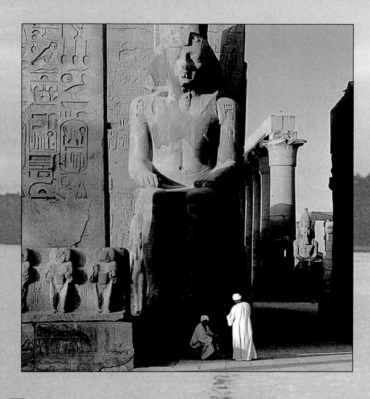

FOR MORE THAN 2,000 YEARS, THE NILE VALLEY
SUSTAINED A SPECTACULAR CIVILIZATION.
IT DEPENDED ON THE WORLD'S FIRST UNIFIED
MONARCHY, CLOSELY ASSOCIATED WITH TEMPLES
AND PRIESTS. WITH NECESSITIES AND LUXURIES IN
ABUNDANCE, THE EGYPTIANS RARELY WAGED WAR
FOR MERE GLORY. THEY PREFERRED TO REMAIN
TRANQUIL, AND TO STEM THE TIDE OF DISORDER
WHEN IT THREATENED. DECLINE CAME VERY
SLOWLY, IN THE FACE OF YOUNGER, AGGRESSIVE
AND TECHNOLOGICALLY SUPERIOR RIVALS.

Main picture The River Nile at Luxor

Inset Colossal statue of Ramesses II at the entrance to the Luxor temple

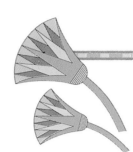
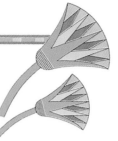

A GIFT OF THE RIVER
Egypt & the Nile

"In their customs the ancient Egyptians seem to have reversed the ordinary practices of mankind. Women attend market and are employed in trade, while men stay at home and do the weaving. Men carry loads on their heads, women on their shoulders; women pass water standing up, men sitting down. Sons are under no compulsion to support their parents if they wish not to, but daughters must. They practice circumcision while men of other nations – except those who have learned from Egypt – leave their private parts as nature made them. When writing and calculating, instead of going from left to right, Egyptians go from right to left."

The Greek historian Herodotus visited Egypt in the fifth century BC and, like most others, was overawed by what he saw. It was not only the magnificence of the art and buildings that impressed him, but the exotic qualities of Egyptian society. He found Egypt as strange a land as China would seem to many later travelers from Europe.

ONE ASPECT of Egypt that most perplexed Herodotus was the great river that formed the backbone of the country.

The Great River of Africa

The Egyptians themselves referred to it merely as *iteru aa*, "the great river"; it was the Greeks who named the river "Neilos". In a sense, the Nile *was* Egypt: its lifeblood and its communication system, its only

TREES AND BUSHES line a garden waterway in this detail of a tomb painting (ABOVE) from Deir el-Medina, near Thebes. Recognizable are the date palm, the doum palm and the sycamore fig. Large trees useful in construction were rare and had to be imported. As with agricultural crops, the Egyptian garden depended on careful management of the nutrient-rich Nile flood. The importance of water is reflected in its presence throughout this painting.

A WAVING FIELD of barley (BELOW) from a sculptured relief suggests the fertility of the Nile valley. Egypt's prosperity was based on fine harvests of grain.

means of survival in an otherwise waterless desert. What particularly intrigued Herodotus was that the waters of the Nile rose in the summer and were at their lowest in the winter, whereas in Greece the summer heat dried out many streams completely. Herodotus tried to explain this and came up with an ingenious, though incorrect, explanation of his own. He argued the sun retreated into Africa in winter and caused the waters of the upper Nile to evaporate; it was therefore not until the summer that the Nile could resume its normal flow.

Herodotus was right in seeing the behavior of the Nile as unique. No other river provides such a predictable source of water to the surrounding land. Each year in May the river begins to rise, swollen with muddy water. Until our own century, when the river has been dammed, the rise would cause the river to burst its banks in June and flood the land. Between July and September the flood was at its height; then the waters began to fall, leaving a rich silt behind them. By November the enriched land could be plowed and sown with crops. From March to June the grain was harvested before the next year's floods began. Sometimes the floods were too high, and villages were swept aside; on other occasions they were too low and famine ensued; but in most years the inhabitants of the valley would harvest a rich crop from the new fertile soil, its yield some four to five times that of normal rainfed soil. It was this magnificent harvest, claimed by the rulers of the Nile valley, which was to sustain the civilization of ancient Egypt, and

IN THE BEGINNING
The Egyptian Genesis

Like most early cultures, the Egyptians had several creation stories, originating in different cult centers along the Nile. All suggest, however, that creation was an ordered process. At the beginning of time, most agreed, the earth had been covered by dark and gloomy waters. Legend says that the sun initiated the first act of creation from this lifeless world from a mound which had risen from the waters. According to one very ancient cult, the sun in this role of creator was Atum, "the all" or "he who came into being of himself", and the reappearance of the land from the floods each year replayed the original act of creation. Heliopolis, the center of the cult of Atum, claimed to be the original creation mound, and the *benben*

(a pyramidical stone in the temple there) was the spot where the sun's rays first touched the earth.

It was from Atum's semen that life was first born. He gave birth to Shu, the god of air, and Tefnut, the goddess of moisture. They represented opposing qualities: air is dry and preserving, and Shu became associated with the cycle of life, renewed annually for eternity; moisture corrodes, so Tefnut was associated with unpredictable events that threaten to upset the ordered pattern of existence. The themes of order versus disorder, and preservation versus decay, pervade the Egyptian philosophy of life. Shu and Tefnut gave birth to Geb, the earth, and Nut, the sky. Shu lifted Nut into her place in the sky, and so the world took shape.

Other gods might also be credited with the act of creation. Ra, the sun-god, gradually became associated with Atum, "the all", so that Ra – among his many other manifestations – was also seen as a creator-god.

In the Middle Kingdom (2040–1640 BC), when Thebes became the political heart of the kingdom, its own cult god Amun, "the hidden one" – the force within the wind, for instance – became prominent and was given a role in creation similar to that of Atum. Ra was too closely associated with the power of the kings and too well established in the north of the country to be replaced entirely by Amun, and so Ra, the visible power of the sun, and Amun, its hidden force, were merged as the powerful god known as Amun-Ra.

Nut, the sky-goddess, arches over the ceiling of the burial tomb of Ramesses VI. Her hands and feet touch the ground, forming the vault of the sky. The top half of the painting represents night, the bottom day. Nut gives birth to the sun in the morning (BELOW LEFT) and swallows it in the evening (BELOW RIGHT). The sun is seen both passing through her "body" (as a disk) and being carried across the sky in the solar bark, which is sometimes towed by jackals. This story of the solar cycle, like the creation myth, was not totally consistent.

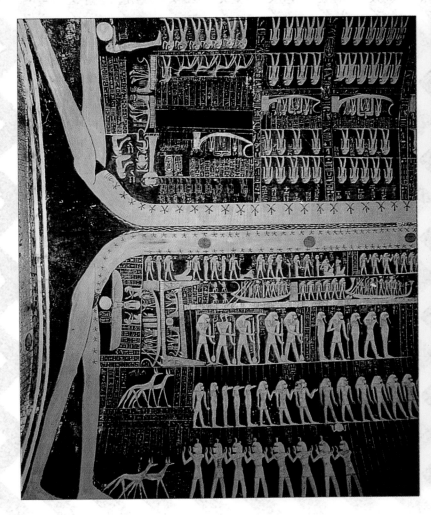
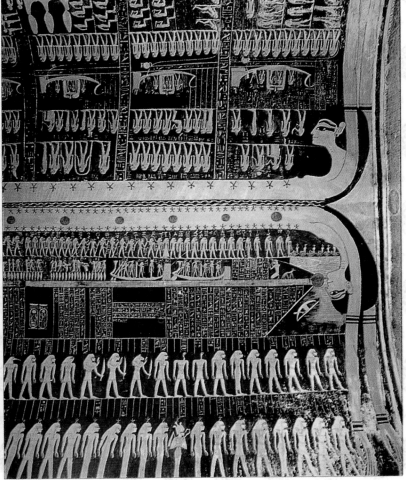

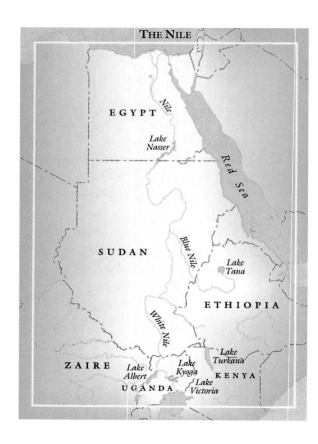

THE NILE

forests. The Nile valley was then so rich in plant life that it would probably have been impossible for humans to live there, and the first settlements in the region were on higher ground above the valley. From about 5000 BC, however, the rainfall began to decline until by 2300 BC there was virtually none, as is still the case today. Gradually the desert became uninhabitable while the valley grew less impenetrable. The valley was settled as the land was slowly cleared of forest and cultivation began.

THE FAMILIAR PATTERN of Egyptian life – human settlement in a long narrow valley, annually

Black Land & Red Land

swollen by floods, desert beyond – was thus established. The Egyptians called the infertile sands that surrounded them *Deshret*, "the Red Land" (sometimes, though mistakenly, said to be the source of the modern word, desert). They were the subject of much fear, the home of bad spirits and malicious animals like the scorpion. Expeditions to the desert were always organized meticulously, both to ensure enough water and provisions were carried, and to escape the evil spirits. The more hospitable valley itself – rarely more than a few kilometers across – was known to the Egyptians as *Kemet*, "the Black Land". They called themselves *remet en Kemet*, "people of the

provide a great attraction for later conquerors, including the Romans and the Arabs.

If Herodotus was correct in seeing the behavior of the Nile as strange, he was wrong in his explanation. The real reason for the rise and fall of the river's waters remained a secret for another 2,000 years. British explorers in the 19th century were preoccupied by the source of the Nile. They discovered that one part of the river, the White Nile, had its origins in Lake Victoria and Lakes Edward and George in modern Uganda, but the secret of its flood was not to be found there. The flow of the White Nile is constant throughout the year, because during central Africa's rainy season much of the extra water is absorbed by the Sudd, a great area of swampland in what is now southern Sudan. The rather shorter Blue Nile, which joins the White Nile at the modern city of Khartoum, holds the answer. The Blue Nile originates in the mountains of Ethiopia and it was in the summer rains here that the floods had their making. The rains start in May and continue through the summer. By the end of May the water reached Egypt, and so the Nile floods began.

Before the rise of the first civilizations, the Nile valley and the surrounding desert had known periods of heavy rainfall in addition to the floods, and the water table was much higher than it was later to become. There are ancient watercourses in the desert, and the fossilized remains of trees have been found, showing that the land once supported

COLORED CANYON in the Sinai desert (LEFT). The Sinai and the Eastern Desert are steep and rocky, rather than rolling and sandy. The Sinai was almost uninhabited in ancient times but was a rich source of copper and minerals.

TISISAT FALLS on the Nile (ABOVE) at the end of the rainy season in September – a force of potentially destructive power as well as a giver of life. The Blue Nile has its source in Lake Tana on the Ethiopian plateau, 31 kilometers (19 miles) away. At Khartoum it joins the White Nile, which has come over a thousand miles from its origins in Uganda.

Black Land", and the word was adopted by the Arabs who conquered Egypt in the seventh century AD and who retained the Egyptian knowledge of and skill at handling naturally-occurring minerals. *Kemet* has survived to our own times, as the root of the words chemist, chemistry and alchemy.

Some 200 kilometers (120 miles) from the Mediterranean, the Nile fans out in six smaller streams and its silt is spread over a larger area. When the Greeks visited Egypt they saw a similarity between the triangular shape of the silted

area and their own letter, delta. The name stuck and the word delta is still used to describe any area of alluvial land formed at the mouth of a river. Although the land here was rich, it was interspersed with swamps and the only way to travel from one part to another was to go down south to the apex of the Delta, and then take a different branch of the Nile to the destination. There was a mass of bird life and fish in the Delta, and the swamps became a favorite hunting ground for the rich. They were also the best source of the papyrus reed, and the Delta was normally referred to as "the land of the papyrus". From about 2500 BC the Egyptians began to reclaim more and more land for cultivation, and by 1400 BC the Delta – or Lower Egypt – had perhaps twice as much cultivable land as the rest of the Nile valley. The entire Delta area is alluvial, which has caused most ancient monuments to disappear under the silt. Far fewer spectacular remains have been found here than in the narrower valley of Middle and Upper Egypt to the south, where most temples and tombs were built on the rocky land beyond the floods.

Further up the Nile valley a branch of the river broke off to the west, then ran parallel with the Nile until running into a large lake, Lake Moeris (now Birket Qarun). Here the strip of cultivation widened to as much as 30 kilometers (20 miles). This area was the Faiyum. It had been the site of some of the earliest human settlements in the region, their inhabitants able to rely on fish from the lake to supplement their diet. Egyptian kings, particularly those of the 12th Dynasty (1991–1783 BC), reclaimed large areas of land in the Faiyum by draining part of Lake Moeris and using its remaining water to irrigate the surrounding soil.

THE ORIGINAL BOUNDARY of the kingdom of Egypt was the First Cataract, 1,100 kilometers (700 miles) from the sea. Granite rocks on the river bed made passage difficult and offered the first obstacle in the great navigation channel which had permitted communication from the mouth of the river to deep inland. Farther up the river were

The Kingdom of Egypt

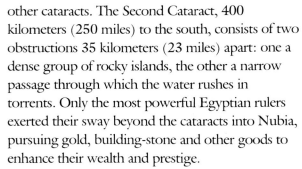

*T*HE HERALDIC PLANT of Upper Egypt was the lotus (ABOVE), also a symbol of renewal. A myth of creation described the new-born sun emerging from a lotus floating on the primeval waters.

*T*HE FIRST CATARACT at Aswan marked the southern border of ancient Egypt. The temple of Philae (RIGHT) is seen from Biga, site of a more ancient shrine and the mythical source of the Nile to the ancient Egyptians.

*A*N AERIAL VIEW of Rosetta (Rashid) on the west Nile delta (BELOW). This small boat-building center was one of Egypt's chief ports when Napoleon invaded in 1798. The Rosetta Stone, a text in three scripts which allowed modern scholars to decipher hieroglyphs, was discovered in a fort in its harbor.

other cataracts. The Second Cataract, 400 kilometers (250 miles) to the south, consists of two obstructions 35 kilometers (23 miles) apart: one a dense group of rocky islands, the other a narrow passage through which the water rushes in torrents. Only the most powerful Egyptian rulers exerted their sway beyond the cataracts into Nubia, pursuing gold, building-stone and other goods to enhance their wealth and prestige.

The ancient kingdom of Egypt therefore was a long, narrow one, made up of a unity of the Delta and the valley as far as the First Cataract and often beyond. Normally the best site for a capital was in Middle Egypt, convenient for both the Delta and the upper valley – at Memphis, for instance, which the first kings of Egypt established as their seat in about 3100 BC. Although other capitals, such as Thebes, were adopted at other times, kings were still maintaining palaces at Memphis two and a half millennia later. It was here that the royal dock-yards, essential for a state reliant on river transport, were based, while close by were the largest pyramids that have been the most spectacular of the monuments of Egypt since their construction around 2550 BC, and were listed among the Seven Wonders of the Ancient World.

Egypt was bound together by the Nile in another crucial way. There was no significant road network (the Egyptians did not develop the wheel, but imported it in about 1650 BC from the civilizations of west Asia) and the river was used for every form of travel. The prevailing northerly wind went against the current, so that a boat without a sail could drift with the current, and a boat with a sail could sail against it. (Local traffic in much of the Nile valley still moves by boat.) The monuments of ancient Egypt could never have been built without the Nile, which made it possible to transport heavy stones. For instance, the nine great slabs of red granite – 400 tonnes in total – that formed the king's burial chamber at the heart of the Great Pyramid of Khufu had to be transported over 800 kilometers (500 miles) from Aswan to Giza. To move them by land would have required between 200 and 250 men, and such a long journey would have been impossible without the river. Even larger stones, like the tall, pointed obelisks that stood outside the entrances to the great temples, could be carried by boat. One granite obelisk, 43 meters (141 feet) long and three meters (10 feet) thick at its lower end, and weighing 110 tonnes, still lies in its quarry near Aswan, abandoned by its ancient quarriers only because faults in the rock were discovered as it was

being shaped. Not surprisingly, the tombs of officials recorded their boasts when they succeeded in bringing such masses of stone to building sites.

There was no lack of suitable building stone. The valley and the surrounding desert provided a rich variety. The oldest rocks in the African continent are granite with veins of diorite (another hard stone) as well as gold concealed within them. These were later overlaid with sandstone. Then, during the Tertiary period, between 18 and 5 million years ago, Egypt was covered by sea, which left a layer of limestone and chalk as it retreated. As the Nile was formed it cut through these layers of rocks, leaving limestone cliffs along the valley sides. In areas such as Aswan, where the river wore down to the foundation rock, granite was available for quarrying; others such as Nubia provided a rich source of sandstone. In addition, especially severe floods about 15,000–10,000 years ago carried a mass of semi-precious stone, including chalcedony, jasper and agate, into southern Egypt.

The valley varied in width – sometimes a few hundred meters across, sometimes a few kilometers, depending on how the river had meandered as it wore its way down through the limestone. The bottom of the valley was deep in silt and was able to support an abundance of plant life. Papyrus grew here, though not in such quantities as in the Delta, along with the lotus flower – the symbol of the valley kingdom and a relative of the water lily. Indeed, one way the Egyptians depicted the unity of their state was to illustrate the god of the annual inundation, Hapy, tying together bunches of papyrus and lotus. It was from the lotus flower that the sun was supposed to have risen at creation, and its sweet-smelling flowers were laid on tombs or on the table at banquets. Flax was also abundant and its fibers formed the threads from which linen, the most usual cloth, was made.

THERE WAS RICH ANIMAL LIFE both in the valley and the Delta. Crocodiles and hippos added to the

Nile Animals & Plants

interest and also danger of everyday life. Herodotus gave a famous description of the crocodile: "It has eyes like a pig's and great fang-like teeth, and is the only animal to have no tongue and a fixed lower jaw." In the desert there

WALL PAINTING from the tomb-chapel of Nebamun (RIGHT), showing him hunting birds in the marshes with his wife and daughter – a popular pastime of the rich. They are standing on a simple papyrus boat that was commonly used for such trips. In his left hand is a boomerang, which was the preferred weapon for hunting birds. Fish were caught with spears or nets. The family is rather elaborately dressed for the outing. In one hand Nebamun's wife holds a sistrum – a musical instrument, similar to a rattle, which made a sound like the rustling of marsh grasses. In the other hand, she holds flowers.

PAPYRUS
Material of Pharaoh

Papyrus, a tough reed originally found in marshes and swamps throughout Egypt (but now grown only in a few areas), was one of the most useful of Egypt's natural products. Its stalks could be made into rope, mats and even sandals. The earliest known Nile boats were made of papyrus reeds bound together, and the reeds also seem to have been used in building. The great hypostyle halls of the temples – which were supposed to recreate the original creation mound covered in lush vegetation – contained a forest of columns in which bundles of papyrus plants were reconstructed in stone. The plant was also a symbol of youthfulness and joy and is shown in offerings to the goddess Hathor. Its distinctive fan-like head was a common decorative theme,

WITH ITS GRASSY LEAVES, papyrus (ABOVE) once grew wild in the marshes of the Nile Delta, but was later cultivated to make paper and other products. Plants can grow up to 4.6 meters (15 feet) high. They flourish in slow-moving shallow water like that along much of the Nile.

and is shown in many paintings and carvings. Its hieroglyphic sign was also used to refer to "green".

The best known use of papyrus was as a writing material, and so papyrus was an essential element in Egyptian statecraft, which relied on thorough administration. The Egyptian name for the plant, *paperao*, probably meant "the

material of pharaoh" and is also the source of the English word, paper.

The earliest recorded use is in a 1st-Dynasty tomb dated at about 3035 BC. The inner parts of the stems were cut into lengths about 50 centimeters (20 inches) long and laid out in rows to form a sheet. Other stems were laid across them at right angles and the square sheet was beaten until the natural juices of the reed bound the whole together. The convention was that there should be twenty squares in a single sheet. This was normally written on only one side, but used papyri were sometimes gathered up by the poor, who would add their own jottings to the blank side. The dry climate of Egypt has allowed much papyrus to be preserved. This is one reason why so many written records of life in ancient Egypt have survived.

had once been gazelles, ostriches, lions, elephants, giraffe and leopards, but the growing aridity, and probably the activities of early hunters, led to the disappearance of many of the larger animals. Hunting gradually ceased to provide an important source of food and became a sport for the kings and their courtiers. Animals were domesticated as agriculture developed, and some – notably cattle – became an important food source. Camels were not used until the start of the Roman period. The Egyptians were famous for their reverence for all kinds of animals. Greeks such as Herodotus found it odd that the Egyptians could worship the cat, baboon or scarab (dung beetle), but the Egyptians saw, in the behavior of each, a telling manifestation of the spiritual world around them.

The most important cultivated product was grain – mainly emmer wheat and barley, from which beer could be made. Grain was the essential commodity of the Egyptian economy. It was not bought and sold within Egypt, but could be stored in temple or royal granaries and supplied to workers and craftsmen. To relieve the monotony of a diet of grain, the Egyptians also cultivated a wide variety of other crops, including vegetables such as beans, lentils and onions. Dates and honey were used to sweeten. With fish, meat from cattle and eggs from ducks and wildfowl, the diet of the better-off Egyptian, at least, was certainly varied.

A BLUE FAIENCE (ceramic) hippopotamus decorated with aquatic plants (BELOW) from a late 20th-century BC tomb at Meir. Hippos were common on the Nile in ancient Egypt, but they were hunted nearly to extinction. They are now found south of the desert, where water is plentiful.

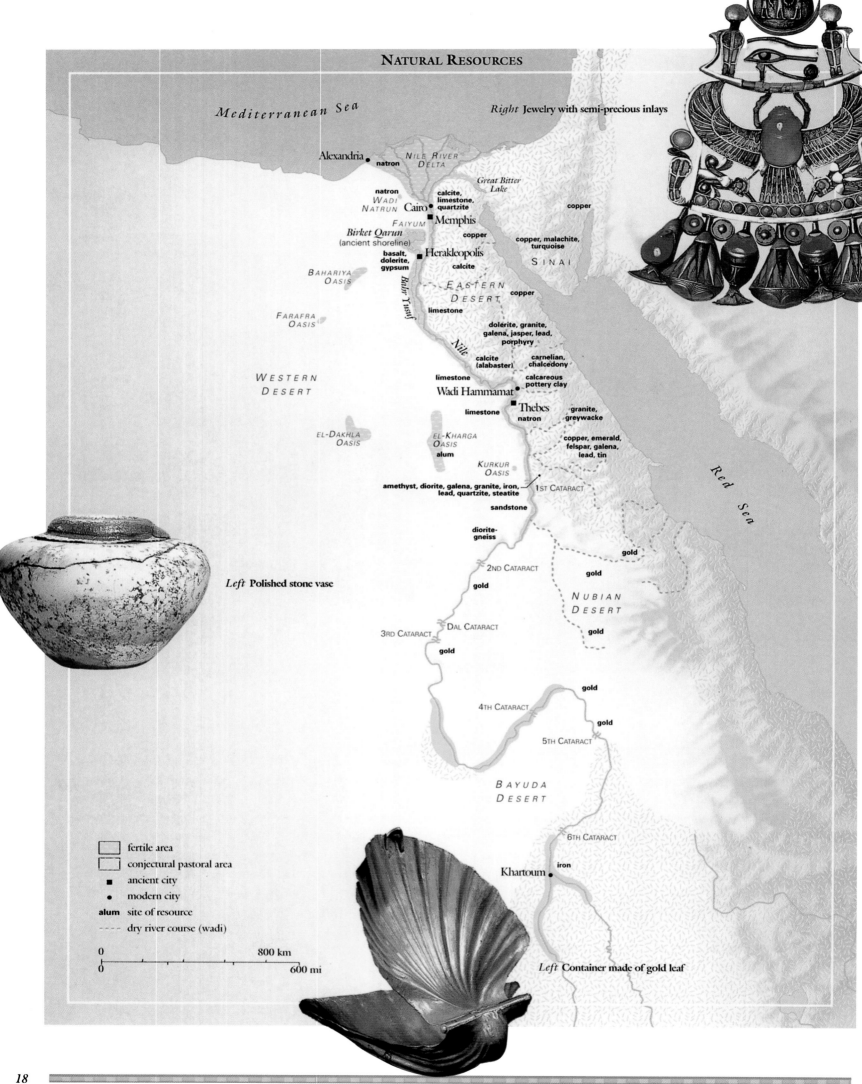

NATURAL RESOURCES

Right Jewelry with semi-precious inlays

Mediterranean Sea

Alexandria • natron

NILE RIVER DELTA

Great Bitter Lake

natron

WADI NATRUN

calcite, limestone, quartzite

copper

Cairo • ■ Memphis

FAIYUM

Birket Qarun (ancient shoreline)

copper

copper, malachite, turquoise

basalt, dolerite, gypsum

Bahr Yusuf

■ Herakleopolis

calcite

SINAI

BAHARIYA OASIS

EASTERN DESERT

copper

FARAFRA OASIS

limestone

dolerite, granite, galena, jasper, lead, porphyry

Nile

WESTERN DESERT

calcite (alabaster)

carnelian, chalcedony

limestone

calcareous pottery clay

Wadi Hammamat •

EL-DAKHLA OASIS

EL-KHARGA OASIS

limestone

■ Thebes

natron

granite, greywacke

alum

copper, emerald, felspar, galena, lead, tin

KURKUR OASIS

amethyst, diorite, galena, granite, iron, lead, quartzite, steatite

1ST CATARACT

Red Sea

sandstone

diorite-gneiss

gold

2ND CATARACT

gold

Left Polished stone vase

gold

NUBIAN DESERT

3RD CATARACT   DAL CATARACT

gold

gold

4TH CATARACT

gold

5TH CATARACT

BAYUDA DESERT

6TH CATARACT

Khartoum • iron

Legend:
- fertile area
- conjectural pastoral area
- ■ ancient city
- • modern city
- **alum** site of resource
- - - - dry river course (wadi)

0 — 800 km
0 — 600 mi

Left Container made of gold leaf

*T*HIS PIECE *of inlaid jewelry from Tutankhamun's world-famous tomb* (LEFT) *incorporates semi-precious materials from Egypt and beyond. Whereas gold was widely available in the Nile valley, silver was mainly imported from west Asia. Lapis lazuli came from farther east, and obsidian from Ethiopia. Carnelian and chalcedony (which form the scarab at the center) were found in the Eastern Desert.*

*P*OLISHED *calcareous stone was used for this vessel with a gold leaf cover in the form of a piece of cloth* (FAR LEFT) *from the tomb of King Khasekhemwy of the 2nd Dynasty. Items for use in the afterlife were made of long-lasting materials, in forms imitating less durable everyday items.*

*G*OLD LEAF *gleams on a shell, possibly a cosmetic container* (BELOW LEFT). *The small quantity of gold used in the earliest period of Egyptian history came from alluvial (water-borne) deposits. As demand grew, gold-bearing rock had to be mined. Egypt's gold was one lure to potential raiders.*

*T*HE OLDEST MAP *still in existence* (RIGHT), *from the 12th century BC, shows mines and storehouses at Wadi Hammamat in the granite "gold mountains" (the topmost of the four mountain ranges drawn) of the Eastern Desert. Workmen's small houses lie below, and to the right is a temple to Amun (white). Stones mark the main road at the bottom. This map was used on an expedition to fetch a statue of a king from the quarries.*

BEYOND THE NILE VALLEY lay the deserts, part sand and part rock. In total covering an area larger than Europe, they left Egypt comparatively isolated. A well-organized king could always fight off intruders. These natural barriers proved crucial to the development of Egyptian civilization and to its maintenance over the millennia. Those few foreign influences that did reach Egypt were quickly absorbed within the traditional life and culture of the country.

Beyond the Valley of the Nile

The deserts also offered opportunities for those kings who were strong enough to reach beyond the confines of the Nile valley. The mountainous regions in the east held important minerals. In the Sinai desert were deposits of turquoise and copper, and along the Red Sea there were other resources, including diorite, gold and tin. The Egyptians dominated the nomadic tribes of the desert, probably using them as laborers for the quarries, and it seems that the first towns arose because of the need for administrative control of trade routes to the Near East. Once Egypt was united as a single state, the kings had the responsibility of overseeing and protecting these routes.

On the edge of the Red Sea there were ports from which ships set out to the East African coast and in particular the mysterious land of Punt (probably on the coast of modern Somalia). These places provided incenses, spices and galena (lead sulfide), which was used as a dark eye-shadow. The desert in the west was less attractive. There were a number of large oases where dates and grapes grew, and these could act as staging posts for expeditions, but they were always vulnerable to attacks by nomads, known to the Egyptians as Libyans. During the New Kingdom (1550–1070 BC) these oases were used as convenient places of exile for political dissidents.

As early as 3200 BC, Egyptian traders were reaching east beyond the Sinai desert into the Levant and linking into a network of trade routes which ran as far east as Afghanistan (the source of lapis lazuli, the deep blue stone much prized by Egyptians). There appears to have been a well-developed relationship with Mesopotamia, the most powerful of the Near Eastern civilizations in the fourth millennium BC. A later important contact was with Byblos on the Levantine coast, from where timber (always in short supply in Egypt) and resin, used in embalming, could be obtained. Otherwise, however, the Nile and its immediate surroundings provided almost everything that the people of Egypt needed, and so there was little incentive for either conquest or trade. Given this, the Egyptians never felt a need to explore further into the Mediterranean.

An important exception to this fortunate self-sufficiency was gold, which the Egyptians found beyond the First Cataract. Nubia was not as rich agriculturally as Egypt, with cultivation restricted to a very narrow band of land along the river, but its important deposits of gold were the targets of the Egyptian kings, especially those of the New Kingdom. Although it was never easy to maintain authority over such distant territory, the Egyptian kings regarded Nubia as an annex of Egypt and had no inhibitions about exploiting the Nubians and their land. Goods were also brought up the Nile from even further south to satisfy some of the most exotic of the needs of the Egyptian market. A flourishing trade in goods such as ostrich feathers and giraffe tails was recorded.

EGYPT REMAINS, as it was in ancient times, a state crowded along the Nile, but in our own times the annual flood has become a thing of the past. Two dams have been built across the river at Aswan, with Lake Nasser (stretching 500 kilometers – 300 miles – south into Sudan) behind them. Their purpose was to provide hydroelectricity and a year-round supply of water to one of the fastest-growing populations in the world. Despite the high hopes engendered by the dam, it has meant that less nutrient-rich silt is carried downstream, with detrimental effects on the fertility of the land in the Delta and the coastal fishing grounds.

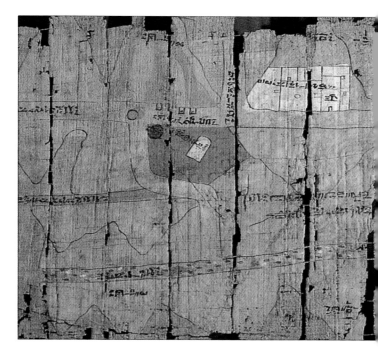

"*I went down to the sea in a boat 120 cubits long and 40 cubits wide. 120 sailors from among the best of Egypt were in it... their hearts were fiercer than those of lions.*"

Tale of the Shipwrecked Sailor

Right A carving of Queen Hatshepsut's famous expedition down the Red Sea to Punt (modern Somalia) shows the detail of her ship's rigging and oarsmen.

The Highway of Egypt

Virtually all Egyptian traffic traveled by the Nile. As early as the fourth millennium BC, papyrus rafts were made of reeds tied together, often with ends decoratively bound and rising from the water. Families used them for trips on the marshes, and hunters are shown harpooning from them. Larger rafts carried a mast and sail specially rigged so that the weight was evenly distributed. Papyrus rafts were easy to make but rotted quickly. Wood was also used, but the supply was limited. The hard-wood acacia, the best wood in Egypt, was only available in lengths of a meter (three feet). Boatbuilders learned to bind the short planks together with dowels or fiber ropes, but larger ships required trunks of cedar imported from Lebanon.

A wealthy Egyptian had his own fleet. The noble Meketre, buried at Thebes about 2000 BC, was provided with ten boats, including four for his personal travel which included kitchens. Boats for everyday work were more robust, less elegant and comfortable. They were broad and flat-bottomed for stability; shoals on the Nile prevented the use of keels. They could drift downstream, but to travel upstream they had to be fitted

Above The owner of the original of this sailing boat commissioned a model of it for his tomb. The pilot is in the bow and the owner rests under a canopy.

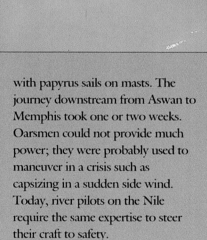

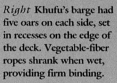

Right **Khufu's barge had five oars on each side, set in recesses on the edge of the deck. Vegetable-fiber ropes shrank when wet, providing firm binding.**

Top and right **Simple lashed-papyrus skiffs were invented more than 5,000 years ago, but their basic design remains completely suitable for traveling on the Nile today.**

with papyrus sails on masts. The journey downstream from Aswan to Memphis took one or two weeks. Oarsmen could not provide much power; they were probably used to maneuver in a crisis such as capsizing in a sudden side wind. Today, river pilots on the Nile require the same expertise to steer their craft to safety.

In 1954, in a pit beside the tomb of King Khufu, a great royal boat was found – the supreme surviving example of early Egyptian shipbuilding. It had been completely dismantled, and reconstructing its 1,200 pieces took ten years. This

boat provided a wealth of information on techniques of ancient boatbuilding. Everything had remained intact, from the two steering poles and ten oars to the enclosed cabin. When put back together, the boat was 43 meters (150 feet) in length, and founded on solid cedar planks 22 meters (77 feet) long. These were bound together on the inside with ropes, so that the hull tightened as the wood swelled in the water. As the boat had been used, the most likely explanation is that it was the very barge that took the king's mummy upriver from Memphis to be buried in his pyramid at Giza. Similar boats, often with the mummy of the owner sitting in them surrounded by priests, are found in later tombs.

Below **Khufu's great boat was mostly cedar. With a wide, flat hull and no keel, it drew little water. It had steering oars at the stern and a cabin behind the canopy.**

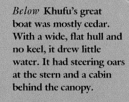

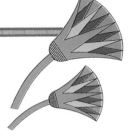

THE FIRST KINGS
Archaic and Old Kingdom Egypt

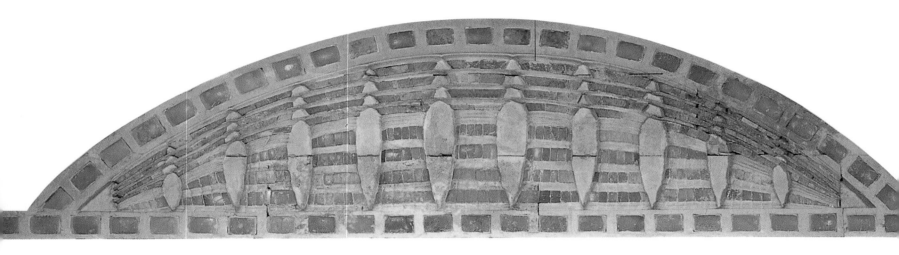

It was not easy to maintain control over the long, thin strip of fertile land that comprised ancient Egypt, but the natural wealth of the Nile valley ensured that the rewards for any sole ruler who could reap the fruits of the entire region would be high. For two millennia after 3100 BC Egypt was ruled as a single kingdom, almost without interruption, by kings who created such an aura of divinity and material power that their supremacy was unquestioned. The mystique of kingship was consolidated and sustained through age-old ritual and enduring conventions of sculpture, carving and painting as much as by physical authority. So powerful were its traditions that when the Roman emperor Titus was portrayed on an Egyptian temple wall in AD 70, it was in a pose very little different from that adopted by Narmer, founder of the Egyptian state, more than 3,000 years earlier. The maintenance of a unified kingship was one of ancient Egypt's great achievements and its civilization could not have survived without it.

THE NILE VALLEY had been settled for thousands of years before the first rulers of a unified state appeared. The earliest Egyptian communities lived in a simple manner along the river or around the desert oases, hunting and gathering what they needed to survive. By 6000 BC, perhaps, they were beginning to collect seeds and cultivate crops. As wheat and barley became an ever more important

Early Cultures of the Nile

STABILITY AND PERMANENCE are represented by the pillars on a faience tiled panel (ABOVE) from the royal apartments in King Djoser's pyramid. The "djed" pillars were Predynastic fetishes, perhaps signifying grain tied to a pole. They became associated with the gods Ptah and Sokar, and finally with Osiris; the "djed" represents his spine.

TIMETABLE	
c.4500–4000	Badarian culture
4000–3500	Naqada I culture
3500–3000	Naqada II culture
c.3100	Unification of Egypt
2920–2575	**Early Dynastic period**
2920–2770	1ST DYNASTY
2770–2649	2ND DYNASTY
2649–2575	3RD DYNASTY
2630–2611	Reign of Djoser
2575–2134	**Old Kingdom Egypt**
2575–2465	4TH DYNASTY
2575–2551	Reign of Snefru
2551–2528	Reign of Khufu
2520–2494	Reign of Khephren
2490–2472	Reign of Menkaure
2465–2323	5TH DYNASTY
2323–2150	6TH DYNASTY
2246–2152	Reign of Pepy II
2134–2040	**1st Intermediate Period**

part of the diet, animals were domesticated – sheep, cattle and goats in particular. Farming developed into a full way of life.

More settled communities emerged. Within a thousand years came the first recognizable culture, known as the Badarian after the modern town of el-Badari in southern Egypt where it was first identified. The Badarian peoples had some conception of an afterlife. They chose to be buried at the edge of the desert with their heads to the south and their faces turned toward the west, and with necklaces and jewelry on their bodies. They may have shared with later Egyptians a ritualistic fascination with animals: dogs and jackals, sheep and cows were buried alongside the human bodies.

By 4000 BC another culture was emerging at Naqada, some 80 kilometers (50 miles) north of modern Luxor. Naqada burials were carried out in the same way as those of the Badarian, facing to the west, but the grave goods were now more sophisticated. Pottery, already known in the region for 2,000 years, was now fashioned into open bowls and tall vases, some in exotic shapes. Stone vases appear, laboriously hollowed out by manual rotary drills. This love of working in stone was to last throughout Egyptian history.

About 3500 BC Naqada culture changed even more dramatically. Settlements became larger and more impressive. Circular huts were replaced by rectangular brick houses and at some sites the communities lived in walled towns. Two of these, Naqada and Hierakonpolis, were well placed to exploit gold deposits in the surrounding desert and trade routes to the Red Sea, and this may have been the reason they became prominent. The furnishing of graves grew more opulent as copper, gold and silver became available. There was pottery decorated with paintings of boats and people, and vases shaped from a wider variety of stones. Stone workers now had the expertise to carve animals and birds. Some of the finest goods of all were flint knives, their blades meticulously shaped.

The communities of the Delta were less developed but seem to have prided themselves on their distinct identity, enjoying their own "capital" at Buto. The remains of Buto have been buried under layers of silt and lay below the water table, but in the 1980s German excavators found the earliest layers of occupation. These showed that the culture of Naqada slowly infiltrated the Delta from about 3300 BC. At first the people of Buto continued their traditional pottery types but adopted styles from Naqada. Within 200 years, goods from Naqada or copied directly from them predominated. For the first time Egypt enjoyed a form of cultural unity.

THE YEARS between 3300 and 3100 BC seem to have been a time of increasing tension and conflict,

Unification of the Kingdoms

perhaps between rival rulers along the Nile valley or against intruders attracted by the wealth of the valley. The evidence comes from ceremonial palettes. Palettes had originally been used as bases on which to grind malachite for eye decoration, but they acquired a sacred quality and were highly decorated. Their reliefs show humans and animals locked in conflict. On one, the so-called Battlefield

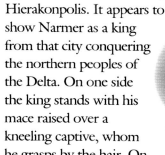

VICTORY is celebrated with religious and military symbols on this pottery vase (ABOVE) from the early Naqada period, about 3700 BC. The large central figure has its arms raised over its head in a gesture associated with a fertility goddess but also used for mourning or to represent the "ka" (life force). Four other figures appear to be captives with their arms bound.

palette, lie slain warriors, their bodies being savaged by lions and vultures. On another, the Hunters' palette, armed warriors go in pursuit of wild animals. On a third, animals, possibly the emblems of warring clans, destroy walled cities.

Another find, a knife from Gebel el-Arak, shows a sea battle on its ivory handle. This battle may have taken place on the Red Sea against Mesopotamian invaders. It certainly appears that some Mesopotamians successfully penetrated the Nile valley at this time, bringing their own culture with them. Mesopotamian culture is represented in cylinder seals, artistic conventions such as the entwined necks of animals shown on the palettes, and palace facades copied from the mud-brick walls reinforced with reeds that were a feature of Mesopotamian architecture. Modern scholars once believed that the idea of writing was also learned from Mesopotamia, but in fact the hieroglyphic symbols in which Egyptians wrote seem to derive from earlier indigenous picture forms. All these innovations were soon absorbed into the mainstream of Egyptian culture.

The first unification of Egypt is dated to about 3100 BC and is traditionally attributed to Narmer, a king of Upper Egypt. His triumph is recorded on a palette which was carefully buried at Hierakonpolis. It appears to show Narmer as a king from that city conquering the northern peoples of the Delta. On one side the king stands with his mace raised over a kneeling captive, whom he grasps by the hair. On

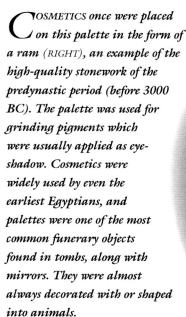

COSMETICS once were placed on this palette in the form of a ram (RIGHT), an example of the high-quality stonework of the predynastic period (before 3000 BC). The palette was used for grinding pigments which were usually applied as eye-shadow. Cosmetics were widely used by even the earliest Egyptians, and palettes were one of the most common funerary objects found in tombs, along with mirrors. They were almost always decorated with or shaped into animals.

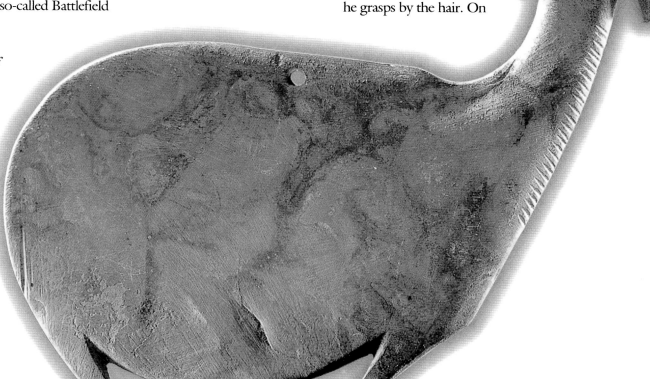

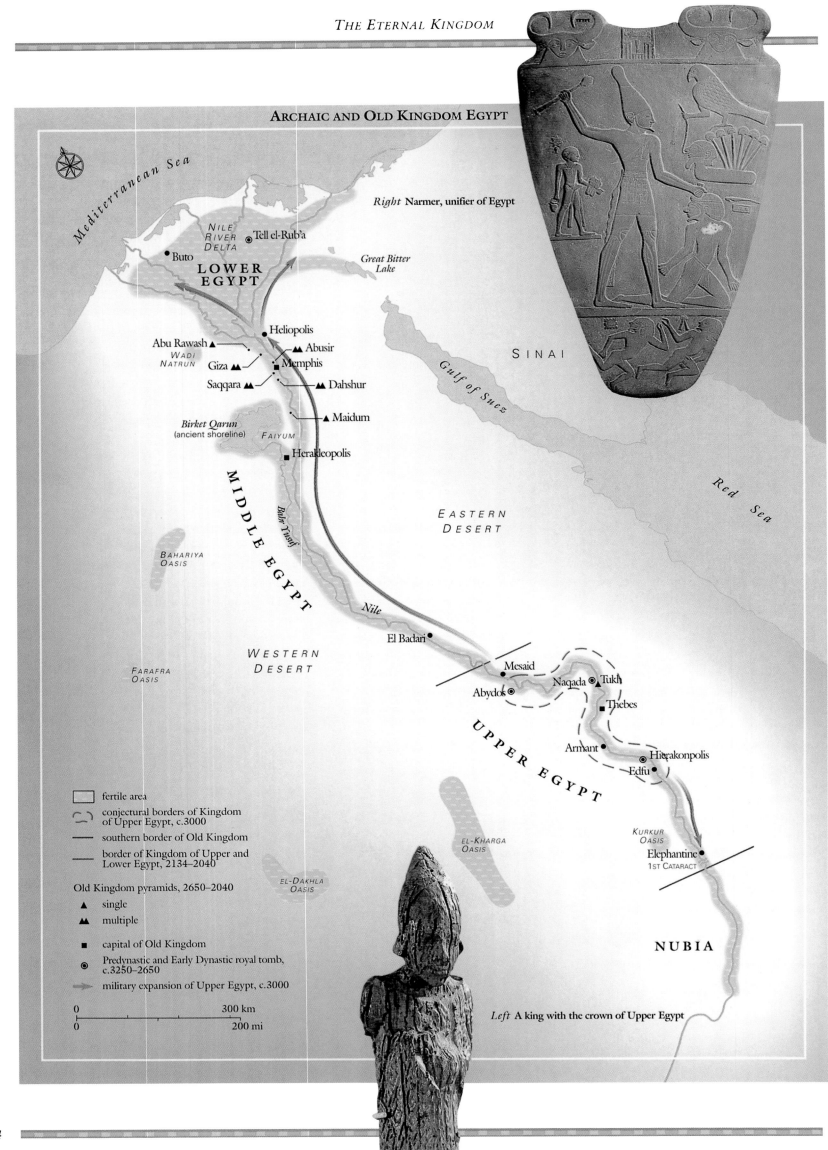

ARCHAIC AND OLD KINGDOM EGYPT

Mediterranean Sea

NILE RIVER DELTA
● Tell el-Rub'a

● Buto

LOWER EGYPT

Great Bitter Lake

Right Narmer, unifier of Egypt

● Heliopolis

Abu Rawash ▲

▲▲ Abusir

WADI NATRUN

Giza ▲▲

● Memphis

Saqqara ▲▲

▲ Dahshur

▲ Maidum

Birket Qarun (ancient shoreline)

FAIYUM

■ Herakleopolis

MIDDLE EGYPT

Bahr Yusuf

SINAI

Gulf of Suez

Red Sea

EASTERN DESERT

BAHARIYA OASIS

Nile

WESTERN DESERT

FARAFRA OASIS

El Badari ●

Mesaid ●

Naqada ◉ ▲ Tukh

Abydos ◉

■ Thebes

UPPER EGYPT

Armant ●

● Hierakonpolis

Edfu ◉

EL-KHARGA OASIS

EL-DAKHLA OASIS

KURKUR OASIS

Elephantine ●
1ST CATARACT

NUBIA

Legend

☐ fertile area

〰 conjectural borders of Kingdom of Upper Egypt, c.3000

— southern border of Old Kingdom

— border of Kingdom of Upper and Lower Egypt, 2134–2040

Old Kingdom pyramids, 2650–2040

▲ single

▲▲ multiple

■ capital of Old Kingdom

◉ Predynastic and Early Dynastic royal tomb, c.3250–2650

➜ military expansion of Upper Egypt, c.3000

0   300 km

0   200 mi

Left A king with the crown of Upper Egypt

*N*ARMER, *traditionally regarded as the first king of the unified Egypt* (LEFT), *is shown on this ceremonial palette "smiting" an enemy, in a pose that was copied countless times over the next 3,000 years. The palette was discovered in near-perfect condition and the king is clearly identified as Narmer by a hieroglyph in front of him. Historians are not sure, however, whether the palette represents an actual military victory or a more general symbol of the king's power.*

the other side of the palette, the same king surveys a mass of headless enemies. It was once thought by scholars that the enemies were fellow Egyptians. However, it has been noted more recently that their hair and beards are curled, unlike those of the Egyptians portrayed on the other palettes of the period; this suggests that the victory celebrated on the palette may have been over outsiders. If so, the unification of Egypt may already have been complete, and on this palette Narmer was exulting in the successful defense of his country.

Narmer is traditionally placed at the head of the 1st Dynasty of Egyptian kings. He and the rest of his dynasty had their capital at Memphis, which was strategically placed between the Delta (Lower Egypt) and the Nile valley (Upper Egypt). According to a list drawn up in about 280 BC by a priest, Manetho, there were 31 dynasties between Narmer's and the establishment of Greek rule over the country in 332 BC. It is not always clear from the list why one dynasty ended and another began. Sometimes "rival" dynasties seem to have existed alongside each other. Manetho's list is incomplete and often confused, but scholars still use it to provide a framework for Egyptian history. Few

dates earlier than about 700 BC are known absolutely, but they can be computed from the king lists coupled with astronomical evidence and inferences drawn from archeology.

Already, at the dawn of Egyptian history, some of the essential characteristics of Egyptian kingship are clear. (The king was not known as the *pharaoh* until much later, in the 19th Dynasty, when the word – which meant literally "great house" or "palace" – was applied to its prime inhabitant.) On Narmer's palette, the king is shown as much bigger than those around him. This artistic convention survived throughout Egyptian history. Once unity had been established, the prestige of the ruler was gradually enhanced by distinguishing and distancing him from his subjects. One way in which this was achieved was by the construction of palaces, which provided a symbolic and physical separation of the kings from the common people. Although these palaces are now long vanished, it is generally assumed that they were surrounded by walls decorated in the Mesopotamian "palace facade" style. The tombs of this early period certainly were ornamented in this way. One of them, the tomb of Queen Neithhotep at Naqada, dating from about 3100 BC, has a block with palace-facade niches superimposed upon the tomb. Kings used a stylized image of a single niche from a palace wall as a frame (known as a *serekh*) within which to have their names written.

*T*HE BATTLEFIELD *palette of about 3100 BC* (LEFT) *shows dead soldiers being devoured by crows, vultures, and a lion, which may all be emblems of the king. The contorted poses of the dead are typical of war scenes, but this example is by far the most grisly. The broken ring in the center of the palette was the cosmetic pan. This palette was almost certainly a votive object offered by a king to celebrate real or symbolic victory.*

*A*N UNKNOWN KING *of the 1st Dynasty* (FAR LEFT), *carved in stone, wears the tall crown of Upper Egypt and ceremonial cloak associated with the 30-year royal jubilee of his reign.*

HORUS & SETH
Gods in Conflict

Geb, the god of the earth, and Nut, goddess of the sky, gave birth to four children, Isis and Osiris, Seth and Nepthys. Isis and Osiris became the first rulers of Egypt. Seth hated Osiris and shut him in a coffin, which he threw in the Nile. Eventually it was found by Isis, who brought the body back to Egypt. Seth, furious at being outwitted, cut Osiris into pieces and threw them into the Nile too. The devotion and healing power of Isis enabled her to gather the pieces and reassemble them. All that was missing was Osiris' penis, which a fish had eaten, but Isis managed to create a new one and breathe new life into Osiris. She conceived a son, Horus, whom she kept hidden in the marshes and protected against all dangers until he was strong enough to overthrow Seth.

In another legend, Seth and Horus were each allotted by Ra half of the world to govern. Horus ruled wisely, Seth unjustly, and a struggle broke out between them. In one encounter Horus lost both eyes, which had to be restored by being bathed in the milk of a gazelle. Hence Horus' eye had special

HORUS and Seth are shown tying up papyrus and lotus, symbolizing reconciliation between them and harmony in the state (Upper and Lower Egypt).

healing powers, and eyes were common shapes for amulets. Eventually Ra intervened to banish Seth. Despite his defeat, the god of chaos remained as a threat ready to bring disorder to Egypt.

Horus, the falcon-god, was the protector of the kings and their power. He was also god of the sky, especially of the eastern horizon, and thus of the sunrise. Though perhaps originating in Hierakonpolis, he had an early temple at Edfu.

The enemy of Horus was another god, Seth, who was probably originally the cult god of a city in rivalry with Hierakonpolis. Seth was presented as a god of mischief and disorder, but from 3000 BC he could be integrated into the king's power as a destructive force to be focused outward at Egypt's enemies. The balance and harmony of opposing forces, shown in the unending battle of Horus and Seth, is a pervasive attribute of Egyptian civilization; it may also explain why the fiction was maintained for so long that Upper and Lower Egypt were two distinct kingdoms, each with its own crown – red for Lower Egypt and white for Upper Egypt. The two crowns could be joined in a single composite form. In the same way, the king was placed under the care of two goddesses, one from each kingdom – Wadjyt, the cobra-goddess of Buto in the Delta, and Nekhbet, the vulture-goddess of Hierakonpolis in the south.

On the open plains of Mesopotamia, where the rivers could change course each year and outsiders from the mountains could easily raid the cities, there was continual struggle between the different communities, and towns were heavily guarded. A successful ruler had to be an effective soldier. Egypt was more stable and the people relished the peace in which to enjoy the fruits of their fields. Their ideal monarch was a king who promised good order and protection against natural and political chaos. It was particularly important for the king to be able to put himself forward as the provider of crops for his people. King Djoser of the 3rd Dynasty described the suffering of his people after a series of low floods: "My heart was in sore distress, for the Nile had not risen for seven years. The grain was not abundant, the seeds were dried up, everything that one had to eat was in pathetic quantities, each person was denied his harvest. Nobody could walk any more: the children were in tears; the young people were struck down; the old people's hearts were sad and their legs were bent when they sat upon the ground, and their hands were hidden away. Even the courtiers were going without, the temples were closed and the sanctuaries were covered in dust. In short, everything in existence was afflicted."

In response, the king prayed to Khnum, the ram-god of Elephantine in southern Egypt, and the god appeared to him in a dream. "I will cause the Nile to rise up for you," he was told. "There will be no more years when the inundation fails to cover any area of land. The flowers will sprout up, their stems bending with the weight of the pollen." Order in the kingdom was restored.

KHEPHREN, fourth king of the 4th Dynasty (LEFT), built the second pyramid at Giza. His temple contained this impressive monolithic statue of the seated king, the back of his head being embraced by Horus in the form of a falcon. Khephren's names, however, included the new epithet "son of Ra", first used by his half-brother and predecessor, Djedefra.

The Protector of the King

THE EARLY Egyptian kings claimed divine support for their authority, and they chose Horus, the god of Hierakonpolis, as their protecting god. Each king took a Horus name as one of his five names, and this proclaimed his ambitions as ruler: "He who Unites the Two Lands" or "Bringer of Harmony". Horus was often portrayed as a falcon perched on a rectangular frame known as a *serekh*. The frame might contain the Horus name of the king, or a palace facade associating Horus with the royal palace. Horus' wings were often shown wrapped protectively around the king's shoulders.

THIS STATUE of King Djoser (ABOVE) was found in a small chapel built against the north face of his step pyramid. Two small "windows" in its facade allowed the dead king to observe, through the eyes of his statue, the offerings laid out before him and the "imperishable" circumpolar stars.

The Immortal Kings

KINGS COULD NOT simply rely on the reappearance of the annual floods – or even their association with the gods – in order to maintain their authority. They had to buy the loyalty of the people, which they did by collecting the surplus crops in the royal granaries and using them to preserve order and to trade for resources from abroad. In addition to providing the luxuries of daily life, more and more of Egypt's wealth was diverted into catering for a fascination with life after death. The furnishing of tombs became steadily more elaborate. Officials were desperate for luxuries that could be buried in their graves to provide for them in their afterlives. It was the king who controlled access to the precious materials that made up grave goods and the craftsmen who fashioned them. The first dynasties saw a dramatic flowering of talent as the kings showered patronage on craftsmen. In doing so, they established styles of art that lasted for generations.

The earliest Egyptian dynasties built grander tombs for the kings themselves. Although they now ruled from Memphis, the bodies of the 1st Dynasty kings were preserved far in the south, at Abydos, the traditional burial place of their line.

They were buried in chambers lined with brick or wood and surrounded by store rooms for grave goods. The later tombs incorporated granite floors. Each tomb was covered by a mound – probably modeled on the mound on which, it was believed, the first act of creation had taken place – and then topped with a flat rectangular superstructure, named in modern times a *mastaba* after a bench of the same shape found outside Egyptian houses. By the 2nd Dynasty most kings were buried in the north in the cemetery, or necropolis, at Saqqara, close to Memphis.

The 3rd Dynasty saw a new phase of Egyptian history: the rulers were now in absolute control of the country and possessed awesome power. Whereas earliest kings emphasized Horus and Seth as the royal gods, now the kings – though not abandoning the earlier gods – were seen as the direct descendants of Ra, the sun-god. Ra, they claimed, would appear in human form to impregnate an earthly mother. This could in theory be any woman, but in practice the king would announce that Ra, disguised as the king himself, had approached the queen and her son was in fact the child of the sun-god. The divinity of the baby was confirmed by Thoth, the messenger of the gods, who had appeared to the queen to tell her of her good fortune. In recognition of this special

🐚 IMHOTEP
Builder and Healer

One of history's first named creative geniuses was Imhotep, courtier and architect of the 3rd Dynasty. It is to him that the building of the Step Pyramid at Saqqara is attributed. By conceiving a massive structure entirely in stone he brought a new dimension to the already ancient tradition of stone-working. Though masons had long made vases from stone and were used to cutting into limestone to carve underground tombs, they had never handled such a vast project, or built so high.

Imhotep's confidence knew no bounds. He envisaged a building 60 meters (197 feet) high, dominating the country like no other building before it, and surrounded it with a complex of courtyards. The columns of the halls are the earliest known fluted stone columns, and the tomb contained the first life-size stone statue of a king.

Imhotep won an enduring reputation that went far beyond his genius as an architect. A thousand years later he was seen to personify wisdom and to be a patron of scribes. He was later known as the son of the craftsman-god, Ptah, and by Greco-Roman times he was worshiped as a local god of Memphis – the only non-royal Egyptian ever deified. Suppliants came for help with daily life and for healing. The Greeks believed him to be the Egyptian equivalent of their own god of healing, Asclepios.

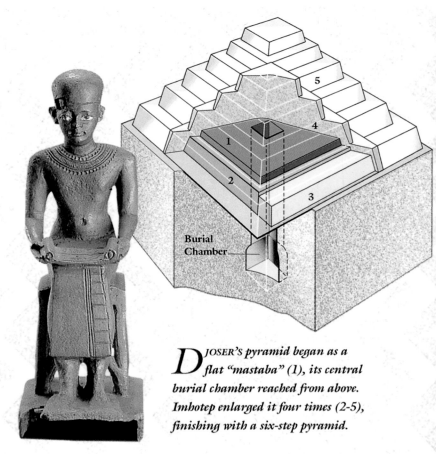

DJOSER'S pyramid began as a flat "mastaba" (1), its central burial chamber reached from above. Imhotep enlarged it four times (2-5), finishing with a six-step pyramid.

A RARE *wooden version of the "false door"* (LEFT) *common to Old Kingdom tombs, which allowed the soul of the deceased to communicate with the living and to receive prayers and offerings. It was important to inscribe all of the person's names and titles on the surface of the door, especially on the tablet at the top, which showed the interior of the dwelling in the afterlife and the deceased sitting at a table piled high with loaves of bread. The owner of this tomb, a royal priest, is sitting with his wife.*

R ELIEF *from King Sahure's 5th-Dynasty temple to the sun at Abusir, outside Memphis, shows the female personification of fertile estates* (BELOW). *Wearing a green dress which represents flourishing plant life, she offers a loaf on a mat. Three "ankh" cords, symbolizing life, are hanging down.*

role, the queen was traditionally known as "the one who unites the two lords".

The ceremony of coronation reflected the new king's ancestry. Coronation was *kha*, the word also used for the appearance of the sun at dawn, and the coronation always took place at the beginning of a new year, July 19 in the Western calendar. Whenever the king left the seclusion of his palace, this too was referred to as *kha*. Every thirty years there was a renewal of his power at the *sed* festival, or jubilee. The local deities from each area were brought to be placed in chapels, and the king was required to run a circuit as if to confirm that he still had the physical stamina to rule effectively. Then he was seated in a pavilion and crowned.

The kings of this period asserted their dominance of the trade routes across the Sinai desert in search of copper, malachite and fine stones, and southward into Nubia. One official boasted of how he brought back 300 donkey loads of luxuries from Nubia – incense, ebony, panther skins and elephant tusks among them. Ships sailed to Lebanon in search of cedar wood. In Memphis the court proliferated, with a mass of officials working under the control of a chief minister, the vizier, who oversaw justice, the royal building works, and the army. Governors were sent out to the provinces (the *nomes* as the Greeks later called them) and regularly moved from post to post so that their primary loyalty remained to the king. As

*R*A, THE SUN-GOD, *travels in his solar bark in this New Kingdom illustration* (ABOVE). *He is shown falcon-headed, in the composite form of Ra-Horakhty, Horus of the Horizon, with the solar disk upon his head. The dead king, as the son of Ra, was permitted to join him on the bark, journeying across the sky every day and returning under the ground each night.*

*M*ENKAURE, *the 4th-Dynasty king buried in the smallest of the three Giza pyramids, is shown* (RIGHT) *wearing the crown of Upper Egypt. He is flanked by the goddess Hathor, bearing her emblem of the solar disk resting between cow's horns, and by a personification of one of the "nomes" or districts of his kingdom, identified by the jackal-god, patron god of the nome. Four similar group statues were found in the pyramid temple.*

written records became essential, the scribes attained a high status, as did the craftsmen who provided the wealth of objects for tombs, furniture, jewelry and pottery. All were in the complete control of the king.

The absolute power of the kings was built on the belief that only they had a right to an afterlife, which could be spent with Ra on the sacred boat (bark) on which he traveled around the Earth. All other people had to endure a shadowy existence in their tombs, unless they could be associated with helping the king achieve his own afterlife. The way to heaven had to be planned with suitable style. The great tomb of King Djoser of the 3rd Dynasty at Saqqara was built entirely in limestone about 2650 BC. No earlier stone monument exists anywhere in the world. Layers of stone were laid over the underground tomb, eventually converting what had begun as a flat-topped *mastaba* into a six-step pyramid, 60 meters (197 feet) high. The idea caught on. At Maidum another stepped pyramid was created, possibly for King Huni. Later its steps were filled in, creating a true pyramid. It was the first king of the 4th Dynasty, Snefru, who planned tombs in the shape of true pyramids from the start, and had two built at Dahshur. The first one, in which he was probably buried, has the nickname "the Bent Pyramid". The angle of its incline was lowered when it began to collapse under its own weight. While a step pyramid may have provided a "stair" by which the king ascended to heaven after his death, the true pyramids probably reflect a change to a solar cult; they may symbolize the sun's rays radiating down. The mortuary temples linked to the pyramids, where the burial rites took place, were often placed on the east side where they would attract the first light of the rising sun.

Old Kingdom Egypt

SNEFRU'S REIGN inaugurated the period known as the Old Kingdom. At first the power of the kings was absolute. Snefru's son Khufu (known often by his Greek name, Cheops) chose a new site for his own pyramid-tomb, a firm limestone plateau at Giza, west of Memphis. Barges could be brought close to the site during the annual flood, allowing limestone and granite blocks to be brought in by water. At this time of year the king's subjects were free from work in the fields and could be pressed into service on the royal tomb.

Khufu's was the largest of the pyramids at Giza. His son Khephren's by its side was slightly smaller and a much smaller one was built for Khephren's son Menkaure. Each pyramid had its own causeway up which the body of the king would be carried to the entrance that led to the tomb chamber deep inside the pyramid. The massive weight of the pyramid bearing down on the roof of the inner chamber was spread by five individual cells within the chamber. Around the

pyramid, space was allocated for the burial of favored courtiers. At the edge of the plateau an outcrop of limestone was fashioned into the Great Sphinx, with the head of Khephren and the body of a lion, the creature believed to guard the gates of the underworld on behalf of the sun-god.

The great complex at Giza remains one of the supreme architectural and logistical achievements of the human race. Yet it also marked a distortion of the harmony which the Egyptians expected to exist between ruler and ruled. Two thousand years later Khufu was remembered as a tyrant, and the Greek historian Herodotus recorded a story that Khufu sent his daughter to work in a brothel to raise money for his building works. Certainly, by Menkaure's reign the kingdom could no longer sustain such massive and costly projects, and by the 5th Dynasty pyramids were no longer entirely built of limestone but had a core of small stones bound together with Nile mud. When later generations removed the limestone coverings, these low-budget pyramids collapsed into piles of rubble.

*O**F THE SEVEN WONDERS** of the ancient world, only the Great Pyramid at Giza* (ABOVE) *remains (with the other, smaller pyramids). The significance of their precise geometry – the largest is 146 meters (508 feet) high, with four equal sides 230 meters (800 feet) long, precisely aligned on the four points of the compass – still excites speculation by enthusiasts. The shape suggests the flaring rays of the sun. There are also associations with the primordial "benben" stone. Man-made mountains, they dominate the horizon, confirming the unity of earth and heaven and the divinity of the king.*

The 5th- and 6th-Dynasty kings built temples to the sun, and in some of their pyramids (much smaller than those at Giza) are found texts – the so-called Pyramid Texts – in which they sought Ra's favor through spells and magic. The Giza pyramids contained no such inscriptions, and the reliance on these texts suggests that the later kings had lost the certainty that they were truly the sons of Ra.

In the years 2400–2100 BC, important shifts of political and economic power occurred. The kings gave grants of land to courtiers, many of whom passed their titles and duties to their sons. The tombs of these hereditary nobles were opulent, exuding the confidence of men who did not fear their superiors. Reflecting – and reinforcing – the dwindling royal glory, the kings gradually lost control of their administrators. In the long reign of Pepy II of the 6th Dynasty, Egypt's frontiers came under threat from Asian raiders, and expeditions for luxuries in Nubia were repulsed. The central authority of the Old Kingdom then collapsed. It remained absent for more than 150 years.

> **"*A staircase to heaven is laid out for the king, so that he may mount up to heaven thereby.*"**
>
> Text inscribed on the pyramid of King Unas at Saqqara

SAQQARA
Royal Staircase to Heaven

Above **The Hall of Pillars was a processional corridor of columns entered through a door at the southeast corner of the Step Pyramid. The fluted pillars are shaped like bundles of reeds.**

Below **The *uraeus*, or cobra, adorned the wall of the offering place associated with a secondary tomb in the great court of the Step Pyramid. The *uraeus* became one of the chief symbols of royalty, frequently shown on the king's headdress to symbolize the power of the king to lash out at Egypt's enemies.**

Saqqara

Saqqara, a few miles from the capital Memphis, became the chief burial place of kings and nobles during the 2nd Dynasty. Its cemeteries and their associated temples remained in use for over two and a half millennia, to the Greco-Roman period. A Coptic monastery (abandoned during the tenth century AD and now ruined) was also built. It is one of Egypt's richest and most important sites.

Dominating the site is Djoser's Step Pyramid, the world's first large stone building and the first pyramid. It is placed within a complex of ritual buildings and surrounded by a wall some 1,600 meters long – almost one mile. These buildings provided the king with a suitable palace for the afterlife – in spite of the fact that many of the constructions were only dummies, their facades attached to structures of solid stone. The architecture, with its decorated and recessed walls and fluted columns, provided models that were to be repeated by later architects over many centuries. Also from the Old Kingdom are some 15 royal pyramids and many associated tombs of nobles, which contain their own wealth of vivid sculpture, painting and texts.

Fine tombs were built again in the New Kingdom, when Memphis was the royal residence – especially during the later 18th and 19th Dynasties. These included a tomb for General Haremhab which was completed before he became king.

Under the Ptolemies, Saqqara flourished as the center of the cult of the god Serapis – a synthesis of Egyptian and Greek gods. It was also the home of the sacred Apis bulls, which were kept in temples as embodiments of Serapis and mummified on death. Sarcophagi of 24 such bulls have been found. A special temple for the bulls was discovered at the end of an avenue of buried sphinxes. Other cults yielded thousands of mummified ibises, falcons, cows and baboons.

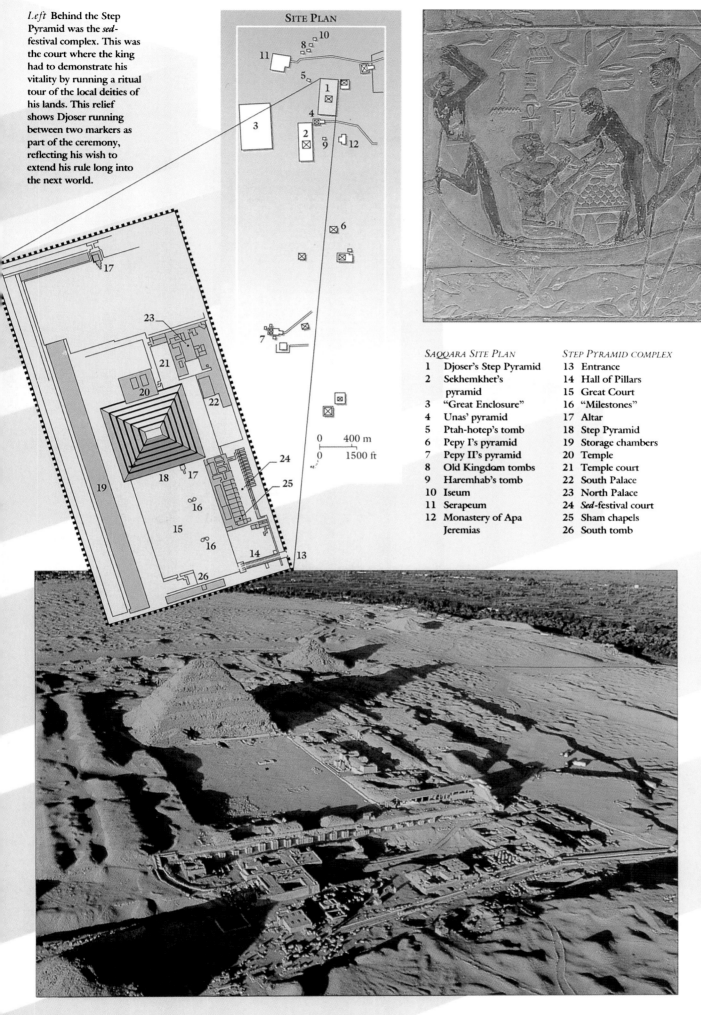

Left Behind the Step Pyramid was the *sed*-festival complex. This was the court where the king had to demonstrate his vitality by running a ritual tour of the local deities of his lands. This relief shows Djoser running between two markers as part of the ceremony, reflecting his wish to extend his rule long into the next world.

SITE PLAN

Above The 5th-Dynasty vizier Ptah-hotep was buried in a *mastaba* (flat-topped tomb) richly decorated inside with scenes of Old Kingdom life. This lively relief shows men on boats returning from a fowling expedition; the seated figure is thought to be a portrait of the overseer of sculptors who was responsible for the carving of the reliefs.

| 0 | 400 m |
| 0 | 1500 ft |

SAQQARA SITE PLAN
1. Djoser's Step Pyramid
2. Sekhemkhet's pyramid
3. "Great Enclosure"
4. Unas' pyramid
5. Ptah-hotep's tomb
6. Pepy I's pyramid
7. Pepy II's pyramid
8. Old Kingdom tombs
9. Haremhab's tomb
10. Iseum
11. Serapeum
12. Monastery of Apa Jeremias

STEP PYRAMID COMPLEX
13. Entrance
14. Hall of Pillars
15. Great Court
16. "Milestones"
17. Altar
18. Step Pyramid
19. Storage chambers
20. Temple
21. Temple court
22. South Palace
23. North Palace
24. *Sed*-festival court
25. Sham chapels
26. South tomb

Left The Step Pyramid and its enclosure as they appear today. In the fore-ground is the causeway leading to the pyramid of the 5th-Dynasty king Unas, bottom left. The causeway, which linked the pyramid's mortuary temple with the valley temple (now lost), was built over several earlier tombs not of royalty. These therefore escaped the attentions of later grave robbers and provided important finds to modern archeologists.

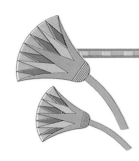

THE MIDDLE KINGDOM
Egypt's Classical Age

W hen central rule collapsed in the First Intermediate Period, social and political structures broke down. Nobles or provincial ruling families carved out territories and maintained order within them as best they could. None of them, however, was able to recreate the vigor of a united kingdom. Trade with Asia ceased, nomadic tribes raided the Delta, irrigation channels were not maintained. Folk memories of the breakdown of order were constantly recalled in the years to come, and recorded in the literature of the period. One man, called Khakheperre-Sonb, lamented how the land was broken up, no one provided for the gods and there was chaos in the council halls. Another, Ipuwer, bemoaned the collapse of social order. Noblewomen were reduced to wearing rags while slave girls were loaded with jewels. Servants were rude to their mistresses and resentful when given orders. Tombs were robbed and documents containing the laws and records of land ownership torn up by beggars.

These "lamentations" probably exaggerated what really happened, a result of the characteristic Egyptian fear of disorder. Some relatively stable states were maintained during this period. The most successful was centered on the city of Herakleopolis and lasted for about a hundred years (c.2134–2040 BC). Herakleopolis was conveniently situated between the Nile and the Faiyum, a rich agricultural area, and was far enough south to be safe from raiders from east or west. The Herakleopolitan rulers had influence as far south as Nubia, and their prestige was enough for two of their dynasties – the 9th and the 10th –

N EKHBET, the vulture-goddess (ABOVE), heraldic emblem of Upper Egypt, clasps in her talons the "shen" sign, a hieroglyphic symbol for eternity and protection. This is a detail of a gold pectoral inlaid with carnelian, lapis lazuli and turquoise, which was found in the Dahshur tomb of Queen Mereret, the daughter or wife of Senwosret III .

TIMETABLE

2134–2040	**1st Intermediate Period**
2134–2040	9-10TH DYNASTIES
	(Herakleopolitan)
2134–2040	11TH DYNASTY (Theban)
2040–1640	**Middle Kingdom**
2040–1991	11TH DYNASTY
	(all-Egypt)
2061–2010	Reign of Mentuhotpe II
1991–1783	12TH DYNASTY
1991–1962	Reign of Amenemhet I
1971–1926	Reign of Senwosret I
1878–1841	Reign of Senwosret III
1844–1797	Reign of Amenemhet III
1783–1640	13TH DYNASTY
1640–1532	**2nd Intermediate Period**
	(14–17TH DYNASTIES)

to be recognized by the chronicler Manetho in the third century BC. Several of their kings asserted their legitimacy by adopting the names of Old Kingdom rulers and an array of traditional titles – Chief of Foreign Regions, for instance – which bore no relation to their actual power. The greatest of the Herakleopolitan kings, Khety II (c. 2050 BC), regained control of the Delta and was able to boast that he had replaced the rule of ten men with the rule of one.

IT WAS FROM THE SOUTH that a challenge came to the Herakleopolitan line. In Thebes, a town far up

The Supremacy of Thebes

the Nile which had enjoyed some modest importance as a staging post for trade with Nubia, a stable dynasty of rulers (the 11th according to the traditional listing) emerged. Thebes and Herakleopolis found themselves in increasing conflict. In about 2040 BC, a famine allowed a Theban king, Mentuhotpe, the second of that name in the dynasty, to break into the north and subdue the Herakleopolitans. Mentuhotpe's first Horus name had been "Divine is the White Crown (of Upper Egypt)". Buoyed up by his success, he was able to take a new one: "He who Unites the Two Lands". This reunification was the beginning of the Middle Kingdom, a 400-year period of peace and prosperity which saw Egyptian civilization reach its height.

Mentuhotpe was a shrewd ruler. He reduced Herakleopolis to the status of an ordinary administrative district but allowed many local

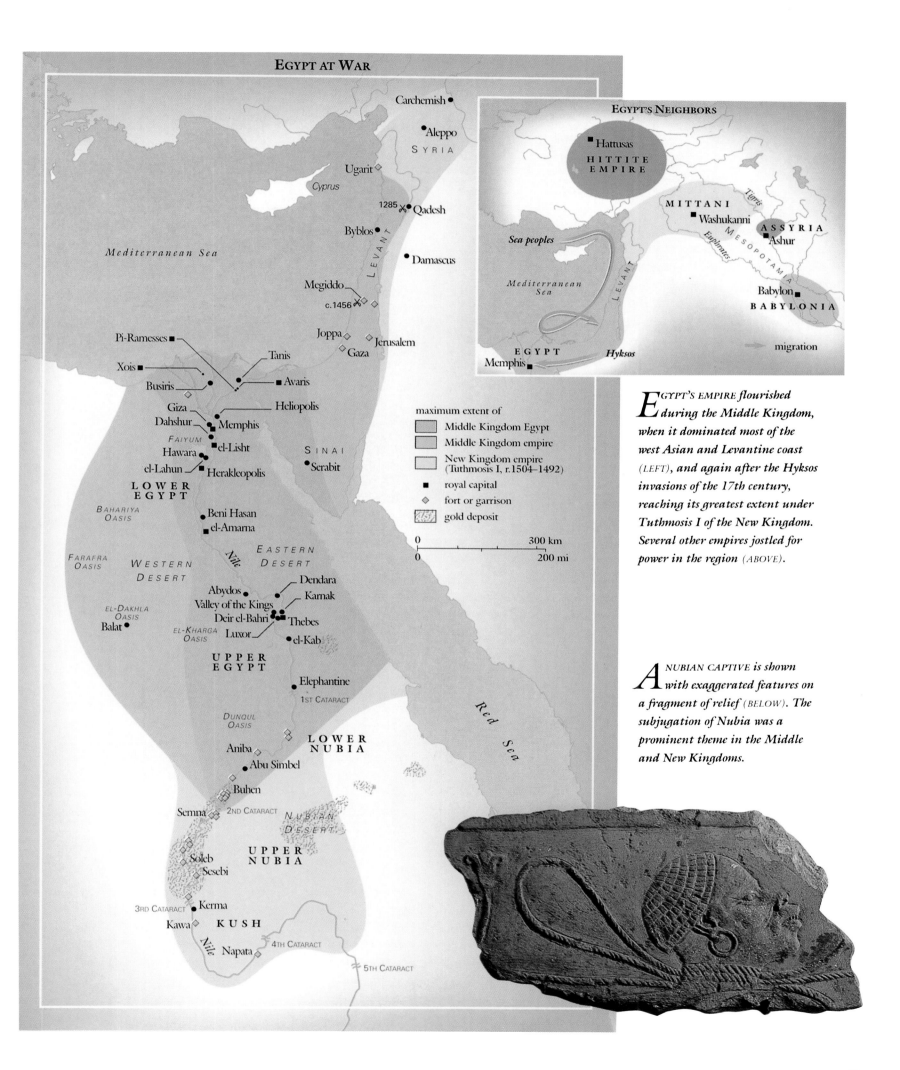

EGYPT AT WAR

Carchemish

Aleppo

SYRIA

Ugarit

Cyprus

1285 ⚔ Qadesh

Byblos

Mediterranean Sea

LEVANT

Damascus

Megiddo

c.1456 ⚔

Joppa

Pi-Ramesses

Gaza

Jerusalem

Tanis

Xois

Avaris

Busiris

Heliopolis

Giza

Dahshur

Memphis

FAIYUM

Hawara

el-Lisht

SINAI

el-Lahun

Herakleopolis

Serabit

LOWER
EGYPT

BAHARIYA
OASIS

Beni Hasan

el-Amarna

FARAFRA
OASIS

WESTERN
DESERT

EASTERN
DESERT

Nile

EL-DAKHLA
OASIS

Abydos

Dendara

Valley of the Kings

Karnak

Deir el-Bahri

Thebes

Balat

EL-KHARGA
OASIS

Luxor

el-Kab

UPPER
EGYPT

Elephantine

1ST CATARACT

DUNQUL
OASIS

Red Sea

LOWER
NUBIA

Aniba

Abu Simbel

Buhen

Semna

2ND CATARACT

NUBIAN
DESERT

Soleb

UPPER
NUBIA

Sesebi

3RD CATARACT

Kerma

KUSH

Kawa

Nile

Napata

4TH CATARACT

5TH CATARACT

maximum extent of

Middle Kingdom Egypt

Middle Kingdom empire

New Kingdom empire
(Tuthmosis I, r.1504–1492)

■ royal capital

◇ fort or garrison

▨ gold deposit

0   300 km

0   200 mi

EGYPT'S NEIGHBORS

Hattusas

HITTITE
EMPIRE

MITTANI

Washukanni

ASSYRIA

Ashur

Tigris

MESOPOTAMIA

Euphrates

Sea peoples

Mediterranean
Sea

LEVANT

Babylon

BABYLONIA

EGYPT

Memphis

Hyksos

→ migration

*E*GYPT'S EMPIRE *flourished
during the Middle Kingdom,
when it dominated most of the
west Asian and Levantine coast
(LEFT), and again after the Hyksos
invasions of the 17th century,
reaching its greatest extent under
Tuthmosis I of the New Kingdom.
Several other empires jostled for
power in the region (ABOVE).*

A NUBIAN CAPTIVE *is shown
with exaggerated features on
a fragment of relief (BELOW). The
subjugation of Nubia was a
prominent theme in the Middle
and New Kingdoms.*

rulers to remain in power. He and his successors concentrated their energies on reopening the trade routes and restoring order to the Delta. To protect the kingdom against intruders from Asia, his son, Mentuhotpe III (r.2010–1998 BC), built a great wall across the desert which remained intact throughout the Middle Kingdom. Mentuhotpe II maintained Thebes as his capital city and designed a great tomb for himself at Deir el-Bahri in the cliffs above the west bank of the Nile nearby. With its causeway leading from a temple in the valley upward to a mortuary temple, it echoed the traditional burial places of the kings of the Old Kingdom. Mentuhotpe II himself was buried in this magnificent temple complex together with six of his queens and royal concubines.

The 11th Dynasty survived until the 1990s BC, when it was overthrown in a coup instigated by Amenemhet, who was probably the king's vizier. Amenemhet was the first king of a new Dynasty, the 12th (1991–1783 BC), which was to prove one of the most powerful in Egyptian history. A new capital was founded near to but separate from Memphis to serve as the center of administration. Known usually as Itjtawy, it has never been found. Its full name could be translated as "It is Amenemhet who has Conquered the Two Lands". Amenemhet then set about building himself a pyramid at el-Lisht, modeling it on the later, smaller, pyramids of the Old Kingdom. It was crucial for him to establish himself as a legitimate ruler. To do so, he composed a series of

prophecies which he claimed had come down from the Old Kingdom. In these, Neferti, a wise man, warned King Snefru that a time of disorder would come but that a ruler named Amenemhet, a southerner of non-royal birth, would restore order after the chaos. "Rejoice, O People of his time," proclaimed the prophecy, "The son of man will make his name for all eternity! The evil-minded, the treason plotters, they suppress their speech in fear of him; Asiatics will fall to his sword, Libyans will fall to his flame!" Knowing that the most dangerous moment for his dynasty would be

*M*ENTUHOTPE II *(ABOVE) reunited Egypt in the Middle Kingdom. He wears the red crown of Lower Egypt. His skin, beard and crossed arms identify him with the god Osiris.*

*F*ORMULAE FOR OFFERINGS *were inscribed on stelae (votive slabs), such as this one (LEFT) addressed to Osiris and other gods of Abydos, and put in temples or tombs. The cult of Osiris became popular in the Middle Kingdom.*

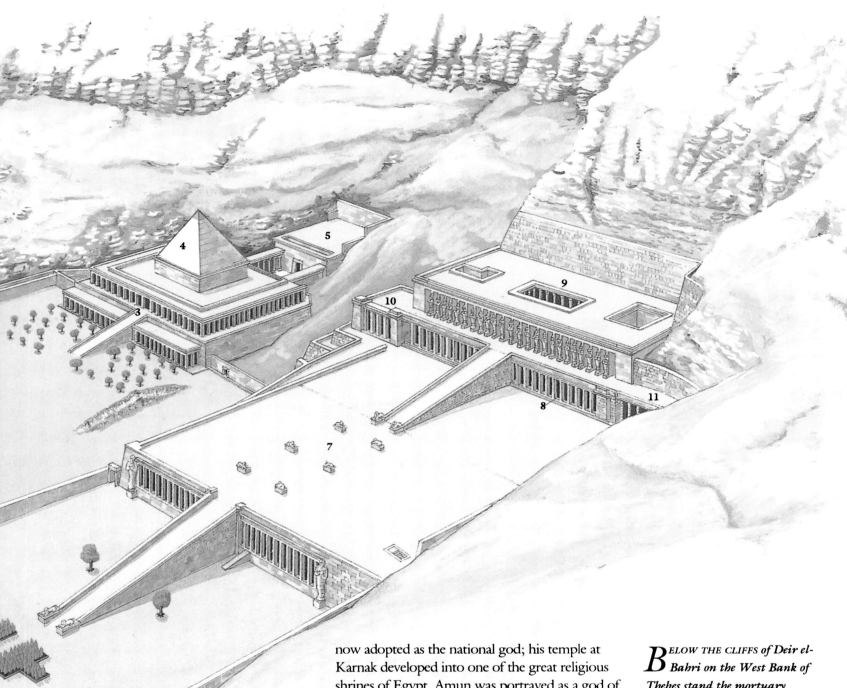

now adopted as the national god; his temple at Karnak developed into one of the great religious shrines of Egypt. Amun was portrayed as a god of creation and was then linked to Ra so that a divine spirit – Amun-Ra – represented a creation force which was both visible in the sun and invisible at the same time. Other gods associated with specific shrines received the special favor of the kings: Ptah, the god of craftsmen at Memphis; the goddess Hathor at Dendara; Ra-Atum at Heliopolis; and Osiris at Abydos. In the Faiyum, where the crocodile-god Sobek was worshiped as a god of water and vegetation, he too became associated with the kings of the 12th Dynasty when they carried out a major program of irrigation in the region. These 12th-Dynasty shrines reached across Egypt, from Dendara and Abydos in the south to Heliopolis in the north, and allowed the provinces to feel that the kings were integrated into the religious life of the kingdom rather than presiding over it as the sole representative of a creator god.

at his own death, Amenemhet made his son Senwosret co-regent, a custom followed by his successors. Even though Amenemhet was assassinated, probably by disgruntled courtiers, Senwosret succeeded without difficulty.

The kings of the 12th Dynasty knew they needed divine support, but their relationship with the gods was no longer solely focused on Ra. The most important god of Thebes was Amun, god of the air. Although little regarded previously, he was

*B*ELOW THE CLIFFS *of Deir el-Bahri on the West Bank of Thebes stand the mortuary temples (ABOVE) of Mentuhotpe (background) and Hatshepsut (foreground). The colonnades and terraced porticoes were important architectural innovations of their time but were not copied by any of their successors.*

TEMPLE OF MENTUHOTPE
1 Forecourt
2 Entrance to earlier royal tombs
3 Terrace
4 Pyramid (conjectural)
5 Tomb

TEMPLE OF HATSHEPSUT
6 Forecourt
7 Terrace
8 Colonnade
9 Sanctuary
10 Shrine of Hathor
11 Shrine of Anubis

OSIRIS
Lord of the Underworld

In Egyptian mythology Osiris was one of the children of Geb, the earth-god, and Nut, the sky-goddess. He became entangled in a legendary struggle against his evil brother Seth. In these struggles he died, but the healing power of his sister-wife Isis always revived him. In other legends Osiris was associated with corn, which each year is buried, rests in the dark and then germinates and flourishes. Death and resurrection thus became inextricably linked. During the Middle Kingdom Osiris became the god of the underworld, shown as a mummy with his hands coming through the wrappings to hold his insignia, the shepherd's crook and flail. He wore a tall white crown with two plumes on either side,

sometimes with the horns of a ram. His skin was shown alternately in green for resurrection, white for the mummy, or black for the fertile soil of the Nile. Embalmers followed the ideal of the mummified form of Osiris, but the deceased could only enter the underworld if he passed the judgment of 42 gods to whom he swore he had behaved properly in life. As a judge of souls, Osiris also had a stern and forbidding aspect, reflecting the Egyptians' ambivalent attitudes to the underworld; he was capable of malevolence. For this reason, the deceased often asked for the additional protection of Ra (the sun-god) so that he could travel to the underworld in the light rather than in darkness. Osiris thus took on

*M*A'AT *(truth) (ABOVE) personified justice and divine order. She was present at Osiris' judgment of the dead when the person's heart was weighed.*

yet another aspect by association: the "night sun", sometimes associated with the moon.

At first, only kings were identified with Osiris, but the afterlife became "democratized" in the First Intermediate Period (2181–2055 BC). From then it was believed that anyone could be resurrected as Osiris, provided that the person was worthy and the correct rituals were followed.

By the Middle Kingdom Osiris had become a major god and many parts of Egypt honored him as their local deity. Myths were developed to allow each city a reason to maintain his cult. The legend that his body had been cut into pieces by Seth and thrown into the Nile enabled many cities to claim part of him. Busiris

THE KINGS of the Middle Kingdom also portrayed themselves as upholders of *ma'at*, harmony

Right Living & Justice

achieved through right living and the provision of justice. *Ma'at* was personified as a goddess, the daughter of the sun-god Ra, who stood at the back of the sacred bark in which Ra crossed the skies. To underline this role a spirit of tolerance and concern was incorporated in stories written under the auspices of the kings. In the Middle Kingdom this literature was of such quality that it was taken as the model of perfection by later generations.

Perhaps the most celebrated of the stories of the Middle Kingdom is that of Sinuhe. Sinuhe was an official who had been sent abroad as a member of a punitive mission against Egypt's enemies in the Libyan desert. While there he overheard the news of Amenemhet's assassination and, for a reason not made clear in the text, took fright and fled across the Delta into Asia. Here he built a successful career keeping order for local rulers. But as he grew old and his strength began to fade, he yearned for home. The king of Egypt heard of his plight and wrote to welcome him back. "Come back to Egypt! See the residence in which you lived. Kiss the ground at the great portals, mingle with the courtiers! For today you have begun to age. You have lost a man's strength. Think of the day of burial, the passing into reveredness." Sinuhe went back, still in fear of royal displeasure. He arrived at Itjtawy and early the next morning ten attendants arrived to escort him to the king's palace. He told how he bowed his head to the ground between statues of sphinxes guarding the palace and was then greeted by the royal children. Led into the audience chamber, he found the king sitting on a great throne enclosed within a canopy of gold. Sinuhe lay flat on his face, trembling before such majesty. But the king reassured him and said how important it was that he prepare for his burial. Then he called in the royal princesses who could not believe it was Sinuhe who had returned. They sang a hymn of praise to the king as protector. "A face that sees you shall not pale, eyes that see you shall not fear!" The king announced Sinuhe would be restored as a courtier and the princesses led him off to be fitted for his robes and anointed with the choice perfumes of the king. Then a tomb was prepared for him, complete with fittings, grave goods and priests. The moral of the story is that the king is a model of forgiveness.

*O*SIRIS *sits in judgment under a canopy* (ABOVE). *The dead man, Hunefer, is presented while his heart is weighed against the feather of Ma'at for purity.*

claimed his backbone, Elephantine his leg. His head was "fought over" by Memphis and Abydos. A thousand-year-old tomb of a 1st-Dynasty king at Abydos was rebuilt as the god's tomb, and there were annual rituals at the shrine in which the role of Osiris as fertility god was reenacted. Nineteenth-century excavators found a statue of Osiris lying intact on a funerary bed. Tombs often contained a model boat to take the deceased on posthumous pilgrimages to Abydos.

A DETAIL OF *the sarcophagus of Chancellor Nakhti shows hieroglyphs of spells to ensure his safety in the underworld. In the Middle Kingdom, Coffin Texts replaced the Pyramid Texts of the Old Kingdom, to which only the king had been entitled.*

A LIFE-SIZED *acacia wood statue of Chancellor Nakhti* (ABOVE) *was put in his tomb. The nobles of the Middle Kingdom gradually eroded the elitist view of the afterlife as reserved for kings.*

Another story, that of the Eloquent Peasant, showed that justice was available for all. This story may have originated a little earlier, but all the copies that survive are from the Middle Kingdom and it must have been popular then. A peasant loaded his donkey with goods to exchange for barley. While he made his way to market, a greedy landowner who was eager to get hold of the donkey and the goods laid a cloth across his path, forcing the donkey into a barley field where he took a wisp of barley. The landowner then triumphantly confiscated the donkey. The peasant was forced to go to court, where the local judge asked the king what was to be done. The king ordered that the peasant and his wife be secretly provisioned with bread and beer while the trial went on, but then required the peasant to plead his own case. The peasant had to make no less than nine petitions to the judge. These were relayed one by one to the king who delighted in the eloquence of the peasant. Finally, when the peasant was exhausted, the king ordered the judge to provide

him with justice in the shape of the landowner's goods. This story was concerned with stressing the importance of fine rhetoric but it also suggested that the king was prepared to listen to the pleas of even the most humble of his subjects. This was the image the kings liked to portray: humanity and attention to justice. When Senwosret III, perhaps the most powerful of the 12th-Dynasty kings, succeeded he was greeted with a traditional hymn that praised him for his role of protector: "How great is the lord of his city: he is a canal that restrains the river's flood water, a cool room that lets man sleep until dawn, a fort that shields the timid from his foe, an overflowing shade cool in summertime, a warm corner dry in wintertime."

Public order depended on efficient administration. Officials were expected to be versatile, at one moment commanding an army, the next organizing an expedition across the desert in search of stone, then returning to supervise local justice. Supervision of the state's resources was meticulous. The carpenters in the royal boatyard

FORTY NUBIAN ARCHERS (BELOW) from the tomb of a prince, Mehesti, are individually represented in carved wood. Soldiers besieging fortresses became a frequent theme in tomb decoration during the First Intermediate Period and the Middle Kingdom, when Lower Nubia became part of Egypt's empire. During periods of disorder the independent chiefs of the provinces (nomes) trained their young men as soldiers and recruited auxiliaries such as these archers from abroad.

THE NUBIAN FORTS

Securing the Frontier

IN THE REIGN of Senwosret III (r.1878–1841 BC) the dynasty achieved its greatest influence.

The Power of the King Extends

Through measures that have not been recorded, Senwosret destroyed the power of the local nobles. The building of provincial tombs stopped abruptly as the direct allegiance of officials to the king was restored. Senwosret also enforced even firmer control over Egypt's trade routes. Far up the Nile at the Second Cataract, a series of forts were built and provisioned so that Egypt's control of Nubia's gold was absolute. Routes down to the Red Sea and across to the mysterious land of Punt (probably on the coast of modern Somalia) were developed so that incense and other exotic produce could be brought back to the royal court. An important trading partner was Byblos on the coast of Lebanon, from where resin (which was used in embalming) and cedar wood were shipped to Egypt. The relationship was so close that local rulers in Byblos adopted Egyptian titles and used hieroglyphs. A cache of treasure found at Tod in Upper Egypt with gold and silver vessels and fine cylinder seals may well have been tribute from a Syrian prince, suggesting contacts deep in Asia. There is also evidence of Asian craftsmen coming into Egypt to share their specialist skills. Craftsmanship now reached new heights of excellence. Finest of all the crafts of this period is the jewelry, much of it found in the tombs of the royal princesses which were created alongside the pyramids of the kings.

The pyramids built by the 12th- and 13th-Dynasty kings

*I*t was from Nubia that the Egyptian kings drew their gold, some of their copper and precious stones such as amethysts. Trade routes brought in exotic goods from the south: leopard skins, giraffe tails and ostrich feathers. Control over these routes was a priority. Senwosret III established Egyptian rule to the Second Cataract, 400 kilometers(248 miles) south of the old boundaries. "I have made my boundary," Senwosret III proudly proclaimed, "I have increased what was bequeathed to me." To control the new holdings, he built forts along the Cataract where the river was only some 400 meters (1,300 feet) wide – easy to

*B*ASTION TOWERS *at Buhen (ABOVE), now under Lake Nasser.*

guard. They were set on rocky outcrops and fitted to the landscape. At Semna a large fort with turreted walls overlooked the river. It had a high command post for spotting any intruders making their way up the Nile. The size of its granaries suggests it might have housed up to 300 men. Across the river a smaller fort was placed on a steep rocky base, and 1,500 meters (5,000 feet) to the south was a fortified observation post. Desert patrols reported the movements of hostile tribes. Nothing was left to chance.

recorded the movement of planks and goat skins. Officials too were expected to act within the spirit of *ma'at*. The so-called Wisdom Literature set out the ideal of the judge. An admonition to officials read, "Do not bring down the men of the magistrates' court or incite the just man to rebel. Do not pay too much attention to him clad in shining garments and have too little regard for him who is shabbily dressed. Do not accept the reward of the powerful man or persecute the weak on his behalf." Everyone had the right to present a case to the vizier, whose title was "priest of *ma'at*". An audience with the vizier, however, was not likely to be granted to applicants of humble status.

*T*HE GRAVE EXPRESSION of *Senwosret III is captured in a red granite head (LEFT). In the Middle Kingdom the serenity of royal portraits gave way to a complex representation reflecting the responsibilities of government and the king's conscientious execution of his duty.*

were highly traditional, although no pyramid of the Middle Kingdom approached the grandeur of those at Giza. They were, however, better protected than earlier designs, with hidden underground shafts leading to the inner tomb, though even these did not save the bodies of the kings from later tomb robbers. On the other hand they were less well built, with a limestone casing over a rubble core, and today they are mostly in a poor state of preservation.

EVEN BEFORE the end of the 12th Dynasty the vigor of the kings was slackening, and in the 13th

Outsiders Move In

it grew weaker yet. Some 70 kings are known in a period of only 140 years (1783–1640 BC). Why there were so many in such a short period is not known, but the administration of the kingdom had reached such levels of efficiency that it seems to have continued to work for a hundred years, regardless of the strength of the ruler. But once another Dynasty, the 14th (which produced 76 named kings), set itself at Xois in the Delta, the kingdom succumbed to the intrusions of outsiders.

Asians had entered Egypt in some numbers during the 12th Dynasty but they had always remained under strict royal control. Now the numbers settling in the eastern Delta increased. The intruders were known to the Egyptians as the Hyksos, "chiefs of foreign lands". The Hyksos were probably a nomadic people pushed into Egypt by population movements in western Asia itself. By 1730 BC they had taken over the city of

A MINIATURE CARVING in ivory (ABOVE) of a sphinx seizing a captive symbolizes, even on this small scale, the archetypal view of the king as the invincible protector of Egypt. The claws are long and sharp, and the sphinx is smiling faintly. The head was once thought to be a portrait of one of the Hyksos kings.

Avaris in the eastern Delta, and then they infiltrated south along the edge of the Delta. By about 1675 BC they had reached Memphis and they appear to have established contact with Nubia. Once the last kings of the 13th Dynasty retreated to Thebes, the Hyksos were able to isolate them. The Dynasty vanished about 1630 BC, and the Hyksos rulers dominated the country, though they never succeeded in unifying it.

Later kings of Egypt, motivated by nationalism, portrayed the Hyksos as barbarians – "invaders of obscure race who burned our cities ruthlessly, razed to the ground the temples of the gods and treated all the natives with cruel hostility", as one account put it. The evidence suggests that the Hyksos actually opened Egypt to a world outside which in some ways was more sophisticated. With them came more advanced methods of warfare, the harnessed horse and the chariot – methods which later Egyptian kings gratefully adopted to spearhead their own conquests. The Hyksos introduced to Egypt the vertical loom, the lyre and the lute, and the apple and the olive. At the same time they were sensitive to Egyptian culture and exercised their rule within Egyptian conventions. They worshiped Ra and even adopted Seth (who may have had similar attributes to one of their native gods) as their patron god; their kings took traditional Egyptian titles and wrote their names in hieroglyphs. Their buildings and sculpture drew on the styles of the Middle Kingdom. They promulgated the great works of Egyptian literature and used Egyptians as administrators. Manetho was able to integrate the Hyksos kings into his list as the 15th Dynasty.

NOT NATIVE to Egypt, horses (RIGHT) were introduced into Egypt from western Asia in the Second Intermediate Period (1640–1532 BC). As status symbols, they were not used for farming but reserved for hunting, battle and ceremonial occasions; they usually pulled chariots instead of being ridden. This pair of horses on a relief block from the 18th-Dynasty capital of el-Amarna may have been part of a royal chariot procession.

Nevertheless, the Hyksos never lost the stigma of being outsiders. In Thebes a new Dynasty, the 17th, had already emerged by 1640 BC. At first it seems to have coexisted peacefully with the Hyksos rulers to the north, and there may have been marriage links between the ruling families. One of the most famous surviving papyri, the Rhind Mathematical Papyrus, was a Hyksos copy of a Theban original, which suggests some cultural interaction. However, the relationship started to break down. There is a story that during one dispute the Hyksos king Apophis complained that

AMENEMHET III, the son of Senwosret III, reigned for 45 years. In this bronze (ABOVE), typical of the Middle Kingdom, he wears a plain headdress (the "khat", similar to the "nemes") of striped cloth pulled away from the forehead and tied with two side flaps hanging down. The "khat" and the prominent ears suggest a sphinx.

he was being kept awake at night by the noise made by hippopotami at Thebes – all of 1,200 kilometers (744 miles) away! Armed conflict broke out between the two dynasties. The skull of one of the Theban rulers has been found to have been smashed with an ax of an Asiatic type. The prolonged struggle involved at least two Theban kings, and the Hyksos no longer had military superiority. In about 1532 BC, they were finally driven from the Delta back into Asia by Ahmose, the founding king of the new Theban 18th Dynasty. Egypt was once again united.

> **"A** *great number of ornaments of gold were at (the king's) neck; his head covering was of gold.***"**
>
> From the confession of a tomb robber, recorded on papyrus in 1116 BC

The Craft of the Jeweler

Jewelry was worn by all social classes in ancient Egypt, and on almost every visible part of the body except the nose. It was not only an indicator of rank, a part of the funerary equipment of the dead, or a charm to protect the living. It also added color to the plain white linen Egyptians wore.

Gold was the material of choice, and was worked to a sophisticated standard by 3000 BC. It took only another few hundred years to develop a full range of techniques. Semi-precious stones such as amethyst, quartz, crystal, onyx,

Below **Sit-Hathor, the daughter of Senwosret III, owned this gold cloisonné pendant. Cloisonné – inlay work – was the Egyptians' specialty. The falcon Horus wears the double crown, flanked by the sun-disk, encircled by a *uraeus* holding an *ankh*.**

Below **A diadem for the princess Sit-Hathor-Yunet is made of a broad band of sheet gold with 15 cloisonné rosettes, based on the design of a flowering rush. It is inlaid with lapis lazuli, carnelian and green faience, and adorned with a *uraeus*, gold streamers and plumes. It was worn with tubular gold wig ornaments, threaded at intervals onto the hair.**

carnelian and jasper were used for color and for their magic properties. Green and blue were the most favored colors; the words for lapis lazuli and turquoise were the same as "joy" and "'delight". Surprisingly, the social status of jewelers was low. They labored with smiths in dirty, hot conditions, passing on their works of art to supervisors who took the credit. In the 12th-Dynasty *Satire on Trades* the scribe Khety complained, "They stink more than fish roe." In tomb scenes, smiths are always dwarfs – a tradition echoed in classical and Western mythology.

The most exquisite examples of the Egyptian jeweler's craft have been preserved in the tombs of five princesses from the Middle Kingdom. By the New Kingdom, some of the delicacy of the design had been lost, and widespread grave-robbing meant that mummies were adorned with faience (glazed ceramic) and glass instead of precious stones. Even the spectacular jewelry found with Tutankhamun has been described by archeologists as costume jewelry compared with the superb workmanship found in tombs of the Middle Kingdom.

Right **The mummy of a New Kingdom noble-woman wears a painted and gilded mask with calcite ear-studs, a broad collar, bracelets and armlets decorated with *udjat* eyes, a pectoral and real finger rings. Dozens of pieces of jewelry were wrapped within the layers of the mummy itself. Some pieces were made specially for the mummy, while others were taken from those worn by the owner in her or his everyday life.**

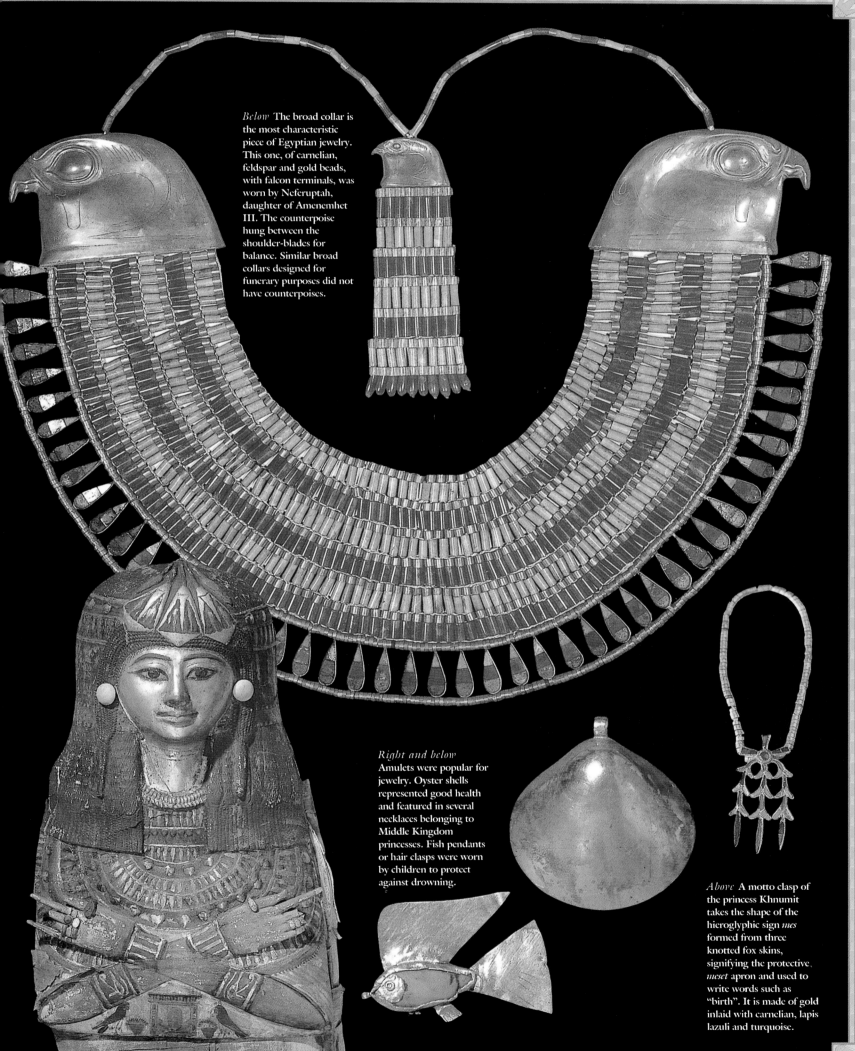

Below The broad collar is the most characteristic piece of Egyptian jewelry. This one, of carnelian, feldspar and gold beads, with falcon terminals, was worn by Neferuptah, daughter of Amenemhet III. The counterpoise hung between the shoulder-blades for balance. Similar broad collars designed for funerary purposes did not have counterpoises.

Right and below Amulets were popular for jewelry. Oyster shells represented good health and featured in several necklaces belonging to Middle Kingdom princesses. Fish pendants or hair clasps were worn by children to protect against drowning.

Above A motto clasp of the princess Khnumit takes the shape of the hieroglyphic sign *mes* formed from three knotted fox skins, signifying the protective *meset* apron and used to write words such as "birth". It is made of gold inlaid with carnelian, lapis lazuli and turquoise.

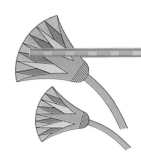
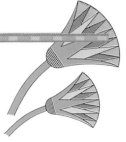

THE NEW KINGDOM
Egypt's Imperial Age

"When His Majesty had slain the nomads of Asia, he sailed south to Khent-hen-nefer to destroy the Nubian bowmen. His Majesty made a great slaughter among them and I brought spoil from there : two living men and three hands. [The hands of dead enemies were cut off as trophies.] Then I was rewarded with gold once again, and two female slaves were given to me. His Majesty journeyed north, his heart rejoicing in valor and victory. He had conquered both northerners and southerners."

So were the exploits of one of the generals of Ahmose I, founding king of the 18th Dynasty, recorded on the walls of his tomb. With Egypt secure against outside attack once more, a new era began in 1532 BC, known as the New Kingdom. The new rulers adopted the traditional stance of their predecessors, offering themselves as semi-divine protectors of their people and upholders of harmony, but they went about their task in a fundamentally new way. Earlier kings had been content to defend the boundaries of Egypt against attack, by building walls across the desert to the east, and forts in Nubia. The kings of the New Kingdom, haunted by the intrusion of the Hyksos, believed that only expansion deep into Asia and Nubia could pre-empt future invasion and bring real security. They asserted Egyptian power as far south as the Fourth Cataract, with a frontier post at Napata under the shadow of the mountain

A DECORATIVE PANEL from a royal footstool (ABOVE) shows Egypt's conquered northern and southern enemies placed under the yoke (and the feet) of the king. In the center is the symbol for the "Union of the Two Countries".

TIMETABLE

1532–1070	**New Kingdom Egypt**
1532–1307	**18TH DYNASTY**
1532–1525	**Reign of Ahmose I**
1504–1492	**Reign of Tuthmosis I**
1473–1458	**Reign of Hatshepsut**
1479–1425	**Reign of Tuthmosis III**
1391–1353	**Reign of Amenophis III**
1353–1335	**Reign of Amenophis IV**
	(Akhenaten)
1333–1323	**Reign of Tutankhamun**
1319–1307	**Reign of Haremhab**
1307–1196	**19TH DYNASTY**
1306–1290	**Reign of Sethos I**
1290–1224	**Reign of Ramesses II**
1224–1214	**Reign of Merneptah**
1196–1070	**20TH DYNASTY**
1194–1163	**Reign of Ramesses III**
1070–712	**3rd Intermediate Period**

Gebel Barkal, which acted as a landmark for traders coming north over the desert. In Asia, Egyptian kings such as Tuthmosis I were to reach as far as the Euphrates, demanding tribute from the chieftains and princes of Syria and Palestine, and risking conflict with larger powers in the north. Gold, silver, precious stones, lapis lazuli, turquoise, and many other luxuries were soon pouring back into the kingdom of Egypt.

Thebes was the undisputed capital of the kingdom once more. Its priests fostered the myth that it was at Thebes that the original mound of creation, from which all life had sprung, had risen from the floods. Amun-Ra became the most powerful god of the country. Amun was no longer simply a god of the air but a god of fertility and war, from whom all creation originated. His temples at Thebes, enriched by the plunder of war, took on new magnificence, their estates stretching across Egypt.

The 18th Dynasty paid special reverence to its queens and princesses. Both the mother and wife of the dynasty's founder Ahmose were worshiped in their own cult temples. And, for the first time there was a ruling queen, Hatshepsut, the daughter of Tuthmosis I and wife of his successor Tuthmosis II. When Tuthmosis II died, his male successor was a concubine's young son, but Hatshepsut seized power as a co-regent. She then claimed to be queen not merely as regent but in her own right as the daughter of Tuthmosis I.

Even a woman as determined as Hatshepsut had a formidable problem in presenting herself as

the ruler of Egypt. All the conventional representations of monarchy were male, and the queen had to decide whether to fit into these conventions or to proclaim herself as a woman. In the end, Hatshepsut compromised. On the walls of her temple she proclaimed herself as the son of Amun and on temple reliefs, perhaps the most conventional settings of all, she is shown as physically male. However, in relation to the falcon-god Horus (who was still seen as the protector of royalty), she took a female title, "The She-Horus of Fine Gold", and in sculpture she was content to be portrayed as unambiguously female.

*T*HE FEATURES *of Queen Hatshepsut* (RIGHT) – *clearly female, but with the false beard of kingship – adorn a sphinx found at her temple at Deir el-Bahri. This duality reflects her anomalous position as a woman who proclaimed herself king. Hieroglyphic texts in the temple and on other monuments emphasized her legitimacy as a ruler. Her successors took equal trouble to erase her name from all records. The story of her only daughter's fate has also been lost.*

A CEREMONIAL AX *of King Ahmose I* (BELOW LEFT), *made of copper with a cedarwood handle, is entirely covered in gold and jewels. The motifs refer to the expulsion of the Hyksos from Egypt and its reunification by Ahmose. The king is portrayed as a sphinx brandishing a severed head. Above are the lotus and papyrus, the vulture-goddess Nekhbet and the cobra-goddess Wadjyt (the "Two Ladies" of Upper and Lower Egypt). Finally, Heh, the god of eternity, offers Ahmose an infinite reign.*

Hatshepsut seems to have encountered little opposition while she reigned. She was well served by her courtiers and had the economic and administrative power to engage in major building programs. The most spectacular was the great temple complex at Deir el-Bahri, whose majestic terraces rose against the backdrop of the hills. The building of this magnificent temple was masterminded by her efficient courtier, Senenmut, who was partly responsible for the overall success of her reign. Uniquely for a commoner, he was shown on the reliefs there, and there were rumors that he was the queen's lover. One survivng statue shows him "nursing" Hatshepsut's small daughter.

One of Hatshepsut's achievements was to maintain effective control over Middle Egypt for the first time and to leave it endowed with a mass of new temples. Outside Egypt's borders, however,

she was less successful. She conducted no significant military activity in Syria or Palestine, and many of the chieftains and petty kings there appear to have broken free of Egyptian control.

ON HATSHEPSUT'S DEATH in 1458 BC, the small boy whom she had pushed aside 20 years before

The Expansion of Power

came to power as Tuthmosis III. He proved a relentless and ruthless military leader, perhaps the greatest that Egypt ever produced. Determined to restore his authority in Asia, he was to conduct no fewer than 17 campaigns there, each carefully planned to increase and consolidate Egyptian power abroad. On one occasion, he defeated a coalition of some 300 princes after the

GOLD FLIES *hang on a chain (FAR RIGHT) from the tomb of Queen Ahhotep, mother of King Ahmose I. This pendant, inspired by a military decoration, was part of an award for valor, given in recognition of her political role in the war to drive out the Hyksos.*

AN AVENUE *of sphinxes (BELOW) links the temple of Amun at Luxor to the Great Temple at Karnak, three kilometers (two miles) away.*

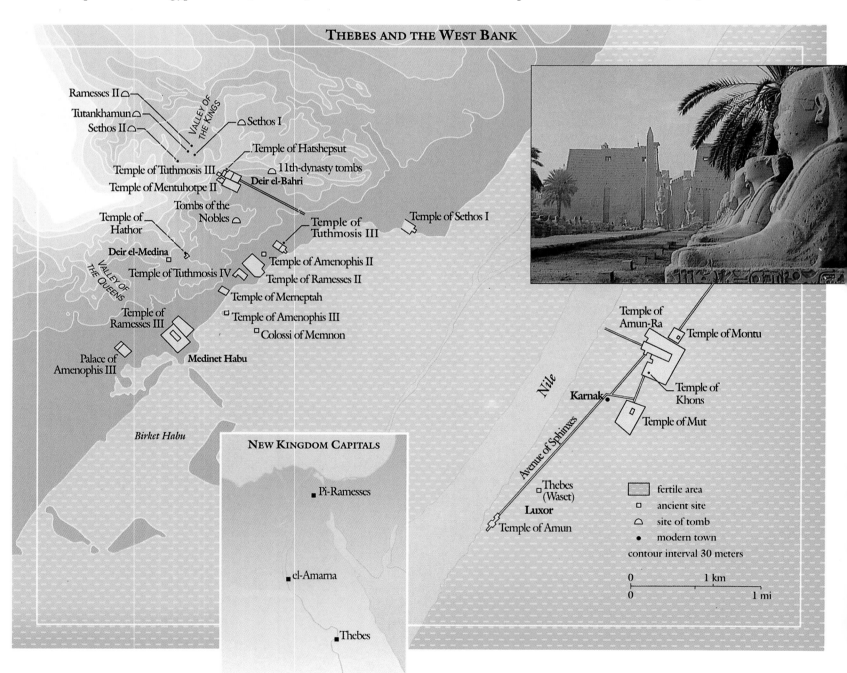

THEBES AND THE WEST BANK

Ramesses II
Tutankhamun
Sethos II
Sethos I
VALLEY OF THE KINGS
Temple of Hatshepsut
Temple of Tuthmosis III
11th-dynasty tombs
Deir el-Bahri
Temple of Mentuhotpe II
Tombs of the Nobles
Temple of Hathor
Temple of Tuthmosis III
Temple of Sethos I
Deir el-Medina
VALLEY OF THE QUEENS
Temple of Tuthmosis IV
Temple of Amenophis II
Temple of Ramesses II
Temple of Merneptah
Temple of Amenophis III
Temple of Ramesses III
Colossi of Memnon
Palace of Amenophis III
Medinet Habu
Birket Habu

Temple of Amun-Ra
Temple of Montu
Temple of Khons
Nile
Karnak
Temple of Mut
Avenue of Sphinxes

NEW KINGDOM CAPITALS

Pi-Ramesses

el-Amarna

Thebes

Thebes (Waset)
Luxor
Temple of Amun

fertile area
ancient site
site of tomb
modern town
contour interval 30 meters

0   1 km
0   1 mi

HATHOR & SEKHMET
Love and War

H athor, the cow-headed goddess, was one of the oldest deities. The cow was a symbol of fertility and as early as 3100 BC Hathor was shown as the head of a cow atop Narmer's palette. Hathor was also associated with the sky, and she was sometimes seen as an enormous cow whose great body straddled the horizon. She was also goddess of the west, and therefore associated with death.

Hathor provided a powerful mother image, and kings were sometimes referred to as the son of Hathor. She was also a goddess of sexuality. One story told how when Ra was in a sulk she appeared to him in the guise of a woman and exposed herself, cheering him up enormously. She was associated with laughter and happiness, music and dance. The *sistrum*, the ceremonial rattle shaken in religious ceremonies, was endowed with her head. Of her many shrines, Dendara (Ptolemaic period) was most important. Later she was associated with Aphrodite, Greek goddess of love.

Another of her aspects was the opposite of all this: fury. It was said that Ra, in a moment of anger at the human race, sent Hathor to destroy it. She took to slaughtering with some enthusiasm and took the name

Sekhmet, "She-who-Prevails". Ra, however, became sickened with the bloodshed, and created a mixture of beer and red ocher, which Hathor mistook for blood. Drinking from it, she was eventually lulled to sleep, and the slaughter ceased. The fury lived on in the goddess Sekhmet, the lion-goddess, who was always worshiped at the edge of the desert where lions came in to find water.

Sekhmet caused destruction. Kings would "rage like Sekhmet" against their enemies, and whenever an epidemic struck Egypt, she was said to be behind it. Sekhmet had to be appeased if healing was to take place. Doctors described themselves as priests of Sekhmet, and the rituals of her worship were among the standard tools of their trade.

T HE GODDESS HATHOR had two aspects: (LEFT) a benign cow in papyrus beds, and (ABOVE) the vengeful lioness Sekhmet.

capture of the major city of Megiddo and replaced them by leaders loyal to Egypt. Their children were taken back to Egypt to ensure the continuing loyalty of their families. On another, he took his army across the Euphrates – a river that astonished the Egyptians, who could not conceive of a river that flowed from north to south ("water that goes downstream in going upstream" was their description). The crossing brought Egypt into direct contact with remote and warlike peoples, the Mittanians, the Hittites and the Assyrians. Its sheer bravado was enough to give Tuthmosis legendary status. His achievements were trumpeted on the walls of the great temple of Amun at Karnak by Thebes. "I cause your victories to circulate in all lands. I shall see that there shall arise none rebellious to you, as far as that which heaven encircles", proclaimed the god. There was also a refined side to Tuthmosis: he ordered the plant and animal life that he had found in Syria to be depicted on one of the walls of the temple.

Tuthmosis and the other warrior kings of the New Kingdom developed Egypt's first professional standing army, applying the new technology introduced by the Hyksos, such as chariots. The army's total strength was probably between 15,000 and 20,000 men. It was divided into units of infantry and chariots (an innovation of the 18th Dynasty), each under a commander and a protecting god. The whole was commanded by "a great army general". A program of continuous recruitment ensured that there would always be a reserve available for the king when he launched a new campaign. When soldiers retired, they were given land on the condition that their male descendants would offer themselves for service. The Egyptians never showed much enthusiasm for soldiering, however, and many kings were content to lead a show of force in Egypt's dominions when they first came to power, leaving garrisons behind them as they returned to their capital at Thebes.

QUEENS & CONSORTS
The Great Royal Wives

The queens of the 18th Dynasty stand out as remarkable figures. The dynasty was founded by Ahmose, whose mother, Ahhotep, shared power with him early in his reign. She was credited with restoring order in Upper Egypt following the Second Intermediate Period. Her military role was unique even among the 18th Dynasty queens, whose power, it has been argued, derived as much from changes in the structure of the religious establishment in Thebes as from their marriages to kings. Ahmose's queen, Ahmose-Nefertari, was the High Priestess of Amun at Karnak before she married, and retained the priestess' title "God's Wife". The power and prestige of the God's Wife were greatly increased in Ahmose's reign. The office was assigned to the queen's heirs in perpetuity, along with rich estates in Upper Egypt, and the title "Heiress" was added. Hatshepsut was such an Heiress. The experience of being high priestess would have given her both a taste for power and the experience to wield it. Down through Nefertiti, all the 18th-Dynasty queens after Ahmose-Nefertari appear to have been God's Wives either by birth or through adoption by the queen.

*TIYE (ABOVE), **the powerful chief wife of Amenophis III, promoted the cult of Nefertari, the first queen and God's Wife.***

HATSHEPSUT'S BURIAL COMPLEX at Deir el-Bahri was never occupied. She must have known that, as

The Valley of the Kings

one who had breached the traditional conventions of kingship, her body would be vulnerable in so exposed a tomb. Instead, she had two tombs prepared in the desolate valleys behind Deir el-Bahri. Even the monarchs of the New Kingdom were fearful of the indignities that might be inflicted upon their bodies after their deaths. No longer were they laid to rest under splendid monuments that invited plunder; now they deliberately chose modest hiding places. On the west bank of the Nile across from Thebes there was an isolated valley below a natural rock formation reminiscent of a pyramid. The valley could be effectively guarded, and it was here that the kings prudently built and subsequently occupied underground tombs. This place became known as the Valley of the Kings. More opulent reminders of their reigns were left in mortuary temples on the open land between the Nile and the hills.

To accommodate the workers the kings set up a workmen's village, now known as Deir el-Medina. Desperate to preserve secrecy, they made Deir el-Medina into a closed community, its inhabitants locked inside the walls at night after they had returned from work in the valley. The site

*TWO COLOSSI (LEFT) **remain at the entrance of the now-destroyed temple of Amenophis III at Thebes. The Greeks called them the Colossi of Memnon, after the Trojan hero slain by Achilles. The statues were much appreciated by the Romans, who thought they heard them sing as wind blew across cracks in the ancient stone.***

has yielded a great deal of information about the homes and daily life of well-to-do Egyptian craftsmen. In addition, a wealth of personal comments and even scraps of gossip have been found there, scrawled hurriedly on *ostraca,* the pieces of broken pottery that were used for everyday writing when papyrus was not available.

The provisioning of this community of 1,200 people reflects the administrative efficiency of ancient Egypt. (Deir el-Medina had no access to water; all had to be carried there by donkey.) In the New Kingdom the peak of this efficiency was reached in the reign of Amenophis III. He ruled

while Egypt's position was secure. Egypt was accepted by its neighbors as a great power, and his name is found recorded as far afield as Greece, Anatolia, and Assyria. Amenophis needed to make only one punitive campaign in his entire reign.

With such peaceful relationships abroad, Amenophis was able to concentrate on a grand building program. Remains of fine temples built by him can be found as far south as Nubia and north as the Delta. At Thebes he commissioned no fewer than 600 statues of the war-goddess Sekhmet; he also built a new temple to Amun at Karnak and planned the approaches to the temples,

THE DESOLATE Valley of the Kings (ABOVE) was the favored burial place of kings from the 18th to the 20th Dynasty. Tombs were cut into the cliffs with corridors sloping down from the surface. By the time the nineteenth-century British artist, David Roberts, painted some tourists and their guides in the valley, all but one of the 62 tombs had been plundered.

with their avenues of sphinxes. On the west bank of the Nile he set up a great mortuary temple with two colossal statues of himself, and placed a huge artificial lake near it. He also took the unusual step of having himself deified during his lifetime.

AMENOPHIS was aware of the exceptional power now enjoyed by the priests of Amun at Thebes.

New Gods for Old

His formidable wife, Queen Tiye, daughter of a courtier, may have been the major influence in encouraging him to patronize other gods in the north of the country. He especially favored Heliopolis, the centuries-old shrine of Ra, the sun-god. When his son, Amenophis IV, succeeded him, he followed his father's example in taking the coronation name "The Transformations of Ra are Perfect". Queen Tiye, who lived on into her son's reign, remained an important influence on him.

Nothing, however, could have prepared Egypt for what happened next. Amenophis IV, who was clearly a forceful individual in his own right, presided over an administration at the height of its power. In the second year of his reign, he abruptly announced that he was replacing Ra by a sun-god in a new form. This was the Aten, always portrayed as the actual disk of the sun with his rays coming downward to earth. If Amenophis had simply promoted the Aten among the other traditional Egyptian gods, there might have been little trouble, but he decided on nothing less than the forceful imposition of the Aten and the complete eradication of the old gods.

In an astonishingly provocative act, the king constructed a major new temple to the Aten in Thebes itself. It must have aroused ferocious opposition. Two years later the king took the more ambitious but less foolhardy course of building a new capital downstream on the east bank of the river, at an uninhabited site where the rays of the rising sun broke through a cliff. It was to be called Akhetaten ("Horizon of the Sun-God"), and when he moved there Amenophis gave himself a new name, Akhenaten ("Agreeable to the Aten"). His wife, Queen Nefertiti, who had been associated with the new cult in Thebes, also took a new title, Nefernefruaten ("Fair is the Goddess of the Aten"). She was given a prominent role in the cult of the Aten, standing alongside the king himself in many of the ceremonies. Fundamental to the reforms must have been the desire to focus attention away from the Theban priesthood to the person of the

king himself. To achieve this, Akhenaten revived the old idea that an individual's afterlife depended on his loyalty to the king, who was the sole intermediary between the human race and the Aten.

The impact of Akhenaten's reforms was profound. In order to finance his building at Akhetaten (normally known by its modern name, el-Amarna) and to destroy rival gods, many temples were closed down and their wealth confiscated in the king's name. This caused massive disruption of the economy.

There were cultural implications as well. The name of Amun was excised from monuments, and the king encouraged new hymns of praise to the life-creating Aten (always presented as a force of light and goodness), which he allowed to be expressed in popular language rather than the classical language traditionally used for such texts. In the visual arts, a new informality and freedom emerged. The king and his family were portrayed in realistic poses far removed from the traditional conventions of portraiture. Tomb decorations placed less emphasis on the hoped-for delights of the afterlife, concentrating on the achievements of the dead man and his role in helping the king.

ONE OF TWENTY-EIGHT colossal statues of Akhenaten (RIGHT) which stood on pillars on the temple of the Aten at Karnak. In the bold expressionist style of the period, he is shown as a living man, with an exaggeratedly long face and nose, slanted heavy-lidded eyes, and large ears. These exaggerated features make his face superbly individual as well as imposing.

THE ROYAL FAMILY offers a libation to the Aten (LEFT) on a fragment of the parapet of the ramp leading to the central chamber of the palace at el-Amarna. They stand directly under the rays of the Aten. Akhenaten (the largest figure) and Nefertiti (behind him) offer libations, while the eldest of their six daughters plays the "sistrum".

PAINTED IN LIMESTONE, this bust of Akhenaten's queen Nefertiti (BELOW) by a celebrated sculptor, Tuthmose, has survived more than 3,000 years to provide one of the most radiant examples of realistic art from the Amarna period. The bust was discovered still in the sculptor's studio.

Return of the Old Gods

AKHENATEN DIED in 1335 BC, after reigning for 17 years. There was probably never much chance that his new god, the Aten, would prove popular. He and his family, in their new capital, were far removed from the mass of population. There was no incentive for ordinary Egyptians to adopt a cult that threatened their conventional way of life. Even the workmen at Akhetaten seem to have continued to worship their traditional gods. Akhenaten's son-in-law, Smenkhkare, succeeded him but died within a few months, leaving the throne to his nine-year-old brother Tutankhaten ("Living Image of the Aten"). Tutankhaten was not strong enough to resist the influence of the courtiers, who now wanted to return to traditional beliefs. Akhetaten was abandoned and the young king was forced to change his name to Tutankhamun ("Living Image of Amun"). It was a time of upheaval which Tutankhamun did not live long enough to

AMUN'S GREAT TEMPLE at Karnak (ABOVE) was built up over more than 1,000 years. The 19th-Dynasty kings made many additions to consolidate their legitimacy and restore the old gods after Akhenaten's heresy.

TUTANKHAMUN (LEFT), the boy king, died at the age of 19. In this gilded wooden statuette from his tomb, he stands on a papyrus skiff with a harpoon in one hand and a cord in the other with which to bind his vanquished foe. The theme of the hunt in the marshes symbolized the forces of order (the king) over chaos (Seth in the shape of a hippopotamus).

*H*AREMHAB, *usurper of the 18th-Dynasty throne, stands between the knees of Amun* (BELOW). *Amun replaced not only the Aten but also Osiris, Horus and Ra as the chief god. He dwarfs the king, reversing the previous convention which showed huge kings with small gods.*

resolve. By the age of 19 he was dead, perhaps of a cerebral hemorrhage. His tomb in the Valley of the Kings was not the most opulent of the New Kingdom, but it is the only one that is known to have survived with its goods intact; its rediscovery by Howard Carter and Lord Carnarvon in 1922 caused a worldwide sensation.

The young Tutankhamun left no male heir, and Akhenaten's unsuccessful attempt to transform the spiritual life of Egypt had left the country exhausted. In a desperate attempt to ensure the

survival of the dynasty, his widow tried to make a marriage alliance with a Hittite prince, despite the ancient tradition that the Egyptian royal line did not marry foreigners. The prince was assassinated on his way to Egypt, however, presumably by opponents of the alliance. As had happened on previous occasions, the man who now seized power was a military commander, Haremhab. He had no inhibitions about taking on the full mantle of kingship. Haremhab wiped Akhenaten and his successors from the record and declared himself a member of the 18th Dynasty. He then ruthlessly set about pulling down the temples to the Aten, including the one built at Thebes. Its stone blocks were used in other temples; some 36,000 of them have been identified.

Haremhab passed on power to an elderly fellow general, Ramesses I, traditionally seen as the first king of the 19th Dynasty. Like Haremhab, Ramesses had no proper claim to the throne. To strengthen his position he appointed his son Sethos as his chief minister. When Sethos succeeded shortly afterward, he portrayed himself as the latest in a line of kings which began with Narmer but which made no mention of either Hatshepsut or the Amarna kings – they were aberrations to be wiped from the historical record. Sethos associated himself with the traditional gods by repairing temples damaged by Akhenaten and building a temple at Abydos, the home of Osiris, and a great hall (which still stands) at the temple of Amun at Karnak. On its walls Sethos is shown restoring control over the princes of west Asia and Libyan raiders. He also made a fine tomb for himself in the Valley of the Kings. Once again a usurping family had integrated itself into the royal line.

THE MAIN THREAT to the Egyptian empire in Asia came from the Hittites, whose empire was based on Anatolia but was now extending southward. It was Sethos's son Ramesses II, the last of the great kings of Egypt, who was to confront them. As the king marched north in the fifth year of his reign, the chroniclers described how he was like the hawk-headed war-god Montu, with all foreign lands trembling before him, their chiefs bringing him gifts, and rebels bowed down through fear of his majesty's might. The objective of the king was the city of Qadesh on the Orontes river, which had been taken by Sethos but then recaptured by the Hittites. The battle of Qadesh is

The Great Days of the Empire

the first in history to be recorded in detail. On the walls of the Theban temples it was proclaimed as a great victory for Ramesses, the culmination of his military career, though Hittite accounts show that the Egyptian army was surrounded and that the "victory" was no more than a successful escape. A few years later, in 1268 BC, the two empires, both aware that their resources were limited and that other empires such as the Assyrian threatened them, made history's first recorded state treaty. It lasted 50 years, during which the royal families maintained close ties. Ramesses even married two Hittite princesses, one of them in a grand ceremony at the city of Damascus at which the armies of the two powers fraternized.

THE YEARS OF PEACE allowed Ramesses to indulge his passion for building. Nearly half of Egypt's

Memorials to Imperial Might

surviving ancient temples were built by him. Perhaps the most celebrated is at Abu Simbel in Nubia, designed to impress the Nubians with the grandeur of the king's power. Four colossal statues of Ramesses, each 21 meters (73 feet) high, sit alongside each other in the rock face. Between them the temple entrance opens into a great hall. Inside are statues of the gods Ptah, Amun-Ra, Ra-Horakhty and Ramesses himself, deified. Twice a year the statues would be illuminated by the rays of the rising sun. Ramesses followed his predecessors in building a tomb, the most opulent of them all, in the Valley of the Kings. As a more visible monument he built a massive mortuary temple, known as the Ramesseum, on the West Bank of the Nile.

The origins of the dynasty lay, however, in the north, and Ramesses sited his capital in the eastern Delta at Pi-Ramesses. Its position helped him to maintain close relationships with Asia. It was at Pi-Ramesses that he built his palace and grand temples to Amun, Seth and Ra. As he neared 30 years of rule he added a massive set of jubilee halls in which to celebrate his *sed* festival. Despite the magnificence of the city, there were signs that the kingdom was now back on the defensive. The city was protected by waterways and three barracks housing soldiers. The truth is that the successors of Ramesses II faced unsettled times over the entire eastern Mediterranean and western Asia. The Sahara seems to have been becoming drier at this time, causing land-hungry peoples such as the Libyans to raid into Egypt.

*T*WO PAIRS *of giant seated effigies of Ramesses II* (BELOW) *mark the entrance to Abu Simbel, his great temple. The temple lay inside the boundaries of Nubia and reminded the Nubians of the king's power. The temple was relocated in the 1960s when the Aswan High Dam was built.*

From about 1200 BC, marauders known as the Sea Peoples were causing havoc from Anatolia to the coast of Egypt. The Hittite empire collapsed under their onslaught; so did the states of the Mycenaean Greeks. Egypt came under direct attack, and battles were fought along the coastline. Although the Sea Peoples were kept out of Egypt itself, the Egyptians could not prevent them from settling along the coast of Palestine, where they remained and became known as the Philistines.

At the same time, Egypt's own wealth was waning. The gold mines of Nubia were almost exhausted and the revenues of the great temples were falling. The Faiyum, a rich source of grain, suffered from Libyan raids. Even the standards of workmanship maintained for so many centuries were in decline.

The 20th Dynasty saw a steady erosion of Egyptian power. All the kings except one took the name Ramesses as if in hope that it would bring back the glory of the previous century, but only

*R*AMESSES II, *the last of the great kings, strikes a very conventional pose to smite enemies* (RIGHT) *on one of his campaigns. Their features and costume identify them as a Nubian, a Libyan and a Syrian. Two of them have raised an arm in a plea for mercy. The names of Ramesses are shown above them.*

one king, Ramesses III, lived up to his namesake and achieved a few last victories against the intruders. Without gold, Nubia now had little to offer Egypt, and the provincial administration eventually withdrew. The empire in Asia disintegrated and was lost by the reign of Ramesses VI. By 1070 BC Egypt was confined once more to its original boundaries along the Nile valley.

Within Egypt the power of the kings now faltered in a series of short reigns of men who were already aging when they came to power. The vigor of the administration was sapped. On one occasion, the workmen at Deir el-Medina failed to get their provisions, and in retaliation they carried out the first recorded strike in history. Worst of all, robbers broke into the Valley of the Kings and began looting the tombs. Local temple officials and workmen at Deir el-Medina were implicated. Some loyal officials collected the kings' bodies and reburied them in the hills above Deir el-Bahri, where they lay until the 19th century AD.

As disorder grew, the words of an earlier banquet song must have been especially poignant: "Those gods who existed aforetime, who rest in their pyramids, and the noble blessed dead likewise, the builders of chapels, their places are no more, like those who never were. None returns from there to tell us their condition, to tell their state, to reassure us, until we attain the place where they have gone."

After this time, a scattering of individual kings reunited the state and revived some of its ancient glories, but the great days of Egyptian civilization belonged to the increasingly distant past.

"He rises in this temple of the Aten at Akhetaten and fills it with His own self by means of His rays, beauteous with love, and embraces me with them in life and power for ever."

Proclamation by Akhenaten on a boundary stela

EL-AMARNA City of the Aten

Left Akhenaten holds an olive branch beneath the sun's beneficent rays, shown as extended hands. This aspect of the sun was called the Aten, in whose honor Amenophis IV changed his name to Akhenaten and dedicated a new capital, Akhetaten.

El-Amarna is every archeologist's dream – a city founded on unoccupied land about 1350 BC and abandoned only 30 years later. Although desecration, cultivation and scavenging have destroyed some areas of the city, enough remains to provide a snapshot of Egyptian society at the height of the New Kingdom.

Amarna was the royal capital of the 18th-Dynasty king Akhenaten, who moved his court there from the traditional site at Thebes. He named it Akhetaten in honor of the god he worshiped. The presence of god and king pervades the archeological finds, reflecting Akhenaten's unconventional approach to art and religion. The site is now known by its modern name, Tell el-Amarna.

The Great Temple of the Aten, the sun-god, dominated the center of the city. Unlike traditional temples, it was open to the sun, and had no shrine or cult statue. Instead, a series of courts led across a huge enclosure to the high altar in the sanctuary. Offering tables in the courts were used by all who were not allowed into the sanctuary. Other temples in the city followed the same design.

Images of the royal family found throughout the city also departed sharply from tradition. Akhenaten himself is shown not only with the trappings of kingship but also as a family man, surrounded by his wife and daughters. The court revolved around the Great Palace, just south of the Great Temple; Akhenaten's diplomatic archive was found intact there. The palace had a special window from which the family appeared before the public and distributed gifts to the crowd. For their private residences, they had a choice of several other palaces.

Government offices and temples were also in the central city, with a business district to the north, and a residential area in the south. From this "suburb" the royal officials and courtiers traveled to the center in chariots. Unlike Thebes, Amarna was

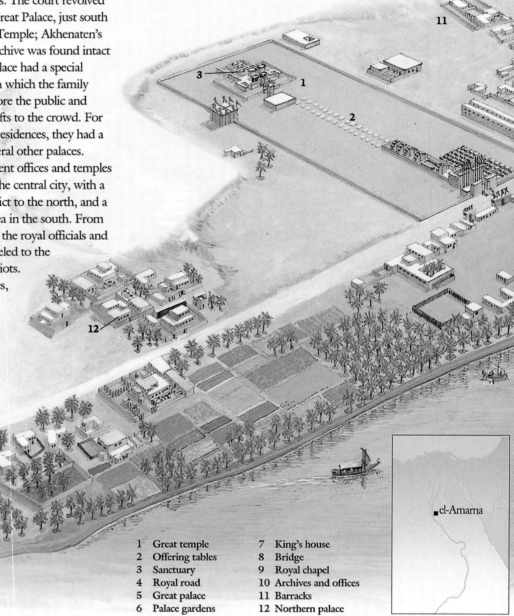

1	Great temple	7	King's house
2	Offering tables	8	Bridge
3	Sanctuary	9	Royal chapel
4	Royal road	10	Archives and offices
5	Great palace	11	Barracks
6	Palace gardens	12	Northern palace

el-Amarna

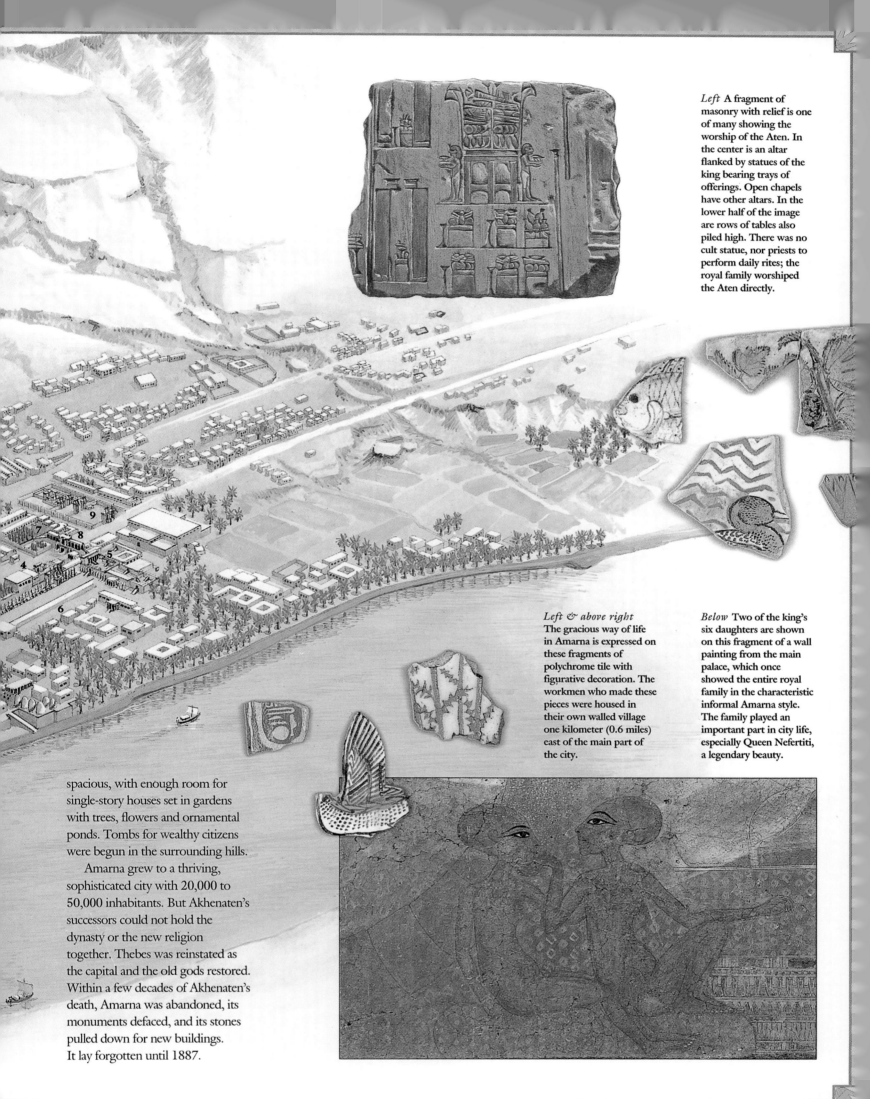

Left A fragment of masonry with relief is one of many showing the worship of the Aten. In the center is an altar flanked by statues of the king bearing trays of offerings. Open chapels have other altars. In the lower half of the image are rows of tables also piled high. There was no cult statue, nor priests to perform daily rites; the royal family worshiped the Aten directly.

Left & above right The gracious way of life in Amarna is expressed on these fragments of polychrome tile with figurative decoration. The workmen who made these pieces were housed in their own walled village one kilometer (0.6 miles) east of the main part of the city.

Below Two of the king's six daughters are shown on this fragment of a wall painting from the main palace, which once showed the entire royal family in the characteristic informal Amarna style. The family played an important part in city life, especially Queen Nefertiti, a legendary beauty.

spacious, with enough room for single-story houses set in gardens with trees, flowers and ornamental ponds. Tombs for wealthy citizens were begun in the surrounding hills.

Amarna grew to a thriving, sophisticated city with 20,000 to 50,000 inhabitants. But Akhenaten's successors could not hold the dynasty or the new religion together. Thebes was reinstated as the capital and the old gods restored. Within a few decades of Akhenaten's death, Amarna was abandoned, its monuments defaced, and its stones pulled down for new buildings. It lay forgotten until 1887.

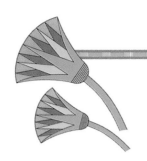
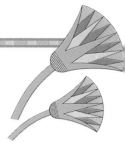

TROUBLED TIMES
The Late Period

With the disintegration of the New Kingdom, the great years of Egypt as an independent power were over. However, this did not mean that its civilization was destroyed, as was that of the Assyrians, for instance, when their empire collapsed. Traditions of religious ritual and art survived – often deliberately revived by kings who felt the need to emphasize their legitimacy as rulers. Occasionally an individual Egyptian ruler was powerful enough to expand once again into Syria and Palestine. However, Egypt was often fragmented and vulnerable to the great imperial powers of the Near East such as Assyria and Persia. At the end of the fourth century BC, Egypt became part of the Greek world and later the Roman empire, whose wealth was underpinned by Egyptian harvests.

AT THE BEGINNING of the Third Intermediate Period (1070–712 BC) the eastern Delta provided

Dynasties of the Delta

the setting for a new dynasty, the 21st, with its capital at Tanis. The succession of Smendes to Ramesses XI – the last king of the 20th Dynasty and of the New Kingdom – was orderly but unusual. During Ramesses' lifetime Smendes had been the ruler of Lower Egypt, with his own capital at Pi-Ramesses, while Upper Egypt and Nubia were dominated by a Libyan priest-general,

ESARHADDON, king of Assyria, storms an Egyptian city (ABOVE). The Late Period saw Egypt almost continuously under attack from all sides.

TIMETABLE

1070–712	Third Intermediate Period
959–945	Reign of Psusennes II
945–924	Reign of Shoshenq I
924–909	Reign of Osorkon II
750–712	Reign of Piye
712–332	Late Period
712–698	Reign of Shabaqo
690–664	Reign of Taharqa
664–610	Reign of Psamtek I
589–570	Reign of Apries
570–526	Reign of Amasis
525-404	27TH DYNASTY (Persian)
343–332	2ND PERSIAN PERIOD
332-323	Reign of Alexander

Herihor. Ramesses himself was sandwiched between the two, with his power base mostly confined to Memphis.

The religious establishment at Thebes, of which Herihor was the head, was the greatest threat to traditional royal authority. In the 19th and 20th Dynasties the temples had acquired additional land, increasing their wealth to the extent that the temple at Karnak virtually controlled the south of Egypt. At about the same time the senior offices of the priesthood became hereditary, making them independent of the king and allowing the priests to establish their own dynasties. It was a short step to set themselves up as rival rulers, sometimes appropriating the titles of traditional Egyptian kingship. One chief priest even adopted a Horus name, "Powerful Bull, Crowned in Thebes and Beloved of Amun." The kings at Tanis could do little to stop them and were obliged to recognize the priest-kings, though the priests in turn recognized the Tanis calendar rather than impose their own. Intermarriage between the two ruling families further confused the distinction between legitimate rulers and priest-usurpers.

Nevertheless, the kingdom was effectively partitioned. The unity of the state was further undermined by the largescale settling of Egypt's continuing influx of foreign prisoners of war in local colonies, creating distinct ethnic groups. The largest of these, originally Libyan, was known as the Meshwesh or Ma tribe. It gradually emerged as the most powerful political force in the country.

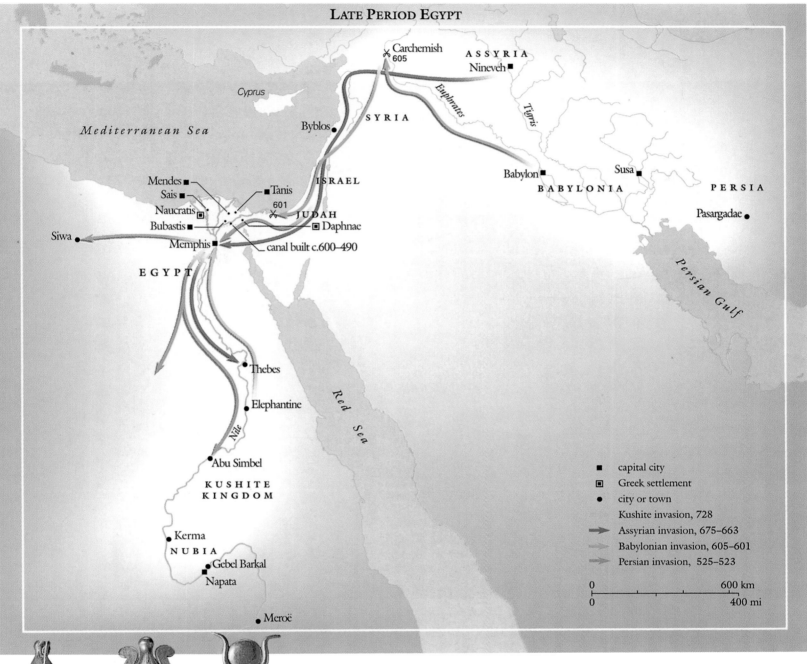

LATE PERIOD EGYPT

capital city

Greek settlement

city or town

Kushite invasion, 728

Assyrian invasion, 675–663

Babylonian invasion, 605–601

Persian invasion, 525–523

IN UNCERTAIN TIMES, especially, the Egyptians looked back to the past for reassurance and stability. The triad (LEFT) of Osiris (in the center), Horus and Isis retained its long-standing prominence among the gods. Egyptian gods were often adopted by foreign rulers such as Osorkon II, one of the kings of Libyan origin of the 22nd Dynasty. The base of this statuette is inscribed with a dedication that puts Osorkon under the gods' protection.

Corresponding to these internal shifts of power, Egypt's prestige abroad declined dramatically. There is a surviving tale of a 20th–Dynasty ambassador, Wenamun, who went to Byblos to obtain wood for a sacred bark to dedicate to Amun. Despite his status he was robbed on the way and then had to bargain for the wood, for which he was eventually charged an exorbitant price. Later the daughter of an Egyptian king was sent to marry the powerful king of Israel, Solomon (c.962–922 BC), breaking the tradition that Egypt's princesses never married abroad.

The last ruler of the 21st Dynasty, Psusennes II – probably the high priest of Amun as well as the king – died in 945 BC, leaving no male heir. His son-in-law Shoshenq, a soldier from a Meshwesh family in the Delta, established the 22nd Dynasty

MEROË
The Last Outpost of Egyptian Civilization

Far to the south of Egypt in the Nubian desert – now known as Sudan – the ruins of an ancient city still litter the landscape. There are palaces, temples and even rows of small pyramids. Huge slag heaps surround the ruins, confirming it as a major center for metalworking. The city was once thought to be the source from which iron spread across Africa, but this is now considered unlikely.

This is Meroë, for some 900 years the capital of the early African kingdom of Kush. Founded by the descendants of the 25th-Dynasty kings, who were driven from Egypt by the Assyrians and dislodged from their early capital at Napata, they were more secure at Meroë.

The kingdom of Kush, like that of Egypt, ran along the Nile. At its height its rulers controlled some 1,000 kilometers (620 miles) of the river, reaching almost to the mountains of Ethiopia. According to the Greek historian Herodotus, the city was a 12-day journey by boat from the Fourth Cataract. However, by modern estimates this appears to be an exaggeration.

Meroë provides a fascinating example of how Egyptian influences integrated with those of Nubia to form a separate, distinct and coherent culture. The Meroitic kings worshiped Amun and Isis, and built pyramids for their tombs. They wrote their formal inscriptions in hieroglyphs. Due to these

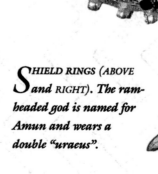

SHIELD RINGS (ABOVE and RIGHT). The ram-headed god is named for Amun and wears a double "uraeus".

MEROË'S kings and queens were buried in pyramids (LEFT) at several sites across the kingdom of Kush. Their burial customs were among the most obvious influences from Egypt.

STONE GARGOYLES of a ram flanked by two lions (ABOVE) represent Amun and two other gods: either Shu and Tefnut or a local god and Amun's son Khons.

similarities, Meroitic culture was dismissed by early archeologists as merely an imitation of Egyptian glory. Now it is accepted that the Meroitic culture had its roots in earlier Nubian civilization dating back to 2000 BC: it did not spring up suddenly with the arrival of the refugees from the 25th Dynasty. It had its own language (Nubian) and its own traditions and ideology in which the king was glorified as a mighty hunter. Another important difference was that inheritance could take place through the female line.

The culture of Meroë did not suddenly disappear due to invasion, as was once thought. Instead, it was gradually transformed and became part of the mosaic of early Africa.

and established his capital at his home town Bubastis. Royal burials were still made at Tanis, however, and these two cities continued to be embellished by the kings, using stone raided from Pi-Ramesses nearby.

Shoshenq used his military expertise effectively and re-established control over the south. The power of the priests at Thebes had begun to decline, and Shoshenq was able to to have his son appointed high priest of Amun as well as commander of the armies and governor of Upper Egypt. In addition, Shoshenq renewed trade with Nubia and led a campaign into Palestine. Egypt's recent unprecedented subservience to Israel was forgotten as Shoshenq carried off King Solomon's treasures from the temple of Jerusalem in 925 BC. Trading contacts were renewed with Byblos.

Such exploits were not to be repeated. In the ninth century BC civil war broke out and Egypt was once more divided. At times during the 23rd and 24th Dynasties there were as many as eleven different local rulers. The 24th Dynasty seems to have held power only in a limited area of the Delta around the western city of Sais, and other local rulers appear to have had similar small enclaves. Fragmentation left the valley open to invasion. This time it came from the south.

THE OLD CITY of Napata, near the Fourth Cataract of the Nile, was the furthest point of the Egyptians' penetration into Nubia. Never as rich as Egypt, Nubia was vulnerable and relatively easy to exploit by any king organized enough to do so. With the loss of Egyptian control a separate state had grown up here – the state of Kush – but it reflected the long years of Egyptian domination. Amun-Ra was revered as its chief god; some scholars even have suggested that Napata was founded by priests of Thebes. In the eighth century BC Kush steadily extended its power as far north as the traditional borders of Egypt at Aswan. Its first great ruler was Piye (also known as Piankhi, 750-712 BC). His exploits were proclaimed on a victory stela which remains at Napata. Claiming that the power of Amun had been insulted by usurping rulers, he marched north to seek revenge. In a gesture of extraordinary arrogance, he took the coronation titles of two of the powerful kings of Egyptian history, Tuthmosis III and Ramesses II, and described himself on the stela as if he was the acknowledged king of Egypt simply restoring

The Kings from the South

TAHARQA, the son of Piye and third king of the 25th Dynasty (ABOVE), was the most important of the kings of Kush. He presided over a reunified Egypt which extended from Napata to the edge of the Mediterranean. He also left his mark throughout Egypt by building and extending temples, including the great temple of Amun at Karnak. He held off the first Assyrian attack in 674 BC but was defeated and forced to retreat to Napata in 671.

order as duty required. Thebes was subdued, and the king took the leading role in the major religious festivals. Piye took Memphis, then went to Heliopolis to enact the rituals of Ra's temple. He stood alone in the temple and broke open the sealed door of the innermost shrine to view his "father". The overawed priests, one account states, "placed themselves on their bodies before His Majesty, saying 'Abide forever without end, Horus, beloved of Heliopolis!'" Then Piye returned south, spending his plunder on building a replica of the great temple to Amun at Karnak. When he died, he was buried in a pyramid near Napata. His dynasty, the 25th, was known as the Kushite. However, with his death, his conquests lapsed. Piye's brother, Shabaqo, reconquered the north, appointed a Kushite governor at Sais and made his own capital at Thebes. His son became chief priest of Amun, although his position was somewhat subservient to that of Shabaqo's sister, who claimed the exalted rank of God's Wife of Amun.

Shabaqo's reign inaugurated what is known as the Late Period, from 712 BC to the coming of Alexander the Great in 332 BC. His successor Taharqa was even more conventional and ruled from Memphis. This was the most glorious of the reigns of the Kushite kings. Taharqa took on the traditional role of the Egyptian rulers, restoring the great temple at Karnak and other temples in Nubia. The classical art of ancient dynasties was revived. It seemed as if the country was once again entering a period of peace and prosperity.

ONCE AGAIN the security proved short lived. To the north had arisen Assyria, one of the most ruthless

The Assyrian Invasion

military powers of the Middle East. Since 900 BC Assyria had been ruled by a succession of strong kings, and they were merciless in their aggression. The Assyrians were now threatening the small kingdoms of Syria and Palestine, who called on their traditional overlords, the Egyptians, for help. Egypt feared that trade routes along the Levantine coast would be disrupted by Assyrian expansion and so was ready to intervene. But the Assyrian king Esarhaddon (r.681–669 BC) was taking no chances. He attacked Egypt in 674 BC and again in 671, when he drove Taharqa from Memphis and sacked the city. Later Assyrian raids reached Thebes, and in 664 BC, in an event which must have seemed to the Egyptians like the return of the primeval chaos which their rulers had done

BASTET
The Cat Goddess

The Egyptians were fascinated by cats. Their name for the domesticated species was *miw* and they would nickname young girls *miw-sheri*, "little cat". One 22nd-Dynasty king was even named "the tomcat". In wall paintings cats are shown sitting contentedly under chairs at feasts. They were trained to go out hunting, and there are reliefs of cats retrieving birds for their masters.

They were kept as pets as early as 4000 BC, but the Egyptians did not regard them simply as pets or mouse-catchers. Herodotus recorded that when a cat died its owners would shave their eyebrows and take the body to Bubastis, the cult center of the cat goddess Bastet, for mummification and burial. Bastet was the goddess of the domestic cat, loving and faithful, in contrast to the lion-goddess

Sekhmet, who stood for all the fury of which the cat family is capable. She was regarded as the daughter of Ra, whose many aspects included that of "the great cat of Heliopolis". Sculptures of Bastet are some of the finest examples of Egyptian art, and they show all the dignity and serenity that the animals possess.

BASTET, the cat-goddess (LEFT), cast in bronze about 600 BC.

TOWERING OVER his defeated foes, Taharqa and a king of Sidon or Tyre, Esarhaddon (LEFT) wears the traditional religious costume of the Assyrian kings. He holds leashes attached to rings through the lips of the defeated.

THE CULT of the sacred Apis bull (BELOW) was revived in the 26th Dynasty under Psamtek, and expanded to include an oracle. Dream-interpretation texts have been discovered with the sacred animals' mummies.

so much to subdue, the great temple of Amun itself was sacked. Despite a vigorous fight, the Kushite rulers of the 25th Dynasty were forced back to Napata.

This was not, in fact, the end of the Kushite kings. At the beginning of the next century they were dislodged from Napata and moved south down the river to the city of Meroë. For the next 900 years Meroë remained the capital of a kingdom which combined Egyptian and Nubian traditions. The kings worshiped Amun and Isis; they were buried in pyramids and wrote their inscriptions in hieroglyphs. Yet their language was Nubian and, since inheritance could take place through the female line, there was a line of queens. They were adept at metalworking and it has been

argued that techniques developed in Meroë spread from there to the rest of Africa. The civilization of Meroë remains one of the most impressive and enduring legacies of Egyptian culture.

Egypt was a long way from the Assyrian heartland north of the Euphrates. Unlike the rest of their empire, which was tightly controlled, the Assyrians were prepared to rule Egypt through local princes. It was not an efficient way of keeping control and the chosen princes intrigued continually. The Assyrians returned in the 660s to wipe out the ruling elites or deport them to the north. The only ruler to be spared was Necho (r.672-664), whose capital was at the town of Sais in the western Delta. When Necho died his son Psamtek (often known by his Greek name Psammetichus, r.664-610) was entrusted with the administration of the country by the Assyrians. His dynasty, the 26th, is also known as the Saite Dynasty after his home city of Sais.

PSAMTEK WAS ONE of the most powerful rulers of late Egypt, and he was one of the shrewdest. He

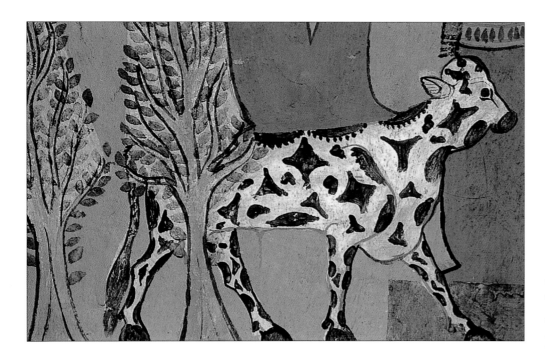

Egypt Gives up Control

subdued the neighboring princes of the Delta towns (many of whom were Libyan in origin, so vulnerable had Egypt become to infiltration) and then forced the submission of the rulers of the lower Nile valley, opening up the Nile and the trade routes across the desert. His next goal was Thebes. In 656 BC he sailed his fleet down to the city and installed his daughter, Nitocris, as the chief priestess ("God's Wife") of Amun, with her own

houses, estates and officials. Her position in this hereditary office which, by long tradition, was always occupied by the king's daughter, reinforced Psamtek's status as the legitimate ruler of all Egypt.

Meanwhile, the Assyrian empire was weakening; it collapsed completely at the hands of Babylon at the end of the century. Its weakness allowed Psamtek to reassert the power of Egypt. The means he used to consolidate his hold on both

PERSIAN SPHINXES shown in glazed brick relief (ABOVE) on the wall of a Persian palace have winged lions' bodies and the bearded heads of kings. Above them is a symbol of Ahuramazda, one of the Persians' main gods.

Upper and Lower Egypt were to be important for Egypt's future. His army was recruited among the refugees – Phoenicians, Syrians and Jews – uprooted by the Assyrian conquests, and above all from the Greeks. Greek mercenaries remained in Egypt for generations, and in the sixth century BC they were 30,000 strong. There was also a Greek trading post established about 620 BC at Naucratis, only a few kilometers from Sais.

By using mercenaries, Psamtek laid himself open to charges of subservience to foreigners. It may have been the need to counter this charge that encouraged him to restore the great monuments of the Egyptian past, such as the Step Pyramid at Saqqara, and to patronize traditional art forms. Psamtek's reign was the last great age of Egyptian craftsmanship. The statues of the Saite dynasty's kings have the calm assurance of the Old Kingdom rulers, and there was a renewed interest in classical language. Psamtek also exploited the popular obsession with animal cults, enlarging the great Serapeum at Saqqara where the sacred Apis bulls were buried.

EGYPT'S FUTURE was now inextricably tied up with the wider Mediterranean world, but only as one of

The Restoration of Power

a number of competing powers. Psamtek's successor Necho II (610–595 BC) accepted the challenges of survival in a wider world. He built the first Egyptian navy as well as beginning a canal between the Nile and the Red Sea. The biggest problem confronting Necho and his successors was that power now lay with the Babylonians, who had defeated the Assyrians decisively in the late seventh century BC and were enjoying a great period of prosperity. In the first half of the sixth century BC the two kingdoms fought repeatedly. To survive, the Egyptians had to reinforce their dependency on mercenaries, which fed nationalist resentment in Egypt. One king, Apries, was overthrown in an uprising after being defeated in Libya. His successor Amasis (570–526 BC) had to confine the Greeks to Naucratis.

*A*MASIS, *a Nubian general (ABOVE), deposed the 26th Dynasty king Apries after a short civil war about 570 BC between Greek mercenaries and native Egyptians in the Egyptian army.*

*T*HE PERSIANS *were defeated in Egypt by Alexander the Great (BELOW) in 332 BC. He spent only one year in Egypt, and died abroad nine years later. He is said to be buried in Alexandria, but his tomb has never been found.*

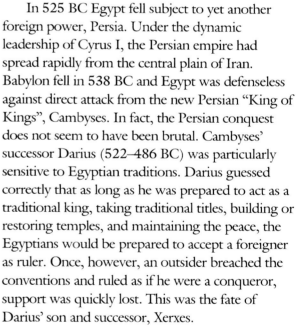

In 525 BC Egypt fell subject to yet another foreign power, Persia. Under the dynamic leadership of Cyrus I, the Persian empire had spread rapidly from the central plain of Iran. Babylon fell in 538 BC and Egypt was defenseless against direct attack from the new Persian "King of Kings", Cambyses. In fact, the Persian conquest does not seem to have been brutal. Cambyses' successor Darius (522–486 BC) was particularly sensitive to Egyptian traditions. Darius guessed correctly that as long as he was prepared to act as a traditional king, taking traditional titles, building or restoring temples, and maintaining the peace, the Egyptians would be prepared to accept a foreigner as ruler. Once, however, an outsider breached the conventions and ruled as if he were a conqueror, support was quickly lost. This was the fate of Darius' son and successor, Xerxes.

From the 460s to 404 BC there were a number of revolts against the Persians. Egyptian independence was even briefly renewed between 404 and 343 BC. Then the Persians regained control with some brutality. When the young Macedonian king Alexander challenged Persia in the 330s BC, he found himself welcomed by the Egyptians as a liberator. Their hopes were dashed as Alexander departed and his officials began to exploit the wealth of the country. The 3,000-year-old kingdom of Egypt had inherited the fate of its numerous former vassals. It was now to be subject to foreign control for well over 2,000 years.

THE EGYPTIAN ACHIEVEMENT

SECURE IN RICH HARVESTS FED BY THE NILE FLOODS, THE EGYPTIANS BUILT THEIR COMPLEX CULTURE. THEY INVENTED A WRITING SYSTEM USED IN THE WORLD'S OLDEST RELIGIOUS TEXTS AND SOME OF THE OLDEST FOLK TALES. THEIR RELIGIOUS MYTHS ADDRESSED PEOPLE'S DEEPEST NEEDS; AND THEIR BELIEF IN THE AFTERLIFE AND THE JUDGMENT OF THE DEAD WAS INCORPORATED INTO WESTERN RELIGION. THE EGYPTIANS' GREAT TEMPLES ALSO INSPIRED LATER CULTURES, ESPECIALLY THEIR ARCHITECTURE AND THEIR REMARKABLE ACHIEVEMENTS IN MONUMENTAL SCULPTURE AND REPRESENTATIONAL PAINTING.

Main picture Aerial view of Khephren's pyramid at Giza

Inset Wall painting from the tomb of Nefertari

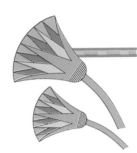
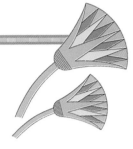

PEACE & PLENTY
Daily Life in Ancient Egypt

"You go down to your ship of fir-wood, manned from bow to stern. You reach your beautiful villa, the one you have built for yourself. Your mouth is full of wine and beer, of bread, meat and cakes. Oxen are slaughtered and wine is opened and melodious singing is before you. Your chief anointer anoints you with ointment of gum. Your manager of cultivated lands bears garlands. Your chief fowler brings ducks, your fisherman brings fish. Your ship has returned from Syria laden with all manner of good things. Your byre is full of calves, your weavers flourish. You are established while your enemy is fallen, and the one who spoke against you is no more."

These words, from a text used by children learning hieroglyphs, summed up the good life for those lucky enough to afford it. Reliefs on the walls of countless tombs present a similar picture: the landowner and his wife watch as laborers gather in crops, store the grain or bring in herds of cattle. These reliefs show only what the landowner hoped he would find in his afterlife, yet the portrayal was rooted in real life on earth. In most years Egypt could expect a rich harvest, and men and women favored by the king could live unusually well.

NOTHING COULD BE achieved without careful management, however. The routines of the

The Pattern of the Year

farming year were fixed by the floods. As the river rose in June, the peasants would guide the water between carefully-prepared dykes. When the floods had reached their height, the farmers paddled around in boats closing the gaps, so that

PAINSTAKINGLY DRAWN by the artist, three species of geese feed together (ABOVE) on a painted plaster panel from the Old Kingdom tomb of Prince Nefer-Mat, a son of King Snefru, and his wife Itet at Meidum. Their wealth procured them vast estates during their lifetimes, and such artistic representations of continued wealth in the afterlife.

the water would be conserved and then seep away slowly into the soil or evaporate, leaving its silt behind. While a low flood always brought the fear of famine, a high one was feared almost as much, as it would sweep away the dykes and prevent the water bringing its full benefit to the soil.

This husbanding of the treasured water was essentially a community activity. When a man died and his soul was presented to the judges of the underworld, he had to swear that he had never diverted water from the fields of others or dammed up water flowing on its way to his neighbors. The

*H*ARVEST SCENE *from tomb of Menna, scribe to Tuthmosis IV (ABOVE). A surveyor measures the crop, and tax collectors beat those who fail their quotas. Below is the threshing floor. The grain is winnowed with wooden paddles, then scribes record its volume. Below that, a row of workers with sickles harvests the grain, which is carried away in nets.*

A SIMPLE TOOL *called the shaduf (LEFT) was used for irrigation from about 1500 BC. Consisting of a pole with a weight and a bucket at opposite ends, it is still used by peasant farmers.*

duties of the individual landowner and local administrators interlocked. Efficient officials would boast of how they prepared new dykes and canals and ensured the water reached onto higher ground. Every ten days they inspected the level of the water, and as it retreated they would be there to establish boundaries between the farms and settle any disputes that arose between the landowners.

Plowing was the first task to be done once the waters had receded. The silt was heavy and needed proper turning before crops could be sowed. Plows were primitive: most of those that survive are little more than sticks with their ends hardened by fire. Some of the tomb paintings show that the poorer farmers had to pull them through the soil themselves, though the richer had oxen to do the job for them. The plows did no more than cut

through the soil. The hard work lay in breaking up the clods of earth so that the seeds – barley or emmer wheat – could be sown. Visiting Egypt in the fifth century BC, the Greek historian Herodotus commented that the peasants reaped the fruits of the earth with less effort than anywhere else in the world, simply sowing the crops and then awaiting the harvest. Another Greek historian, Diodorus (first century BC), wrote of how the peasants enjoyed feasting and recreation during the floods. However, texts from earlier periods suggest that life was never quite so relaxed. There was much back-breaking work to be done, and during the months of the floods peasants might find themselves conscripted as labor on the great building projects of the kings – though in famine years these projects may have offered effective relief by employing thousands of laborers.

▼ KHNUM & HAPY
Gods of the Flood

K hnum, one of the oldest gods of Egypt, came from the area of the First Cataract, to the far south. He became associated with the annual Nile flood, which seemed to originate from his domain. As a symbol of the fertility which the flood brought, he was depicted with the head of a ram and given the role of a creator-god. A temple of the Roman period portrayed him as creator of all, even of the other gods.

Khnum created the human race from clay, which he made by mixing earth and water with air. Many reliefs show him with his potter's table and the small figures into which he was to breathe life. As he did so, he gave each individual his or her allotted life span, "that-which-is-ordained". However, Khnum tired of this work and placed a potter's wheel in the womb of every female creature so that creation could continue without him.

The god of the inundation itself was Hapy. It was believed that he

K HNUM, god of floods, shown as a ram-headed man in this 18th-Dynasty sandstone relief.

dwelt among the rocks of the First Cataract. He too was a symbol of fertility and was shown with a pot belly, pendulous breasts and a headdress of aquatic plants, thus combining male and female aspects of fertility. Akhenaten may have drawn on this image when he allowed himself to be portrayed with a distended stomach.

As the crops grew, the overseers came back to calculate the yield, so that a preliminary assessment of taxation might be made. Then the harvest would begin. The harvesters worked in groups, advancing in rows to the rhythm of harvesting songs, wielding their flint sickles in time to the tune of a flute. The heads of the grain were cut off, leaving the stalks to be collected later. These were used to make bricks or baskets, or as fuel for the pottery kilns. Farmers with oxen would then use them to stamp the gathered corn so as to separate the chaff from the grain; it was winnowed by being thrown in the air. Clearing the fields had to be done quickly. There are accounts of peasants hurrying to get in the last of the crop before the new floods came to drown the fields.

Barley could be transformed into bread and beer, the staples of the Egyptian diet. The beer was made from the mash of fermented barley-bread and could be sweetened by adding dates. Wine was

preferred by the rich, and there were vineyards in the Delta. Vegetables could be grown as a second crop (they replaced the nitrogen which the first crop had taken) or in separate garden plots. Onions, garlic, leeks, cabbages, cucumbers, peas, beans, even asparagus were grown. Flowers were cultivated in the gardens attached to the houses of the prosperous, providing a haven for bees. Domesticated bees were known as early as the Old Kingdom (they were believed to be the tears of the sun-god Ra), and their honey was used for sweetening food and drink. The hives were made from bundles of reeds. When the time came to extract the honey, the bees were smoked out.

The larger landowners owned herds of cattle. The herds of the temples were often huge. The temple of Amun at Karnak, the richest in all Egypt, had no fewer than 421,000 recorded in the reign of Ramesses III. Their meat was used as offerings to the gods. For the individual landowner, a large

A HAND REACHES for figs on a table (ABOVE) in this detail of an 18th-Dynasty Amarna period wall painting from Sheikh Abd el-Qurna, West Thebes. The realistic style of the art from this period was beautifully suited to everyday scenes. A sense of ease and plenty comes through clearly.

CATTLE ARE DRIVEN before a landowner and his son while four scribes count the number of animals (BELOW). Guards with sticks stand ready nearby. This wooden model was made for an 11th-Dynasty tomb.

herd seems to have served as a status symbol, with the cattle counted and paraded in front of him perhaps once every two years. This "census" was so important that in early Egyptian history the reign of a king was measured by the number of biennial cattle counts that had taken place. Sheep and goats were also farmed. Although the pig was associated with Seth, the god of chaos, pork was not taboo; it was eaten by the poor, and there seem to have been separate pig farms.

For clothing, linen was preferred to wool, and so flax was another important crop. The plants were pulled up by the roots, and the seeds were taken off and crushed to produce linseed oil. Linen cloth made from the fibers of the stalks, which were twisted into balls and the fibers pulled out of them for weaving. Weaving was always done by women, often under supervision by a male overseer in workshops. The Egyptians preferred simple clothes. Anything too elaborate would have been unbearable to wear in the long months of intense heat. Linen was praised for whiteness and for a delicate, nearly sheer texture. Colored cloth was worn only by foreigners.

Many farmers were tenants. The temples, for instance, often rented out their vast estates, demanding a fee of some 30 percent of the crops. At the end of each harvest the temple barges could

*G*RANARY SCENES *are painted on the tomb of an official from the First Intermediate Period* (BELOW REAR), *who obviously managed to provide for himself in spite of the disorder. A donkey carries two baskets of grain. Porters carry further baskets up the stairs to the top of the dome-shaped granaries.*

*S*UCCESSFUL DIGNITARIES *could expect to be well rewarded for their efforts. The 5th-Dynasty vizier Ka-aper* (BELOW FRONT), *carved in wood and found at Saqqara, displays the universal result of keeping a rich table.*

be found journeying up and down the Nile each year in search of their dues. Once the rent had been paid, the tax collector had to be satisfied. The officials visited each landowner with standard-sized tubs to measure out their exactions from whatever was spare. A famous account from the *Book of Advice to Scribes* (which attempted to persuade trainee scribes of the advantages of their profession, which did not depend on the land for a living) talked of tax collectors arriving with bailiffs armed with sticks, beating up the hapless peasants and throwing them into a pond when they could not provide what was due. Even women were tied up and children put into shackles; neighbors disappeared rather than staying to offer support. It is impossible to know whether this was typical, but life in ancient Egypt was certainly harsher than the idyllic paintings on tomb walls suggest.

On the tomb walls of the 18th-Dynasty vizier Rekhmira at Thebes, the mayors of towns are seen presenting the accumulated revenues of these visits by the tax collectors. They include everything from barley to honey, from cattle to pigeons, from grass mats to ingots in gold or silver. There could be other predators on the surplus produce. When the general Haremhab was trying to restore order to Egypt after Akhenaten's reign and began listening to complaints, he discovered that the queens and the royal harem, making their leisured way down the Nile, had seized grain from the local mayors. Other decrees show that the forts in Nubia had acquired a habit of siphoning off some of the exotic goods passing on boats from the south on the way through to temples in Egypt. In the future, one decree warned, any official who was caught stealing would be subject to a hundred lashes.

JOSEPH
and the King's Dream

JOSEPH fills the pyramids (thought in medieval times to be granaries) with grain, on a mosaic from the cupola of St Mark's Cathedral, Venice.

One of the most familiar stories set in Egypt is that of Joseph, from the Old Testament. Joseph was an Israelite brought into Egypt as a slave when his brothers sold him to traders. He served as a household slave but soon became a steward to the commander of the guard. When he rebuffed his mistress's attempts to seduce him, she had him thrown into prison. His abilities again became apparent and he was placed in charge of the prisoners. He was particularly gifted at interpreting dreams. News of his skill reached the king, who was troubled by a dream in which seven thin cows ate seven plump ones and seven lean ears of corn swallowed seven fat ones. Joseph explained that the dream predicted seven years of plenty followed by seven of famine. A man of wisdom should be appointed to govern the country and call in a fifth of all grain in the years of plenty to keep for the years of famine. Joseph was given the job.

When famine eventually struck, outsiders came to Egypt in search of grain. All Joseph's brothers except the youngest, Benjamin, came to

beg from Joseph but he treated them as spies; keeping one as a hostage, he asked them to bring Benjamin as a sign of their integrity. The others returned with Benjamin. At last Joseph revealed himself and called them all, including his father, to settle in Egypt. The Israelites become prosperous and grew in numbers, but their status gradually fell. Their descendants, led by Moses, left Egypt in the Exodus.

The story is apparently set in Egypt's New Kingdom. But some scholars argue on stylistic grounds that it is a late addition to the text of *Genesis* (which was compiled in 800–700 BC) and that such tales of rags-to-riches and of men achieving power through their wisdom are typical of literature of the seventh and sixth centuries BC. If so, then Joseph, if he truly existed, was of far later date than the Jewish presence in Egypt that ended with the Exodus.

Overseers, Officials & Order

EGYPT'S POPULATION during the New Kingdom has been estimated at about three and a half million, a large figure for this early period. The effective administration of the kingdom therefore required a bureaucracy which, when driven by the motivating force of a strong king, was able to exercise strict supervision so that the surplus of crops, produced by peasant labor up and down the Nile valley, was passed on to the king and the ruling classes. Entrance to this bureaucracy was only possible after 12 years of a rigorous education which centered on mastering the hieroglyphic script. Successful students became members of the ruling elite, as the scribe was far more than just a clerk who was able to write and did not have to dirty his hands in the soil. As one text put it: "When you call one, a thousand answer. You will walk unhindered on the road and not become an ox to be handed over. You will be at the head of others". A scribe might be required to supervise justice, lead expeditions into the desert and oversee building projects. However high an official rose in the service of the king, he always took pride in his status as a scribe, and this achievement was included among his other titles, no matter how many he attained.

The peak of a successful career was to become the king's vizier. The New Kingdom vizier Rekhmira (c.1450 BC) boasted on the walls of his tomb at Thebes that there were no secrets that were hidden from him, even those of the gods. He was the heart, the eyes and the ears of the king. Viziers had such power that they could keep the country functioning at times when the kings themselves were weak, such as during the Second Intermediate Period.

Other senior officials were managers of the king's personal estates, commanders of the armies, head of the building works, chief priests (who might be former royal officials). Each of these spheres of responsibility had its own department headed by a core staff of 20 or 30 leading officials. Among the posts was that of supervisor of the state granaries, responsible for preserving the grain surplus. The granaries owned by the state and the temples could be huge. The mortuary temple that Ramesses II built for himself at Thebes, for instance, could store enough to feed perhaps 20,000 people for a year. The granaries were the "banks" of the state, with the grain its "capital" supporting the king's building projects.

AN ALABASTER CUP in the shape of a half-open lotus flower (LEFT) was found at the entrance of Tutankhamun's tomb. The handles also take the form of a lotus flower and buds, on each of which perches a spirit of "millions of years". The cup is inscribed with a wish for the king's eternal happiness. Such exceptional beauty and craftsmanship were reserved for royalty and for the very rich.

Grain also provided the essential resources for Egypt's trade, though granite and diorite were also traded into Mesopotamia. Ultimately it was the king who oversaw Egypt's trade. A successful ruler sent expeditions into the desert in search of gold, copper, turquoise, and further afield for exotic goods: incense from Somalia, animals from central Africa, timber and resin from the Levant, copper from the Mediterranean and lapis lazuli from Afghanistan. Much of this was passed on to the elite to enjoy during their lifetimes, or to place in their graves after death. There is no more potent symbol of Egypt's wealth than its capacity to create a vast array of sophisticated goods, many of them exquisitely crafted, which were intended simply to be shut away forever with the dead.

TUTANKHAMUN'S TOMB also contained a ceremonial chair (BELOW). Its gold-plated wood is decorated with geometric motifs and hieroglyphs inlaid in ebony, ivory, semi-precious stones and faience. The seat is of ebony with an ivory inlay imitating a spotted animal skin. The legs are carved as ducks' heads. The frieze shows the usual icons of royalty such as the solar disk and the vulture-goddess. Bound foreign captives appear on the footstool – literally under the king's feet.

EVEN AFTER so much of the wealth had been squirreled away in tombs, the wealthy – who with their families made up possibly some 5 percent of the population – enjoyed a fine lifestyle. Surviving pictures of houses and daily scenes within them show that ancient Egyptian life could be orderly and civilized. Houses were probably built in mud-brick but plastered and painted white. Outside the towns, the country villas of the rich had gardens and pools surrounded by trees. The houses themselves were often raised from the ground, presumably to give protection from high floods, with the best reception rooms placed on the second floor. Excavations at

A Prosperous Lifestyle

el-Amarna show how the more opulent residences were decorated. In one there is a ceiling of brilliant blue, columns painted in brown, and white walls with a frieze of blue lotus leaves against a green background; there are bathrooms with slabs on which a bather stood while water was poured over him. On the top floor, the roof had openings through which the breeze could blow, bringing some relief from the stifling summer heat.

Homes of craftsmen, the class immediately below the bureaucratic elite, were found at Deir el-Medina, the village that built and serviced the royal tombs in the Valley of the Kings. These houses

*T*HE GROUND PLAN *of a Theban villa set in a garden (ABOVE) is painted on the wall of an 18th-Dynasty tomb – that of Minnakht at Sheikh Abd el-Qurna, Thebes. Inside the mud-brick walls, which were often 3 meters (10 feet) high, there was also room for granaries and a well. The largest villas had enough space for a shrine and enclosures for animals.*

were more cramped. Entering from a narrow alley, visitors were received into a small room dedicated to household gods. Next they came to a larger reception room graced with a column and a couch. Underneath this room was a chamber for storing valuables – the owner would often place his bed over its entrance at night. Beyond were the living rooms, including the kitchen. A staircase at the back of the house led up to the roof, which was used for relaxation in the warm evenings.

For the well-to-do, a large staff was essential: if there was anything that the rich truly feared, it was having to do manual labor or domestic work

themselves. On the ground floor below the reception rooms, a small army of servants carried out the business of daily life: weaving, brewing, kneading dough, baking and waiting on their master and mistress. Even when simply walking through the streets, a wealthy Egyptian was accompanied by two servants, one shielding him from the sun and the flies, the other carrying a spare set of sandals for him to put on when he had washed the dust from his feet. It was a sign of status that the landowner and his wife had light skin. They clearly did not have to endure the hot sun every day, unprotected, as their laborers did.

*T*HE YOUNG *Tutankhamun and his wife Ankhesenamun are depicted on an ornamented chest (LEFT). The queen wears a fine, transparent robe of pleated linen and a heavy bejewelled wig, topped by a perfume cone. She offers her husband bunches of lotus and papyrus decorated with mandrakes, the fruit of love.*

*F*EMALE SERVANTS *and dancers were often shown wearing nothing but a thin girdle like this one (RIGHT) from the 12th-Dynasty tomb of Princess Sit-Hathor-Yunet. The cowrie shell had talismanic significance, with its supposed resemblance to female genitalia, and would protect the wearer, especially in pregnancy.*

*O*NE OF THE PRINCESSES *of Amarna (BELOW) is sculpted wearing an asymmetric ringleted wig. Wigs, like jewelry and perfume, were worn by both sexes and were often heavily decorated.*

*T*HERE IS some written evidence surviving of the ways the personal relationships of

Courtship and Marriage

this leisured elite evolved. Among the young there seems to have been a surprising amount of social freedom. The love poetry of the New Kingdom reveals young lovers bantering with each other and making no secret of their sexual desire. In one song a seductive girl told her lover how, if he came with her to the river bank, she would let him see her undress and bathe. Another song contained a frank admission of desire from the girl who stayed awake all night longing for the body of a young man.

However, there is no doubt that more serious relationships, such as marriage, were not chosen at will by young people but were arranged formally by their parents, usually between families of equal social status when the girl was just at the onset of puberty. Only rarely did the Egyptians marry within their own immediate family, though from very early times the king frequently married his sister or step-sister, following the example of Isis and

Osiris. (This was usually a symbolic marriage for religious purposes; the king's children were almost always born to a wife other than the one who was his sister, or to one of his numerous royal concubines.)

Once married, women took the traditional role of overseeing the house and its activities, and men were specifically warned not to interfere with their wives' management. Women were portrayed in ancient texts as an asset best enjoyed through good treatment. "If you are excellent," one text runs, "you shall establish your household, and love your wife according to her standard: fill her belly, clothe her back; perfume is a prescription for her limbs. Make her happy as long as you live! She is a field, good for her lord." A good husband installed his wife in style and encouraged her to take care with her appearance.

A cosmetic set surviving from the New Kingdom has eye paint, a mixing palette, an ivory comb and pink leather sandals. In many cases married couples appear to have lived in genuine affection. The naturalistic style of art developed at el-Amarna showed many informal moments in the lives of Akhenaten and Nefertiti with their three children, offering an intimate picture of domestic bliss.

Civilized living depended on social and political stability. If ever the long lines of communication along the Nile valley weakened or broke, the surplus harvest could not be passed on to the centers of power and the whole structure of society was threatened. Despite Egypt's long history, its structures were often fragile. This explains why there was a deeply-rooted, almost pathological fear of disorder at all levels of society. One of Egypt's greatest achievements was maintaining social stability for so long, in spite of brief periods of disruption. Rulers were able to rely not only on their divine status but also on a model of order which stretched back over many generations.

However, there was a price to pay for such stability. The ultimate weakness of this system was that it proved all too easy for outsiders – Persians, Greeks and Romans – to appropriate the well-established framework of royal power and rule for themselves, claiming that they too were legitimate rulers of the country they had come to exploit.

" *Let husband and wife therefore live blamelessly together, observing all the duties of marriage.* "

Marriage contract, AD 260

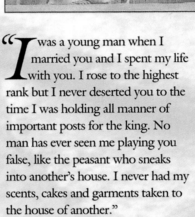

Men, Women & Children

" *I* was a young man when I married you and I spent my life with you. I rose to the highest rank but I never deserted you to the time I was holding all manner of important posts for the king. No man has ever seen me playing you false, like the peasant who sneaks into another's house. I never had my scents, cakes and garments taken to the house of another."

This letter, written by a man to his wife after her death, sums up the ideal of Egyptian family life. Young men were expected to marry as soon as they had the financial means. By the age of 15, most girls were married and had given birth to one child. Husbands and wives were expected to live in equality and to show care for each other.

Of course, the ideal was not always the reality. On pottery fragments from the workmen's village at Deir el-Medina are accounts of arguments and

Above A faience statuette of a woman, possibly Nubian, nursing a baby. A small monkey sits on each shoulder and a third on the ground. Children were suckled till their third year and wet-nurses were often employed.

Above The dwarf Seneb and his family from their 4th-Dynasty tomb. It was usually the wife who was shown embracing the husband (as here) rather than the opposite, but the portrait clearly shows mutual affection. This reflected the cultural expectation of marriage as a state of earthly bliss.

Right The royal builder Sennedjem and his wife Iynefert plow and sow seeds together in the mythical fields of Iaru. Wives were entitled to their own personal graves and complete funerary equipment, but they were almost always buried with their husbands if the couple were wealthy enough to afford a tomb. A divorce meant that the wife's name and image would be removed from the husband's tomb.

Left A squatting woman gives birth, aided by two figures of the goddess Hathor who, alongside Taweret, was called on to ensure safe delivery. Providing a male heir was the primary duty of a wife, and failure to conceive was grounds for divorce. A husband might take a concubine either as a remedy or simply because he wished to do so. Concubines were usually slaves, and their children were also slaves until freed by legal adoption by their father.

Left A father grooms his daughter while two younger siblings sit at their feet – one of many representations of affectionate family life that have survived in tomb paintings. Young children often went naked, and their heads were shaved except for a sidelock. This was so much the symbol of childhood that it came to stand as a hieroglyphic for child or youth. Puberty for girls usually occurred at age 12 or 13, a year later for most boys.

separations. Adultery was a serious crime punishable by public flogging, branding, or banishment, and the infidelity of a wife was grounds for divorce. (Husbands were not held to the same standard.) Although the marriage ceremony was a private matter, ungoverned by church or state, divorce was discouraged by financial penalties. A woman who divorced her husband could claim back her personal property and her share of joint property, but no more. A man who divorced his wife to marry another woman might have to pay out two-thirds of his personal estate as well as paying back the dowry and handing over all joint assets. Court interviews of cast-off wives exposed husbands to embarrassment and censure.

Children were perhaps the most important part of family life, and most families had between four and six. Infant mortality was high, particularly around the age of three, when the protective power of breast milk was lost to solid food. Affection for children was reflected in their names: "This is the boy I wanted", "Welcome to you". Children were not expensive. They went naked, and according to one account they could thrive on toasted papyrus shoots. They had toys and years of play before they grew old enough to work. As adults they were expected to support their aging parents.

Background Akhenaten and his daughter

Above A toy horse from the Greco-Roman period. Animal toys were very popular, including models of crocodiles that could open their mouths and shake their tails. Dolls, rattles, spinning tops and other toys were also made, sometimes by the children themselves.

> **"** *Enjoy yourself while you live, put on fine linen, anoint yourself with wonderful ointments, multiply all your possessions on earth, be joyful and make merry.* **"**
>
> Harper's song, from the tomb of Inyotef

Pleasures & Pastimes

Ancient Egyptians were sociable and knew how to enjoy their leisure. In the evenings they often gathered together for dinners or banquets. There were elaborate rituals of welcome by the host, who was complimented in turn by the guests on the prosperity and good order of his house. On informal occasions men and women sat down together to eat, on formal occasions apart. Men were not the only ones who became intoxicated: "Bring me 18 goblets of wine," a wealthy woman commands a servant in one tomb scene, "can't you see I am trying to get drunk?" After the meal, singers and dancers would perform.

Music pervaded everyday life, and by the New Kingdom there was a wealth of instruments: oboes,

Above Swimming was popular with everyone, as this cosmetic spoon shows. The handle is a naked young girl, and the container is in the form of a duck. Girls undressing to swim were also a common theme in Egyptian love poetry.

Below An 18th-Dynasty banquet is captured in a tomb painting. Wealthy guests sit in chairs above; the lower register shows dancers and musicians. One is playing the double flute, with the words of the song written above. Rhythmic hand-clapping and nodding the head in time to the music are clearly shown. This painting is unusual for showing a full face view.

Left In his short life Tutankhamun played *senet* ("passing") on this gilded ebony gameboard, inlaid with ivory, which was subsequently buried with him. The two players sat opposite each other at either end of the board and moved pieces similar to chess pieces. *Senet* was frequently depicted on tomb walls and came to symbolize passage through the underworld.

Right A royal fly whisk made of wood covered in gold. Its curved edge is pierced with holes for attaching ostrich feathers (the whisk). The scene on the upper handle shows Tutankhamun hunting ostriches in the desert with bow and arrows. Hunting, fishing and archery were all competitive sports for young men.

> *Toil no more than is required nor cut short the time allotted for pleasure; it offends the spirit to be robbed of its time...wealth will come even if you indulge your own wishes, it will be useless if you thwart them.*
>
> *Instruction of Ptah-hotep,* 5th Dynasty

Right This faience (ceramic) bowl of the 20th Dynasty depicts a girl playing a mandolin. Its long-necked oval body was made of wood and covered partly in wood and leather for resonance. Singing and music went together; the voice was almost always heard accompanied, and straight instrumental music did not exist at all. Ensembles were most common in the New Kingdom.

flutes, lyres and harps. The dancers were kept in time by the beat of a hand rattle called the *sistrum*, which is still used today in the rituals of the Coptic (Egyptian Christian) church. Storytelling was also valued. One papyrus records the sons of Khufu entertaining their bored father with tales of the exploits of magicians. Those who were less affluent could drop in at the local inns, which seem to have stayed open all night. Brothels catered to young single men. Such establishments were the bane of teachers who tried in vain to impose sobriety on the young scribes they were training.

Board games were popular for entertainment at home. Most of them involved moving counters around squares, some of which had lucky or unlucky associations like the luck of the draw in modern board games. Children preferred to play outside, often inventing their own activities. Boys appear to have enjoyed competitive games such as wrestling or fighting with sticks. Girls preferred dancing, which was not only a pastime but also a necessary accomplishment for any well-bred young woman. One dancing game involved a whole group whirling around together. Both men and women danced, but not together. To cool off after sports or dancing, there was swimming.

Throughout all these pursuits was an awareness that there is more to living than toil and the burden of office, and that relaxation among friends is one of the joys of existence.

Background **Tomb painting of wrestling**

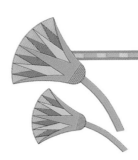
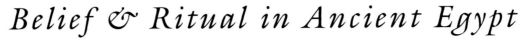
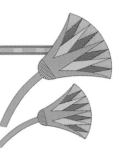

AMONG THE GODS
Belief & Ritual in Ancient Egypt

The Egyptians had a powerful sense of the creation of the world as an act that had brought order out of disorder, and abundant fertility from the mournful waters that had originally covered the earth. They set out an orderly story of creation by which the land, the earth and the sky, the ruling gods and finally the human race appeared. However, even after centuries of evidence that the Nile would annually deliver the sustenance they needed, the Egyptians never felt truly secure. They lived as if they were continually under threat from the forces of disorder that persisted in the deserts around them, in the possibility of the floods failing, or in the natural hazards of life. Order on earth could be preserved only through an active relationship with the gods. Complex rituals and practice were developed to achieve this.

The king, always believed to be wholly or semi-divine, acted as the intermediary between humans and the gods. He was responsible to the gods for maintaining order on earth. The goal of all worship and daily living was *ma 'at* – harmony and balance – and the Egyptians believed that this could be achieved eternally in an afterlife where all would be harmonious and serene.

GODS STRIDE in a line across the sky in the tomb of Sethos I at Abydos (ABOVE). They include Horus (with the falcon head), Thoth (ibis head) and Anubis (jackal head). Horus and Anubis were the sons of Osiris, and Thoth was the son of Horus. From the time of the Old Kingdom, all three were associated with the west – the land of the dead.

Our knowledge of Egyptian religion comes mainly from inscriptions and carvings in tombs and temples. Written myths about the gods were set down not by the Egyptians themselves but by the Greeks and Romans. Also, most archeological evidence has to do with the official religion practiced by the king and his priests. It is difficult to know to what extent the ordinary Egyptian believed in or practiced the official religion – in addition to folk religion – because there are so few records of the common people.

FROM HERMOPOLIS, Memphis and Heliopolis, three principal cults contributed their own particular myths to the creation story. The Hermopolis cult dealt with the creation of being out of non-being, beginning with the emergence of a sun-god from four pairs of male and female primeval forces. The Heliopolitan cult was based on the belief that life was produced by the sun-god (Atum), who had created himself, and then created air (Shu) and moisture (Tefnut), who mated and gave birth to Nut and Geb, the sky and

The Family of the Gods

the earth. Finally, the theology of Memphis centered on creation by the spoken word of the creator-god Ptah. After unification, many of the myths were merged, leading to inconsistencies. Unlike the modern Westerner, who considers truth to be an "either/or" proposition, the ancient Egyptians were not troubled by the apparent contradictions. Creation, for them, was not a single definitive act but a continuous process.

In addition to the different religious centers, there were many local deities. Horus was associated with Hierakonpolis and Seth with Naqada. After unification these gods were gradually formed into a family, complete with marriages, alliances and feuds. Horus and Seth remained enemies as their home cities had been. Newcomers were simply fitted in. Anubis, the jackal-god, was introduced as the offspring of Nephthys, the wife of Seth. It was said that Nephthys fell in love with Osiris and visited him at night. Thinking she was his wife Isis, Osiris made love to her, and Anubis was the result. Much of the success of Egyptian religion lay in the creation and development of story lines such as this, so that new gods – who expressed new aspects of the world – could always be catered for.

The stories themselves answered spiritual needs. Osiris offered a parable of suffering, death and resurrection, while Isis became the archetype of the protective mother as she cared for her child Horus and protected him from serpents and other evils. The longevity of these stories shows that they satisfied some of the deepest needs and hopes of the ordinary Egyptian: for the triumph of order over disorder, life over death and for the protection of a mother figure.

In a country not far from the Equator and one where rainfall was virtually nonexistent, no one could

escape the presence of the sun. Its disappearance each night in the west and miraculous reappearance each day in the east was bound to have a powerful effect on all who depended on its warmth and creative powers. By the time of the Old Kingdom (2575–2134 BC), the sun-god Ra was the unchallenged chief god of Egypt. His most important shrine was at Heliopolis, near the junction between the Nile and the Delta, and centered on the *benben* stone, which was believed to mark the spot where the rays of the sun had first touched earth. Ra's journey on a boat each night through the darkness under the earth was seen as a hazardous one, and so each sunrise was greeted with joy that he had survived its dangers. Seth, god of the underworld, was often shown on the prow of the boat, warding off the powers of darkness.

The forces associated with the sun were too varied to be shown in a single form. Ra himself came to be linked to other gods. Horus, the falcon-god of the sky and protector of the

A RMS RAISED in adoration, a woman prays before Ra-Horakhty, the sun on the horizon (BELOW). The god holds the "was" scepter in one hand and an "ankh" in the other. The sun's rays in the form of lotus buds pour down on the woman in blessing. An offering table stands between them. Each god had a conventional "portrait" as human or animal or a combination. Ra was portrayed as a falcon-headed human with a sun-disc headdress.

A RAM-HEADED SPHINX from the entrance to the temple of Amun at Karnak shelters a king between its paws (LEFT). Rams' heads were associated with the sun-god, Amun, who was regarded as the father of the divine king. The image represents the god's protection of the king.

kings, was associated with the horizon, which was also believed to be the home of Ra – the place from which the god climbed each day and to which he returned each night. Ra and Horus merged to form Ra–Horakhty, meaning "Ra as he appeared on the horizon". An even more significant merging came at the beginning of the Middle Kingdom. The chief god of Thebes, Amun ("the hidden one"), became prominent due to the success of the Theban kings in restoring order to Egypt following the First Intermediate Period. As in any country with an official religion, church and state went hand in hand. It was politically shrewd as well as spiritually satisfying for the Theban kings to link their southern god with the northern Ra, forming a composite god Amun-Ra: the sun as both a visible and invisible source of divine power. In the New Kingdom, Amun-Ra was the spearhead of Egyptian imperialist expansion.

*T**HE KING** offers incense to the sacred barks of Amun-Ra, Khons(the moon-god) and Mut (the vulture-goddess) on a painted relief from a temple of Sethos I at Abydos* (ABOVE). *The god's bark was kept in the inner sanctuary of his temple. On the prow and stern of the bark is the aegis (Greek for shield or breastplate) of the god, in this case the ram's head of Ra. The cabin on the bark has been replaced by a "naos", the innermost part of the shrine that contained the god's cult statue.*

The local gods of the area around the First Cataract – Khnum and Hapy in particular – had always had the aspect of creators; Khnum, the god of the Nile silt, was believed to have shaped the first humans on a potter's wheel. Their individual characteristics soon became associated more specifically with fertility. This attribute was not confined to female deities; there were male or androgynous fertility gods such as the pot-bellied, bearded Hapy with large breasts. In contrast, an important male fertility god was Min, the local god of the ancient trading center of Gebtu, north of Thebes, where trails across the desert from the Red Sea met the Nile. Min is instantly recognizable on artifacts by his flail and his erect penis. At the beginning of each harvest season, his statues were taken from the temples and paraded before the public. They offered him lettuce, whose milky sap was thought to have aphrodisiac powers.

The King & the Gods

AS THE SON OF RA, the king was the representative of heaven's rule on earth. On his shoulders fell the awesome task of maintaining order and right, *ma 'at*. This required more than steady administration. Harmony on earth – the security of Egypt as a stable and prosperous state – could only be maintained through strong kingship.

The king took responsibility for infusing the gods with the divine energies needed to keep order. This was done through the temple rituals. Egypt was full of temples. Each god had his or her main shrine plus a host of secondary ones. In addition, there was a profusion of small shrines for local gods. Sometimes a "family" of three gods had adjoining temples. At Karnak, Amun was associated with his consort, the vulture-goddess Mut, their temples linked by an avenue of ram-headed sphinxes. The moon-god Khons was supposed to be their son, and had his own temple in the precinct of the temple to Amun.

The king was also responsible for building and maintaining the great temples. Some were in a state of continuous rebuilding as kings showered their munificence on favored gods. Kings had their own cult temples at which they could be worshiped alongside the gods. The temple of Abu Simbel is dedicated to Amun, Ra and Ptah and to its builder, Ramesses II, whose queen Nefertari was portrayed in a smaller adjacent temple as the mother goddess Hathor. The king's semi-divine status is indicated by showing him as equal in size to the gods to whom he makes offerings.

At the heart of every temple was its cult statue of the god. This was not believed to be the god itself but a medium through which the god could be approached. It was kept in seclusion in a locked shrine in the darkened center of the temple, approached through a series of halls, each with a higher floor and lower

ceiling than the last. So sacred was a cult statue that the king alone had the right to approach it in the daily ceremonies. These involved breaking the seals that protected the shrine of the statue, changing the clothes that it wore, rubbing it with oils and leaving it food. The purpose of the ceremonies was to renew the energy of the god so that his power could be used to fight off the forces of disorder.

The king himself could not officiate at more than a tiny proportion of these ceremonies. He delegated his responsibility for performing the rituals to senior priests. The priests were not an elite with expertise in theology, but officials who took charge of the temple's building programs, properties and revenues as well as its ceremonial

P ENMA'AT, *a priest at the temple of Amun* (LEFT), *makes an offering of incense in this scene from his own "Book of the Dead". His shaved head identifies him as a priest – he was the head archivist of the temple. Most priests were either specialists (as scribes, astronomers or embalmers, for instance) or were in the lower ranks of administration and maintenance. As such, they often had little to do with direct service of the god. Priests served in one-month "watches" three times a year; for the rest of the time they were entitled to live with their families and pursue a career.*

T HE TEMPLE OF KHONS *at Karnak* (BELOW) *was typical of cult temples in its layout. An avenue of sphinxes representing Ra led to the huge pylon (gateway) at the entrance. From here, a series of processional corridors led through the courtyard and main hall, the height of the floor rising along the way to the god's cult statue in the inner sanctuary.*

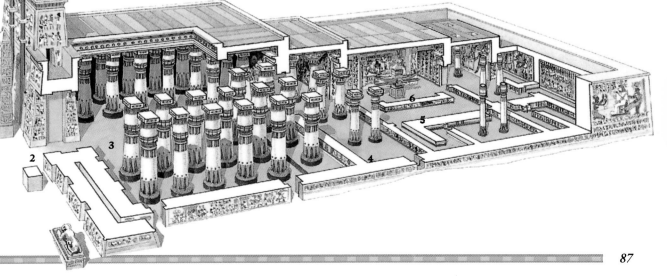

1 Avenue of sphinxes
2 Pylons
3 Courtyard
4 Hypostyle hall
5 Gallery
6 Sanctuary

life. Nonetheless, in their ceremonial duties they had to observe strict rules of purity. They were required to keep their bodies completely shaven (even their eyelashes) and to wash themselves and their vessels thoroughly in the sacred lakes that stood alongside most temples. Although they could marry, they had to abstain from sexual intercourse during their term of duty before approaching the cult statue.

The cult was an exclusive affair. The general public was never admitted through the great pylons and into the temple precincts. Opportunities for mass involvement came only at the great festivals, which centered on the journey of a cult statue from its home temple to another nearby. In the annual *opet* festival at Thebes, the god Amun, weighted with jewelry and gold, was taken by the king in a ceremonial boat and carried on the shoulders of the priests from Karnak to Luxor 2 kilometers (1.25 miles) away. This festival celebrated the god's sexual union with the mother of the reigning king. Crowds lined the route, dancing to drums, with the women shaking rattles known as *sistra*. Some members of the crowd fell prostrate in the path of the god. This was the moment when they might ask questions of the god. His "answer" was shown by the way the priests tilted the statue toward or away from the supplicant.

SEVERAL PAIRS of ears decorate a stela (ABOVE) from a temple at Deir el-Medina. The stela is dedicated to Ra, shown at the top as a pair of rams, by the supplicant, Bai, kneeling at the bottom. The ears represent an aspect of the god, "He who listens to prayers".

Folk Religion & Ritual

FESTIVALS OF THE GODS were rare, and only a tiny proportion of the population could have attended them. In everyday life, less grandiose methods had to be found to preserve the individual from the ever-present threats to a secure life. Largely excluded from the state religious cults, the typical Egyptian relied every day on magic, superstition and ritual. At childbirth, a particularly dangerous moment, a woman had to be protected by ritual. Even the brick over which a mother crouched as she gave birth could be personified as a goddess. Among the protecting deities were Bes, shown as a dwarf figure with a grotesque mask on his face, and Taweret, who took on the guise of a pregnant hippopotamus. Neither had temples but existed at a much less formal level. Pictures of Taweret are found on bed posts and on the amulets worn by all Egyptians to ward off evil.

The chances of survival in life could be enhanced by the use of spiritual forces. The gods were asked to provide every kind of protection for a child at its birth, and an oracle was consulted. Once a favorable response had been gained, the god's promises were listed on a papyrus worn in a tube around the child's neck. Typically the child

AMULETS
Protection & Health

One of the most common ways of attracting good luck or protection was by wearing charms called amulets. Some amulets, in the shape of a bull or a lion, for instance, may have given special strength, courage or potency; others may have been designed to protect limbs or organs or even aim to replace them if they had been damaged. Favored gods were worn for good luck. There were also many symbolic shapes: the *udjat* (Eye of Horus) warded off evil; the *djed* pillar represented stability and endurance; and the *ankh* symbolized life itself. Semi-precious stones were thought to have healing properties, which could

be reinforced by wearing them in particular combinations and colors: green for joy, blue for protection (and for joy too). Red was powerful but could also be unlucky.

Amulets were also wrapped within the layers of mummies to ward off any evil which could threaten the afterlife. They could be of the funerary gods such as Anubis, the god of embalmers, or the four

COMBINED "ankh", "djed" and "was" scepter (TOP LEFT), scarab (BOTTOM LEFT), girdle of Isis (TOP RIGHT), "djed" pillar (BOTTOM RIGHT) and the "udjat" eye of Horus (FAR RIGHT).

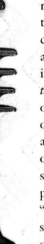

Sons of Horus. (Osiris himself, lord of the underworld, was rarely used.) They could also be parts of the body, designed to replace anything that was missing or damaged. The heart amulet was the most important of these. The *Book of the Dead* stipulated that it be made of cornelian (red, for power), but other materials were also used. As amulets were placed on specific parts of the body, they were activated by spells and incantations. Scarabs, powerful amulets of life, had to be "killed" (their eyes and mouths smashed) before being put in tombs, or they could harm the dead.

A POPULAR DEITY, associated with marriage and domestic happiness despite his grotesque appearance, Bes (LEFT) protected the household from misfortune. He was one of the gods of folk religion rather than official religion. Having no temple, Bes was worshiped by people at home.

TAWERET, goddess of childbirth (BELOW), was invoked by expectant mothers of all social classes. This statuette, carved from green schist, was found outside the temple of Amun at Karnak. Taweret is shown as a female hippopotamus with human arms, lion's legs and a long crocodile's tail formed by her wig.

might be given protection from collapsing walls, from disease and malevolent gods and even from foreigners. Also worn around the neck were amulets, small charms in the shape of gods or parts of the human body, perhaps a part that had been damaged. A favorite design was the "eye of Horus". A legend told how Horus had lost his left eye in one of his battles with Seth. Hathor had restored it, and so the eye became the symbol of healing and making whole.

In the original act of creation it was said that Atum had been aided by a divine creative force, *heka* (often translated as "magic"). This same force was available to ordinary humans. *Heka* could transform one thing into another, inflict harm on enemies, cure illness or offer protection against every form of danger. The most effective way of using *heka* was through incantations. To ward off attacks from animals, for instance, a list of every kind of scorpion, serpent or worm was recited. The incantations did not have to be intelligible. In fact, those that could not be understood by the speaker were believed to have particular power. One papyrus listed a whole collection of sayings that had been borrowed from the languages of the Middle East and Aegean.

OPENING THE MOUTH was the most important ritual of the funeral (RIGHT) – an elaborate ceremony of 75 individual acts that restored living senses to the mummy. Special priests called "sem" priests touched the face twice with an adze and once with a chisel, and rubbed its face with milk. They then embraced the mummy to bring back its soul. These rites might also be performed by the son and heir of the deceased. In this scene from the "Book of the Dead" of Hunefer, another priest in an Anubis mask holds the mummy upright, and a third priest, in a leopard-skin robe, swings the censer. Hunefer's wife mourns in front. The funerary chapel to the right has a pyramid-shaped roof.

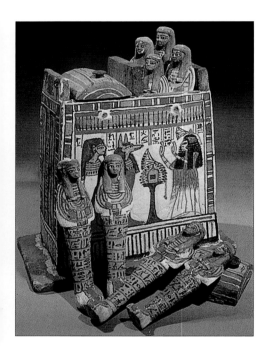

MODEL SERVANTS called shabtis could be delegated to do manual labor in the afterlife. The standard number provided for a wealthy man was 365, with 36 supervisors. Even their tools were included. They were sometimes kept in boxes such as this one (ABOVE) belonging to a Theban princess.

THE EGYPTIANS BELIEVED that human beings were made up of different spiritual elements. In addition to the body itself, there was its shadow and two other forces: *ka,* the divine energy which gave the body life and *ba,* the personality unique to each individual. All of these elements were crucial for participation in the afterlife.

In Search of Eternal Life

Death was an utterly consuming part of Egyptian religion – perhaps more so than in any other religion in the world, reflecting the deep-seated Egyptian horror of unpredictability and lack of control. For the average person, the most predictable thing about death was that it came soon: the life expectancy of the general population was about 29 years. The rich, benefiting from a superior standard of living, might expect to live to 35 or 40. Whenever and however it happened, death was always considered a tragedy. The Egyptians loved life and did not depart it gladly.

However, death was not an end but a pathway into an eternal existence. From their earliest history, the Egyptians believed in an afterlife, burying their dead with the tools they might need in the next world – a practice common to most ancient cultures around the world. The Egyptians regarded the Nile valley as paradise on earth, and they invented a version of paradise that was just like home, with the Nile flowing, the grain

growing, the sun shining, and all the necessary material goods – plus servants for the wealthy – readily at hand. Anyone unfortunate enough to die abroad was brought home to Egypt for burial if this was at all possible.

All the forces that made up an individual – the body, the shadow, *ka, ba* and name – had to be preserved if the individual was to undergo the transformation into *akh,* the form in which a body was able to live in the afterlife. The rituals of mummification and burial were designed to preserve the integrity of the individual. The techniques involved in mummification began early and crudely, with corpses in predynastic times dried in the sun and wrapped tightly before being buried in hollow tombs. Old Kingdom bodies were plastered and painted, with no attempt to control decay underneath. Evisceration was introduced in the 4th Dynasty when bodies began to be buried in an extended position, rather than curled up as ritual had previously dictated. Slowly, over thousands of years, the procedures were refined and elaborated, until mummification reached its height in the Third Intermediate Period. From then on, the level of skill declined, although the practice went on until Christianity became dominant in Egypt.

Once the mummy was complete and had been solemnly escorted to its tomb, the funeral could begin. The mummy was placed upright in its coffin

▼ANUBIS
Jackal God of the Dead

In ancient Egypt jackals wandered along the edges of the desert, just in the places where the Egyptians buried their dead. As scavengers, jackals aroused the fear that they might uncover bodies and feast on them, thus destroying the chances of an afterlife for the deceased. The need to conciliate the jackal must have been behind the appearance of Anubis, a god of the dead with the head of a jackal. His distinctive black coloring did not have to do with the jackal but with the color of rotting flesh and with the black soil of the Nile valley, symbolizing rebirth.

Anubis was the most important god of the dead in the Old Kingdom, but he was replaced during the Middle Kingdom by Osiris. Anubis was given a place in the family of gods as the bastard son of Osiris and Nephthys, and in this role he helped Isis mummify his dead father. In this connection he became the patron god of embalmers, who are believed to have worn jackal-headed masks while preparing mummies. Illustrations from the *Book of the Dead* often show a priest wearing the jackal mask supporting the upright mummy during the funeral rites. And at the judgment of the dead, it was Anubis who read the scales on which the heart of the deceased lay and reported whether the heart was too heavy in evil to allow it into the afterlife. Along with Osiris, Anubis was known as "Foremost of the Westerners" – the west being the land of the dead. His cult became assimilated with that of Osiris.

When Tutankhamun's tomb was opened in 1924, a life-sized figure of Anubis in wood was found in it, complete with carrying poles. As guardian of the dead and overseer of the burial rites, it can be assumed that Anubis was carried in the final processions towards the burial chamber. His image was on the seals of the entrances to the royal tombs in the Valley of the Kings, a symbol of protection for the occupants.

ANUBIS in the form of a black jackal guarded the "Treasury" chamber in the tomb of Tutankhamun, where the canopic chest was kept. It faced the burial chamber, watching over the door.

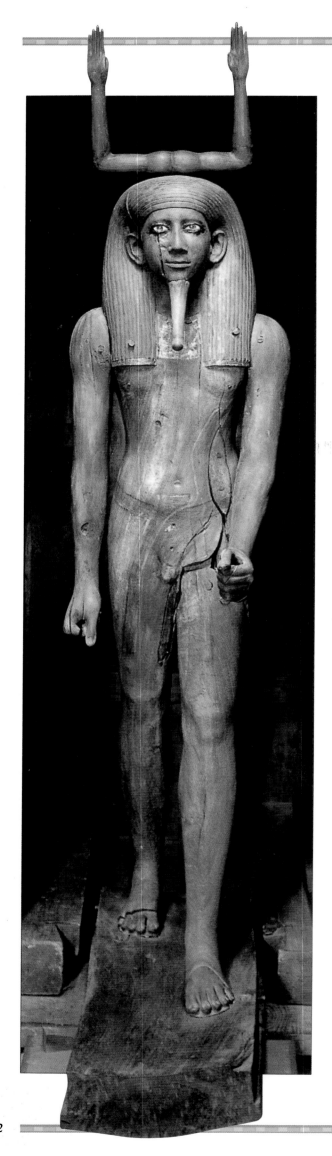

at the tomb door. Mourners fell prostrate before it while priests recited eulogies and sacred texts to assist the deceased in making the transition to the afterlife. The earliest collection of these, called the Pyramid Texts, have been found inscribed on the inner walls of several pyramids of the 5th Dynasty. Some were specifically aimed at bringing the *ba* back into the body; others at protecting the deceased from any misfortune in the life to come. By the Middle Kingdom the texts had changed to give more prominence to Osiris, the god of resurrection, and were inscribed on coffins; they became known as the Coffin Texts. This change reflected far more than just the location and nature of the texts: a private citizen, with no connection to the king, could now gain access to the afterlife.

The texts were also used to ensure that all the comforts of life accompanied the deceased. Anyone who had lived righteously was eligible for the afterlife, but the quality of eternal life depended on the provisions available. Goods were presented in paintings on the walls of the tomb; in actual objects, including favorite jewelry; and in models. The rich were buried with tables, beds, chairs, even chariots and boats. Tutankhamun's tomb boasted a throne of gilded wood, clothes, writing palettes, game boards and fans. Offerings of food were also left in the tomb to sustain the *ba* and the *ka*. Priests, retained in advance, continued to conduct prayers and make offerings to kings. For everyone else, offerings by the family on feast days were sufficient. The tomb paintings, by depicting a life of plenty in the hereafter, could magically substitute for the offerings if these should stop.

BY THE TIME of the New Kingdom a book with some 200 spells was left in the tomb beside the

The Realm of the Dead

mummy, or even bound into it. Collectively called the *Book of the Dead*, these books spelled out the procedures through which the deceased had to pass before being admitted to the Field of Reeds, the eternal realm of Osiris. His heart was weighed against a feather representing *ma 'at*, the harmony which depended on living righteously. Next, he had to promise that he had dealt well with his fellows, respected the gods and never interfered with the offerings made to the dead. Fundamental to these promises was respect for the community, bearing in mind the need to share the good fortune brought by the annual rising of the Nile. The judgment was recorded by Thoth, the scribe-god,

THE BOOK OF THE DEAD of the scribe Ani (ABOVE) guides him through his life in the underworld: making the river crossing from the world, inspecting farms in the Field of Reeds and worshiping Ra, the seven celestial cows and the bull of heaven.

KA was the force that animated the living and distinguished them from the dead. It remained alive but separate when a person died, and was guided back to the right owner by a funerary statue (LEFT) of the deceased with the "ka" symbol – upraised arms warding off evil – over its head. Food offerings and spells were addressed directly to the "ka", which required them to sustain its life force.

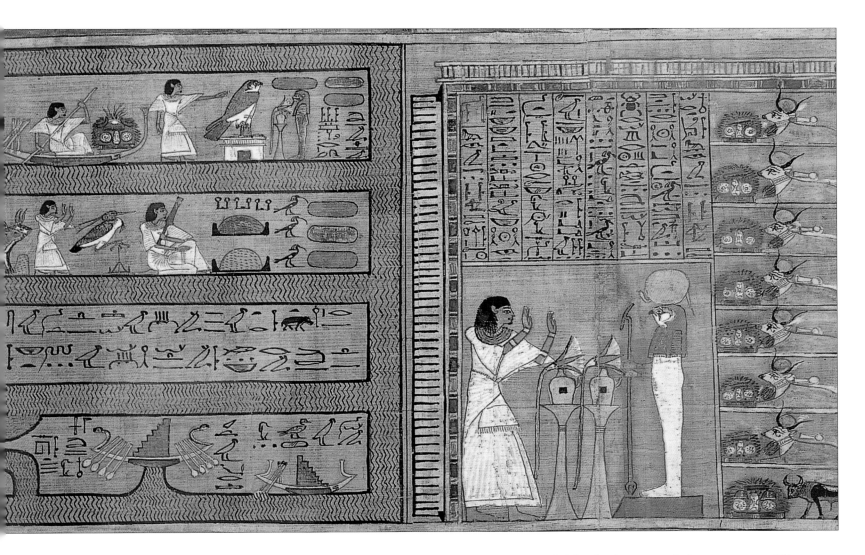

and the successful petitioner could then take up his permanent abode in his tomb, or travel around the underworld as a spirit, one of millions in the solar boat with Ra. In the Old Kingdom this privilege was reserved for kings, and ordinary souls could merely "walk on the perfect ways of the west" (the realm of the dead).

Not everyone who appeared before Osiris could truthfully declare that he had lived a decent life. Some of the spells in the *Book of the Dead* were magic incantations against an unfavorable judgment. A hybrid monster with a crocodile head, known as Ammut or the Eater of the Dead, stood at the scales ready to devour the heart if it proved too heavy with misdeeds. Those condemned to this second death existed as demons in a separate underworld, threatening the forces of order and harmony. It was against these demons that so much protective daily magic and ritual was directed by commoners and nobles alike, and against whom the gods served by the king continuously struggled.

*E*YES LOOK OUT *on the world from a sarcophagus* (BELOW). *Inside, the body lies with the head turned to align with the view. The sarcophagus is decorated like a house, with a painted door to allow the spirit of the deceased to come and go at will.*

Spiritual values pervaded every aspect of Egyptian life. They show a sophisticated desire for balance and harmony on earth as in the afterlife, and the disposition to enjoy both the temporal and the eternal existence. There was little room for personal guilt or feelings of oppression by the gods. Yet the physical and supernatural worlds of the ancient Egyptians remained threatening, and security could only be assured by constantly renewing the energies of the gods. With chaos and disorder never more than a slight mis-step away, it is little wonder that the afterlife was always portrayed as one of ordered harmony. This coherent system of belief came to terms with the deepest human need for meaning and purpose in life and in death. Later, when Egypt's Greek rulers opened the country to the Mediterranean world, the wider wisdom of its most ancient religious heritage fed into other spiritual traditions, including those of the Roman Empire and, still later, those of emerging Christianity.

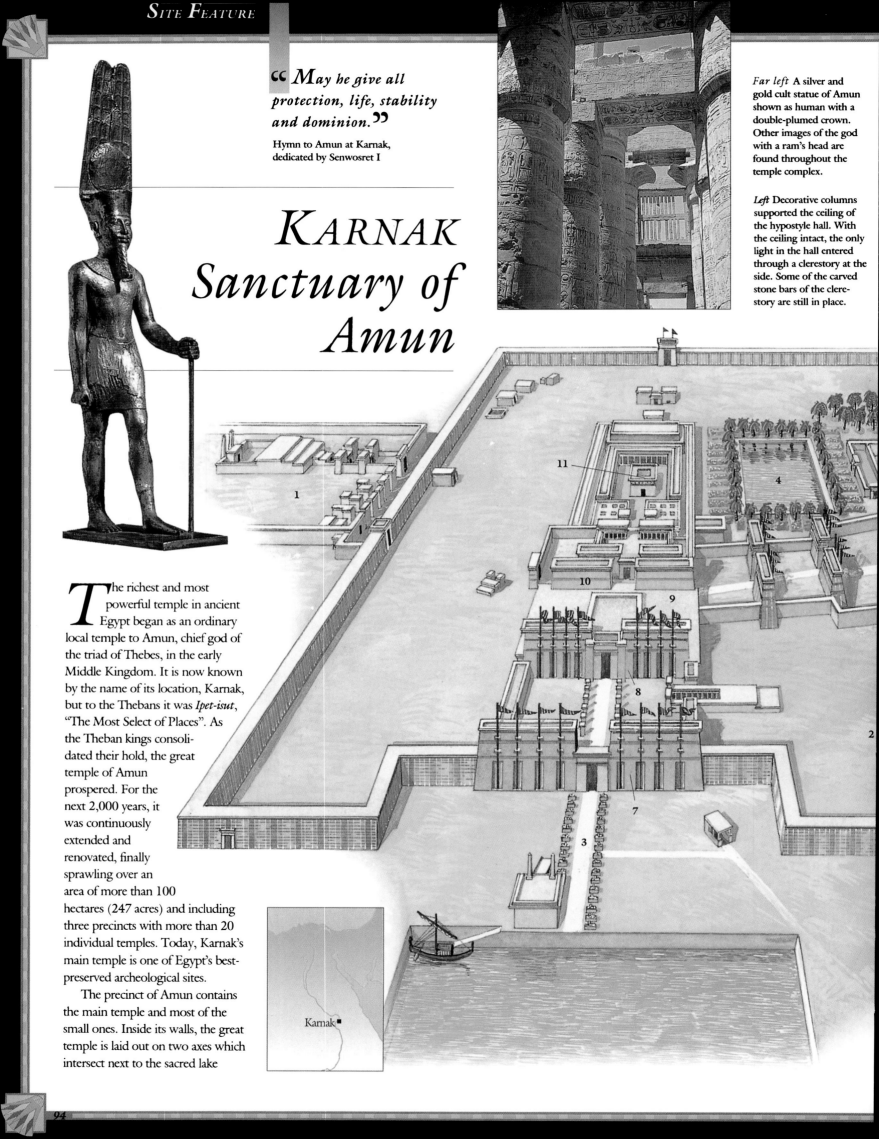

"*May he give all protection, life, stability and dominion.*"

Hymn to Amun at Karnak, dedicated by Senwosret I

KARNAK Sanctuary of Amun

Far left A silver and gold cult statue of Amun shown as human with a double-plumed crown. Other images of the god with a ram's head are found throughout the temple complex.

Left Decorative columns supported the ceiling of the hypostyle hall. With the ceiling intact, the only light in the hall entered through a clerestory at the side. Some of the carved stone bars of the clerestory are still in place.

The richest and most powerful temple in ancient Egypt began as an ordinary local temple to Amun, chief god of the triad of Thebes, in the early Middle Kingdom. It is now known by the name of its location, Karnak, but to the Thebans it was *Ipet-isut*, "The Most Select of Places". As the Theban kings consolidated their hold, the great temple of Amun prospered. For the next 2,000 years, it was continuously extended and renovated, finally sprawling over an area of more than 100 hectares (247 acres) and including three precincts with more than 20 individual temples. Today, Karnak's main temple is one of Egypt's best-preserved archeological sites.

The precinct of Amun contains the main temple and most of the small ones. Inside its walls, the great temple is laid out on two axes which intersect next to the sacred lake

Karnak

Above Before entering the sanctuary, priests bathed ritually in the sacred lake. They also held ceremonies in which the barks of the three Karnak gods were sailed.

KARNAK
1 Precinct of Montu
2 Precinct of Amun
3 Avenue of sphinxes
4 Sacred lake
5 Temple of Khons
6 Precinct of Mut

TEMPLE OF AMUN
7 First pylon
8 Second pylon
9 Hypostyle hall
10 Third pylon
11 Sanctuary
12 Tenth pylon

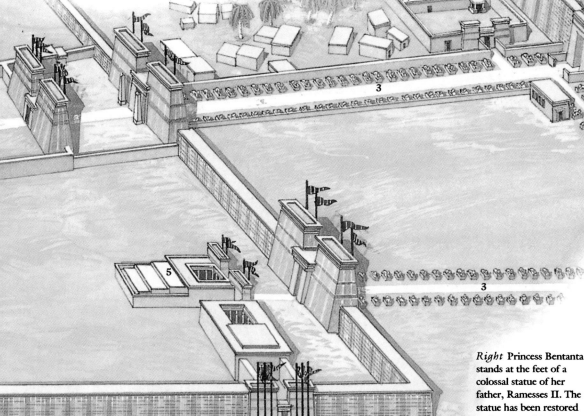

Right Princess Bentanta stands at the feet of a colossal statue of her father, Ramesses II. The statue has been restored and re-erected in the courtyard between the first and second pylons.

found at all Egyptian temples. The temple began with an east-west axis, and the later north-south axis extended south towards the precinct of the goddess Mut. Ten massive gates, or pylons, mark the major extensions. (The third precinct, that of the god Montu, lies outside the north wall.) Between the pylons are huge courtyards filled with statues,

shrines, altars, obelisks, and the minor temples. The original temple lay between the fourth and fifth pylons, erected by Tuthmosis I in the New Kingdom. Four giant obelisks behind the third pylon once marked the original entrance, but only one remains. The surviving sanctuary, containing the bark shrine of Amun, lies behind the sixth pylon

of Tuthmosis III and was built by the early Greek ruler Philip Arrhidaeus (brother of Alexander the Great). Tuthmosis III built a festival hall in the court beyond the sanctuary. Between the second and third pylons is the great hypostyle hall of Ramesses II, which itself covers more than 5 hectares (12 acres). A densely-packed group of

134 colonnades, decorated to look like marsh reeds and papyrus, once created the impression of a primeval forest in dim light. The center of the "forest" is dominated by a dozen towering columns 21 meters (69 feet) high. Outside, avenues of ram-headed sphinxes lead away from the first and tenth pylons, the boundaries of the temple wall.

Far left Protective amulets were laid in ritual order between the wrappings of a mummy. The heart scarab was the most important. The underside was usually inscribed with a formula from the *Book of the Dead*, to prevent the heart from testifying against its owner when it was weighed in the balance.

The Defeat of Death

Fearing death, the Egyptians developed a belief in the afterlife very early in their history. They buried their dead in the hot sand of the desert, with objects that might be needed in the next life. They noticed that if a body was dug up years later, it looked very much as it had looked in life. Preserving the body thus became linked with the afterlife. The poor could never afford anything more elaborate than burial in the sand. But when the wealthy began to be buried in deeper, more elaborate chambers, mortal decay set in.

The first attempts to save the bodies of the dead were crude: wrapping them in linen stiffened with plaster. Embalming was not fully developed until the New Kingdom. The complete process took 70 days; a choice of two abbreviated procedures was available at reduced cost. The full treatment involved cleaning the body, removing the organs, cleaning it again, drying it with natron (the most important aspect of preservation), scenting it, oiling it to keep the skin supple, replacing missing external parts such as eyes, and finally wrapping it and placing it in a coffin. Removing the organs was not a

precise operation; the bladder was often missed, the kidneys almost always. The heart, believed to contain the soul, was left in. The Greeks thought that the brain was removed through the nose – a physically impossible task. In fact, it was liquified by exposure to warm air through a hole in the nose, out of which the liquid then drained.

Every step in embalming and burial was accompanied by ritual. The most important burial ritual was the elaborate ceremony of the Opening of the Mouth, in which a priest restored "life" to each part of the mummified body by touching it with a sacred instrument and rubbing its face with milk.

Left The mummy of an unnamed Theban priestess was buried in this coffin about 1000 BC. By this time, tombs were so often violated that burial caches were used instead. Without tomb walls on which to depict the afterlife, the coffins themselves were decorated with the ritual scenes, as well as with the face of the deceased.

Background Star motif from burial chamber of King Teti

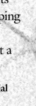

Left The unwrapped mummy of Ramesses II. Resin used in embalming has deteriorated and turned his skin black. Arab observers attributed this to the use of bitumen – *mummiya* – from which the mummy got its name.

" *May your soul live in the sky before Ra, May your ka be divine at the fore of the gods, May your body rest in the underworld before Osiris, May your mummy be a transfigured spirit at the fore of the living, Your name secure on the mouth of those who are on earth.* **"**

Document for Outlasting Eternity
10th century BC

Right The embalmed organs were originally stored in canopic jars placed near the mummy. The stoppers were the four Sons of Horus. Human-headed Imsety guarded the liver, ape-headed Hapy the lungs, jackal-headed Duamutef the stomach, and falcon-headed Qebehsenuf the intestines. Later the organs were put back into the body cavity in packets and the canopic jars became purely symbolic.

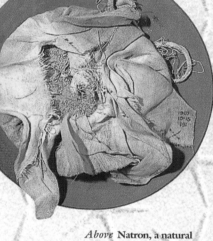

Left The tomb was where the essence of a person – his *ka*, *ba*, shadow, name and body – were reunited after death. It was his eternal home in the afterlife. Men began building their tombs as soon as they reached maturity and established themselves financially. By then they were married; tombs included provisions to bury their wives.

Above Natron, a natural salt, was packed in and around the body to dry it out for embalming. It caused up to 75 percent weight loss by dehydration. Plain salt was used before the 4th Dynasty, but it destroyed the skin.

Left Tutankhamun's solid gold coffin was found inside two larger, richly-ornamented wood coffins inside a massive quartzite sarcophagus. All the inner coffins were anthropoid – shaped and decorated to resemble the king. This practice began in the 12th Dynasty as extra insurance against the destruction of the mummy itself. The king is posed as Osiris, arms crossed, holding two sacred insignia. The feathers engraved on the coffin represent the *ba*, usually shown as a bird.

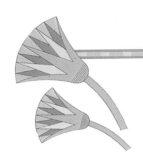
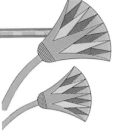

IMAGES OF FOREVER
Art & Architecture in Ancient Egypt

The artists and architects of ancient Egypt were creators of one of the finest cultural traditions the world has known. In their buildings they achieved the monumental without losing a sense of mystery. In their art they developed a style and imagery which fulfilled the complex needs of the Egyptian religious system at the time, and which the modern observer never ceases to find engaging and absorbing. Egyptian art is instantly recognizable, and maintained a unity of style that hardly altered over 3,000 years. Whether as sculptors, painters, workers in gold and precious stones, or craftsmen in wood and rock, the Egyptians reached levels of skill that have seldom been rivaled by any other civilization, and they sustained these levels over many centuries. It was an extraordinary accomplishment.

Only a small proportion of this astonishing art was designed to be seen by living eyes. Art was lavished on the dead and on glorifying the gods in temples which only a tiny number of priests were allowed to enter; the mass of the populace was kept outside the gates. Any art that was visible to the general public invariably had a didactic or propaganda purpose. All Egyptian art reflected the overriding desire to create and preserve the ideal order brought into being at the beginning of creation. Maintaining serenity and order was particularly important for

Eyes of horus watch over a tomb (ABOVE), accompanied by two jackals representing Anubis. Protection by the gods was one of the themes most widely invoked in Egyptian art.

Wedge slots in granite blocks can still be seen in a quarry at Aswan (BELOW). The slots were cut with copper chisels and wooden wedges hammered in and soaked with water. The resulting swelling of the wood split the rock along the lines marked out by the senior mason.

the afterlife, which was, after all, eternal. Tombs – including the pyramids of the Old Kingdom – helped the king reach his rightful place in heaven just as temples allowed the gods to be given their due honor. Sculptures and paintings, similarly, were placed in the tombs of kings and commoners alike – not as frivolous decoration but to create the possibility of an afterlife for the deceased, whose mummified body lay within those walls.

ART WAS RARELY JUST DECORATION or a simple representation of nature. Sculptures were more

The Magic Power of Art

than mere portraits in memory of the dead; paintings in tombs of the hoped-for delights of the afterlife were there for a specific purpose. The images produced through art could be brought alive. A sculpture of a man, placed in his tomb and with the correct rituals enacted over it, was thought to provide a permanent, undecaying abode for his soul after death. A painting of food could magically become the actual food itself; the columns of a temple heavy with leaves could be a forest, or even the very first forest that sprang up at the moment of creation. Similarly, negative images could become very powerful. A hippopotamus or a snake, which might pose a threat in life, could be equally threatening after death. Artists tried to avoid depicting such negative figures altogether, in hieroglyphs as well as in painting or sculpture. Where they could not be avoided, they were often neutralized by being shown in mutilated form, such as a hippopotamus with a harpoon in its side.

Artists were concerned with creating pictures and monuments that were suitable for being brought to life in this way, and therefore they observed artistic conventions that seemed to have been successful in the past. As a result, very few artists were innovators. In this sense, therefore, they were more craftsmen than artists, and it is perhaps less surprising in this case that they rarely signed their work – unlike the much later Greek masters, for instance. Instead, the most important identification to be made was that of the subject, in order for the art to fulfill its ritual function. The hieroglyphic inscriptions that explained the significance of a piece were absolutely crucial, and equal care was lavished on their execution.

The building of tombs and temples was essentially a royal enterprise, and all artistic activity ultimately derived from the king. The king probably had a monopoly of access to the fine metals and stone that were required for building. Only he had the resources to organize quarrying and trade missions – their resumption after a period of weak central government was one of the first signs of a return to order. Another sign, in the Middle and New Kingdoms in particular, was an explosion of temple building. A powerful monarch might build at several sites throughout the kingdom at the same time. Craftsmen were in effect royal employees, and nobles often could not prepare their own tombs unless the king released skilled men to work on them. In the *Tale of Sinuhe*, royal craftsmen were ordered by the king to start work on Sinuhe's tomb after his return from exile.

The trainee craftsman was often the son of a craftsman father. He had access to a large reservoir of collective knowledge. Standards were extraordinarily high. This, together with the fact that the artists and craftsmen formed a cohesive workforce constantly subject to the dictates of royal authority, was another reason why Egyptian art was essentially conservative. There was little opportunity for individual expression, except in the most informal context, and relatively few occasions when significant developments in artistic styles took place. The most important was during the early dynasties when there was an explosion of talent. Later, in the New Kingdom, there was the

short-lived revolutionary approach of Akhenaten at el-Amarna. This religious reformer also appeared to have a passion for art, and may even have personally instructed the royal craftsmen to ignore convention in the representation of the royal family. Oblique disclaimers survive on several pieces in which craftsmen claim to have been "taught" their art by the king. Their bold experimentation showed the king not only informally posed with his family but also drawn in a fashion so exaggerated as to seem deformed: his characteristic long face, prominent chin, and full stomach and thighs, which have suggested a hormonal disorder to modern observers, although at the time it may have been meant to represent the king as the ultimate androgynous fertility figure. No Egyptian craftsman who valued his life would have dared to portray a divine monarch in this way without the monarch's explicit permission, which may have been expressed as a direct order.

IMAGES OF A LIFE of labor survive on tomb paintings such as this stuccoed and painted sandstone (BELOW) from the 19th Dynasty . It depicts two carpenters working on a building site (part of the scaffolding is shown). The lower man holds a tool called an adze. His uncombed, unshaven appearance identifies him as a laborer, in contrast to the idealized representations of the Egyptian upper classes.

THE PYRAMID is, along with the mummy, the most common association that the tourist makes with Egypt, but pyramid-building was mainly concentrated in a relatively short period of the Old Kingdom. In the long history of Egypt, it soon proved an architectural dead end. The towering structures served as a beacon for grave robbers, and not every king was strong or prosperous enough to command the labor of tens of thousands of men for long enough to complete such a project. Later kings chose to be buried more discreetly – though perhaps more lavishly in terms of the contents and decoration of their tombs. Instead, the effort of the royal builders was redirected to be concentrated on temples. Every temple was a shrine to a particular deity, whether local or national, though kings were also regarded as deities even before they died. In their shape and function, the mortuary temples resembled the temples at the traditional religious centers, and after the age of pyramids had passed, the mortuary temples became just as imposing.

The Shrines of the Gods

No early temples or shrines survive, but small mortuary temples dedicated to the cult of the king were built at the bottom of the great causeway that led to the pyramid and its burial chamber. From the Middle Kingdom the temple became the major form of public architecture. Few survive even from that period: kings had no inhibitions about pulling down or rebuilding the temples of their predecessors. The most complete of the surviving temples are those of the New Kingdom or later.

The origins of temple architecture are found in the simple reed shrines of predynastic times, at which a local deity was worshiped by a provincial ruler. These simple shrines had gateways made of bound reeds, courtyards within, and then the shrine proper. This simple layout, reproduced in stone on a majestic scale, was preserved through the centuries in almost all the great temples.

At the front of a temple stood a massive gateway, known as the pylon (from the Greek word for gate). The mass of the population were never allowed beyond the pylon, which consisted of two tapering towers linked by a corniced doorway. At Karnak the pylons were oriented

MASSIVE COLUMNS dominate the portico of Philae (RIGHT), one of the major temples of the Greco-Roman period, in this picture by the nineteenth-century British painter David Roberts. Built mostly between 250 BC and AD 300, on a lush island in the First Cataract of the Nile, the temple has many marsh and aquatic themes. The capitals of the columns were carved to look like papyrus, while the long shafts were decorated with carved and painted relief. These elaborate composite columns were common in the Greco-Roman period.

PTAH
Patron of the Crafts

"O mighty Ptah, life-giving spirit of the world, we invoke thee." The great concluding chorus from Verdi's opera *Aida* pays tribute to the great creator-god of Memphis.

The earliest Egyptian capital had its own creation story in which Ptah, who had existed at the dawn of time, personified the primeval mound. The priests of Memphis considered Ptah superior to other gods of creation because he created through the power of his mind and words. Every heartbeat and sound manifested his creation. It followed from this that every kind of work and handicraft was also his, and so he became the god of craftsmen.

Ptah was shown as a mummified figure, his hands sticking stiffly out and grasping a *djed* pillar, symbol of stability and endurance. His temple at Memphis, now vanished, was

known as *Hoot-Ka-Ptah*, Mansion of the Soul of Ptah. The name was taken by the Greeks to refer to the country as a whole; it became corrupted to "*Ai-gy-ptos*", from which "Egypt" in turn derived. Ptah was also associated with the bull. A live one was chosen to live as his "deputy" in a stall near his temple. The Apis bull, as it became known, excited great reverence. On its death it was mummified and buried in a great vault in Saqqara. Shrines to Ptah were found in other parts of Egypt. The craftsmen at Deir el-Medina had one by their village, while Ramesses II chose Ptah as one of the gods honored at Abu Simbel.

DETAIL from a papyrus (LEFT) shows Ramesses III before Ptah, patron of craftsmen – and thus of royal building projects.

east–west so that the sun would rise or set between them. On the outside the pylons were carved with reliefs, frequently dominated by a formidable figure of the king who built the temple. A temple facade was sometimes created in other ways. Ramesses II fronted his great temple at Abu Simbel, carved from the cliff-face, with four colossal statues of himself, but behind in the rock the temple was set out in a conventional manner, with inner chambers leading to the cult statues of the gods.

The pylon might also be decorated with flags. At the entrance to the temple – as at the great temples of Luxor and Karnak – huge granite obelisks were erected, their tops capped with gold to catch the first rays of the rising sun. The obelisk, a tall needle-like stone, originated at Heliopolis, the cult center of Ra. Its pyramidical top echoed the *benben* stone – the object on which the rays of the sun first settled after the act of creation. By the New Kingdom obelisks were erected in pairs in front of temples, though not even one complete pair now remains in place.

A QUEEN'S HEAD, probably Nefertiti, is a serene and lovely piece of portraiture (ABOVE). Prince Rahotep and his wife, from the Old Kingdom, are reproduced in painted limestone (BELOW).

The temple and its surrounding buildings for the attending priests were enclosed with a mud-brick wall. The wall was worked with wavy lines to represent the waters around the original mound of creation. The temple itself usually had a simple axial plan, and consisted of a processional way through an open courtyard into covered halls, dark except for the light percolating through small grills at the tops of the walls. These halls, called hypostyles, were full of columns ending in palms, lotuses or papyri to represent the sense of the original creation. Below them were carved instructions for the temple rituals. Plants were painted along the dados. As the way moved through the halls toward the sacred enclosure in which the cult statue was held, the floor level rose in imitation of the original mound of creation cited in Egyptian religious doctrine. At the center of the mound stood the cult statue of the god.

The column, whether freestanding or engaged (partially attached to a wall) and with its decorated capital supporting a beam or lintel, became a major structural element of Egyptian architecture. In its design, sometimes with swellings, flutings and ties, it echoed the bundles of reeds of the earliest temples. Nevertheless, with a lack of suitable timber and with limestone roofing blocks able to span no more than three meters (nine feet) without breaking, the Egyptians were unable to explore the possibilities of column-based architecture as freely as the Greeks and Romans did later.

Temples of related deities might be linked to each other by processional rows of statues. These were usually of sphinxes, with the head of a king, as on the avenue of king Nectanebo between Karnak and Luxor, or the animal form of a god: a ram for Amun at Karnak, for instance. Along these routes were smaller shrines (kiosks) where the cult statue of the god would be rested on its way from one temple to another when paraded on feast days.

There were exceptions to this model of the enclosed temple protected by wall and pylon. One was the great terraced complex of Mentuhotpe II at Deir el-Bahri. Set against its backdrop of towering limestone hills, the causeway to the temple rose among trees to columned porticoes, one set above the other. There were parallels in the design of the tombs of earlier Theban kings, and some Egyptian houses had stairways leading to second-floor porticoes; but as a temple the design of Mentuhotpe's was original, and it inspired the temple of Hatshepsut alongside it. Another variation is found in temples to Aten, the sun-god of el-Amarna. Here the normal order was reversed:

the temple was entered through a hall but, instead of having a small enclosed shrine, it was left open to the sky.

ARCHITECTS RELIED ON an expertise in the carving of stone. Whether working in soft

Glorifying the Body in Stone

stones such as limestone or sandstone, or the hardest – granite, dolerite or schist – Egyptian sculptors showed real mastery both in the round and in relief. The softer stones could be worked with chisels or saws; the harder had to be pounded and scraped with flint tools, using quartz as an abrasive. A master sculptor drew lines on a block from which his assistants worked. Mistakes could be corrected with pieces of stone fastened back on with wooden dowels, but craftsmen were skilled at working around any blemishes.

Sculptures in the round were created within well-established conventions. Royal figures were normally shown seated in a square pose, looking directly forward, or standing with the left foot slightly advanced, the fists clenched at the side or clasping the trappings of office across the chest. Some were produced for tombs, but other royal sculptures might be made for public display, and in these the kings usually presented themselves as youthful and serene. Their faces, in particular, were idealized to display their dignity and majesty. This does not mean that there was no attempt at a likeness. Statues of kings have been compared with their mummified corpses and show that some features, at least, were copied from life. Occasionally the sculptor departed from the conventions and attempted to portray deeper feelings: the Middle Kingdom statues of Sesostris III, for example, show the king as an older man, with a much more somber gaze than was usual. It is hard to be sure of the aims of the artist in such cases – it is easy to read in emotions that were never intended – but there is occasionally no mistaking a more human approach, as in a statue of Menkaure and his queen, or of Hatshepsut's vizier Senenmut nursing a royal princess.

The king's sculpted image was an expression of power or propaganda. Yet a cache of more than seven hundred non-royal statues, found at Karnak

NEFERTITI, queen of Akhenaten, was glorified in 18th-Dynasty art almost as a love-goddess. This torso (ABOVE), carved in quartzite, is typical of the exaggerated yet realistic style of the Amarna period. Painting and sculpture became even more vivid, expressive and beautiful as the stiff formality of convention was deliberately ignored – almost certainly by royal command.

ISIS, mother of Horus, sister-wife of Osiris, and goddess of healing (BELOW), was one of the nine most important gods involved in Egypt's creation mythology. Such classical themes were revived in the Late Period as the Egyptians looked to their more ancient past for assurances of stability. This statue from a tomb of about 530 BC shows her wearing the crown of Hathor and holding an ankh. Beautifully carved in schist, with harmonious proportions, it is finely polished. The inscription at the bottom is an invocation by a chief scribe.

❖ PROPORTION
and Harmony

Figures in painting and relief work are instantly recognizable as Egyptian. This is partly due to the use of a standard canon of proportion – ensuring harmony and the correct positioning of the parts of the body – through almost all Egyptian history.

The basic unit of this canon was the fist (hand plus thumb). A grid was drawn up using this unit, and the figure arranged so that the hairline was 18 units high, the shoulders were six units across, the arm from elbow to fingertip was 4.5 units and the foot 3 units long. If the figure was to be drawn sitting, the same proportions were used, but the part of the grid relating to the thigh bone was placed horizontally. Similar grids were used when drawing animals.

Because images were symbolic rather than naturalistic, figures of gods and humans were given props (clothes, headdresses, objects to carry such as the royal crook and flail) to denote their status or meaning in a particular context.

As there was no way to show perspective, a problem often arose in

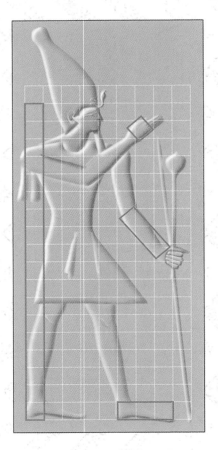

depicting the relationship between a figure and inanimate objects such as furniture. Two people sitting on a chair might appear to be on each other's laps. Only in work done in el-Amarna or immediately after (such as some of the objects in Tutankhamun's tomb) are figures posed more naturally.

in 1904, shows that sculptures of individuals, priests and donors, could sometimes be found in a public setting. Most, however, were designed for tombs and here the sculptor seems to have been free to present a true likeness.

TOMB SCULPTURE emphasizes the essentially magical role of so much representation in Egyptian art. The sculpture, however crudely done, was inscribed with the name of the deceased, without which his reanimation could not be complete. In the Opening of the Mouth ceremony, the face of the sculpture was stroked in a ritualistic way so that its subject could live again in the next life. There were set types of tomb sculpture. Family groups are common and scribes are often shown seated, with a papyrus roll across the knees. Many of the tomb sculptures of the Old Kingdom are considered among the finest of all Egyptian work, with their simplicity and lack of superfluous detail.

Preparing for the Afterlife

Wood, ivory or metal were sometimes used for sculpture. The few remaining wooden sculptures (most have been eaten by termites) show what a wealth of fine art in wood has been lost. Metal statuary reached the heights of excellence in the Late period, but for centuries the Egyptians had been experts in handling precious metals. The gold innermost coffin of Tutankhamun weighs over 110 kilograms (243 pounds). In a typical piece of jewelry, gold was used as a base, hammered into sheets or cut into wires, and precious stones were inserted or attached to it. The range of stones used was wide: lapis lazuli, amethysts, jasper, cornelian and turquoise were all popular.

The best jewelry has been found in secret recesses of tombs, or as protective amulets on the bodies themselves. The tombs of ancient Egypt, like so much else, were built according to traditional models. A tomb was a pit or subterranean chamber where the body was preserved within its coffin for ever. Sometimes grave goods were placed beside the coffin, but usually these filled a number of store rooms above the burial chamber. The most important room was the offering chapel, where the rituals designed to restore energy to the deceased and his belongings took place. The arrangement of a tomb depended on the environment – it could be built or tunneled into rock, with the roof held up by pillars of rock – and the need for security, with trapdoors, false entrances and pits to deter robbers.

*T*HE IDEALIZATION, *formality and rigidity of Egyptian tomb art, designed to perpetuate a perfect world in the hereafter, could be abandoned in private residences. The impressionistic ducks (BELOW LEFT) are from the palace of Amenophis III.*

*A*UNIQUE *wooden chest (BELOW) from Tutankhamun's tomb was painted in a style that influenced the great triumphal murals of the next dynasty. The chest's sides portray his military victories, real and symbolic. The Egyptian army is arranged in the strictest order, while the enemy is shown in a chaotic jumble.*

A Treasury of Ancient Painting

TOMBS WERE TREASURE-HOUSES of painting. More paintings have survived in Egypt than from any other ancient civilization. Many are astonishingly well preserved due to the dry climate and the pigments used. Blue was made from a carbonate of copper found in the Sinai desert, green from powdered malachite, red from iron oxides. Black was derived from carbon or soot.

The earliest paintings, from about the fourth millennium BC, are of scattered groups of humans and animals. By unification, figures were shown on base lines and status was expressed by size. Although many paintings show conventional poses, in the best works there are also striking expressions of intimacy, character and movement.

Tomb art provides our most accessible images of the ancient Egyptians at work and at play. Because the objects and figures in the paintings were meant to come to life, they were drawn with as many features as possible, ensuring that these would be included when they were reanimated. The subjects were always shown as youthful and serene. Their faces were drawn from the side with one eye showing, but this always had its pupil drawn centrally. The torso was shown frontally but with the legs and feet in profile, usually showing the big toe on both feet. Physically this was an impossible pose, but it was designed to ensure that the most important features of the body were present when it was brought to life.

There was no attempt, or need, to show perspective. The contents of a box were shown above the box to make sure they would be included, and similarly a house and its gardens were shown as a diagram. The Nile was drawn from above, teeming with the fish that the deceased hoped would be available in the afterlife. The scenes and the figures within them were arranged in rows or registers, and the whole composition was planned with the geometrical regularity of all the Egyptian arts.

THERE WERE A NUMBER of standard scenes for tombs, and the tomb owner could choose which of these he wanted, in consultation with the master craftsman. Such things were planned well in advance, especially for royalty; to die without a tomb ready and waiting was a disaster. Sketches were prepared on papyrus before being transferred in outline to the walls of the tomb. A landowner might be shown viewing his estates at the different seasons or having his herd of cattle paraded before him. The owner was shown as the largest figure, his wife and family next in size, and those working for him as smallest of all. An official might prefer to be shown carrying out the duties of his office. The tomb of the vizier Rekhmira shows him in one scene surrounded by craftsmen whose work in jewelry and stone he appears to be supervising. In another scene he is shown welcoming men from Nubia, Syria and Crete bringing tribute. Often the owner might be shown enjoying leisure activities such as hunting, fishing or banqueting. Finally, there would be scenes from the funeral itself, with the key ceremony of the Opening of the Mouth prominently featured.

There was limited opportunity for innovation in tomb painting. Apprentices learned their trade by copying and recopying the paintings of the Old Kingdom. Provincial centers evolved their own styles to a degree, and sometimes a distinct approach by different teams of craftsmen can be spotted. The main figures on the paintings had to be done according to convention. Royalty and the upper class were shown as young and perfect. There was more scope for realism in the painting of servants and animals, which could be shown as they were in life. To modern eyes, these are the most animated and attractive pieces.

The Artistic Legacy

EGYPTIAN ART is overwhelming in volume and scale, and so familiar to us that it is easy to forget its importance in terms of the development of visual arts worldwide. The Egyptians produced some of the earliest and greatest-ever individual portraits. Despite their formality and rigid adherence to the established conventions, their artists achieved a directness – particularly in their free-standing sculptures of men and women – that was unequaled in the ancient world until the Greeks. During the Old Kingdom, at a time when outstanding sculptures were made (such as those of Khephren and Rahotep), Egyptian sculptors and painters were by far the most technically skilled in the world. Naturalistic detail combined with simple though sophisticated composition mean that their work has retained its immediacy for more than 4,000 years. This achievement – especially when seen in conjunction with that of the construction of the pyramids – was so complete that their descendants had no need to introduce more than superficial influences from abroad, until the arrival of the Greeks in the Ptolemaic period.

Despite the naturalism of the best work, all Egyptian art has an intellectual quality that has often distracted the viewer. Every detail – the arrangement of the elements, the pose of the characters, the headdresses of the gods – was selected for its meaning more than for its appearance: an Egyptian painting or sculpture is meant to be read rather than merely looked at. Once the original intentions of the artists had been forgotten, the image was often

RICHLY LADEN with offerings, a table stands between Nebamun (seated) and his son, who offer clusters of flowers (LEFT). Fresh plants cool the wine jars under the table. The objects are drawn without the modern technique of perspective, so that they appear piled together.

remembered for its oddness rather than for the beauty of its elements. As a result, later observers sometimes found Egyptian art outlandish and incomprehensible, particularly the art of the Amarna period.

There is little sign that Egyptian art had any significant influence on that of surrounding cultures. The Mesopotamian ziggurat, comparable in its outline to the step pyramid, was not a copy of an Egyptian model but a local development – an attempt to raise the height of the temple above the surrounding plain. The rich royal tombs of Ur, similarly, seem to owe little to the Egyptian example. There is no evidence of Egyptian craftsmen working outside their country, or of Egyptian art leaving the Nile valley, until the Late Period, when invaders conquered the kingdom. A few images, such as the sphinx, were adapted in the Near East during the imperial age, but in general, Egyptian artists kept their secrets to themselves – adding to the awe experienced by those who visit the country even now.

THE TOMB CHAPEL of the noble Sennefer, mayor of Thebes (ABOVE), is also known as the "tomb of vines" because of the richly decorated ceiling. The offering chapel, the interface between the living and the dead, was more the focus of artistic effort than the burial chamber itself.

> **"*Everyone fears Time but Time fears the Pyramids.*"**
> Egyptian proverb

GIZA Mountains Made by Men

Above The Egyptians had no pulleys, yet they lifted millions of stone blocks into place – up to several hundred a day. White limestone and pink granite formed the casing.

Of the more than 90 pyramids discovered at 12 major sites up and down the Nile, those at Giza are the largest. Visible for miles across the desert, they overshadow the smaller structures built around them, for the pyramids were never stand-alone structures but part of burial complexes. The step-pyramid complexes of the 3rd Dynasty consisted of the main pyramid, a mortuary temple, and one or more subsidiary pyramids for relatives and favored courtiers, all enclosed within a wall. By the 4th Dynasty, when the pyramids at Giza were built, a long causeway had been added outside the wall, leading to a valley temple with landings for boats. The pyramid itself was aligned on a north–south axis, with the mortuary temple built against its east face, and the subsidiary pyramids in the southeast corner. The causeway was also built on the east side, creating an axis along which the king's mummy was carried to be laid to rest in the westernmost structure, the pyramid.

The pyramids show the technical mastery and clear vision that underlie the Egyptian achievement. However, although they are the most intensively studied structures in the world, it is not clear exactly how they were built, or even what they represented. The change from step pyramid to true pyramid must have reflected a shift in religious doctrine that made the cult of the sun dominant, and the shape of the new pyramid echoed the rays of the sun slanting down.

This much is known. The king chose the site and helped calculate the dimensions for the architect. Astronomers laid out the north–

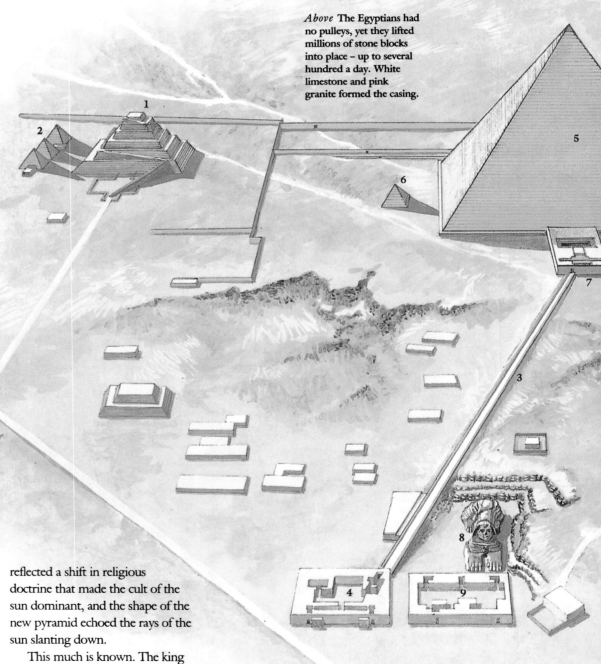

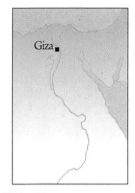

GIZA COMPLEX
1   Menkaure's pyramid
2   Subsidiary pyramids
3   Causeway
4   Valley temple
5   Khephren's pyramid
6   Subsidiary pyramids
7   Mortuary temple
8   Great Sphinx
9   Sphinx temple
10 Great Pyramid
     (Khufu)
11 Boat pits
12 Pyramids of queens

Above A huge block of stone makes its way by boat along the Nile. The most distant quarry was at Aswan, 950km (589 miles) from Giza, and the trip took one or two weeks. One quarrying expedition used 17,000 men for ground transport when the stones came ashore. They were far more numerous than skilled stonemasons.

Above The ceiling of the Grand Gallery in the Great Pyramid is 6.7 meters (22 feet) high. The design was altered twice while in progress, and the gallery was built to extend an ascending passage to the uppermost of its three burial chambers. The gallery may also have been used to store the huge blocks that were pushed down the passage to seal it after the king's funeral.

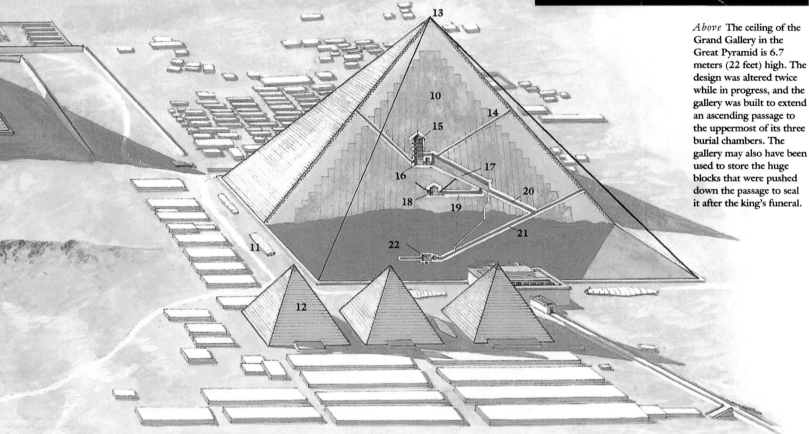

south axis, surveyors measured the site (within 131mm or 5.16 inches of accuracy for the Great Pyramid) and leveled it. If the alignment of the sides was wrong, they would not meet at the apex. The king drove the first stakes with a golden mallet. Underground rooms were built first, followed by the core. Stone for the core was quarried as close to the site as possible. For the exterior, two-and-a-half-tonne blocks were dragged on sleds from specially-built river harbors and up the growing pyramid on ramps. As the core grew, inner passages and chambers were added in layers. There were also shafts which were once thought to be for air but may be linked with astronomy. Fitting the exterior was the finest work. Each block was cut and set so perfectly against the next that a knife-blade could not fit between them. Casing began at the top, after the capstone was in place. The ramps were dismantled as the casing worked its way down.

THE GREAT PYRAMID
13 Gilded capstone
14 Astronomical shaft
15 Load-bearing chamber
16 "King's chamber"
17 Great Gallery
18 "Queen's chamber"
19 Level passage
20 Ascending passage
21 Descending passage
22 Subterranean chamber

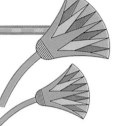

THE DIVINE WORD
Wisdom & Knowledge in Ancient Egypt

The power of words was enshrined in the earliest Egyptian creation myths, in which the creator used three forces to produce matter from nothingness. The first force was *heka*, which gave life and could be invoked as magical protection; the second was *sia*, which allowed the creative force to be focused on a goal. The third force was known as *hu*, the divine word. It allowed *heka* and *sia* to achieve material form. This aspect of their creation myth gave the Egyptians a deep reverence for words, which was reflected everywhere in their culture: in the importance of names, and of identifying the images with which the Egyptians decorated their tombs; in the visual artistry of the writing system itself; and in the social status of scribes, which was exceptional in an almost totally illiterate society.

GREEK VISITORS were the first of many outsiders to be fascinated by what they called hieroglyphs,

Writings of the House of Life

"sacred carved letters", which adorned all of Egypt's many temples and monuments. The Egyptians themselves knew their writing as "the writing of the divine word" or "the writing of the House of Life" – the name of the temples where scribes and priests were trained.

Egyptian hieroglyphs originated around 3200 BC. Although they came slightly later than the development of the world's first writing in Mesopotamia, the Egyptians seem to have invented hieroglyphs without copying the Mesopotamian system. The need for writing was

HIEROGLYPHS WERE finely carved in stone as on this frieze from the temple of Karnak (ABOVE). The "sacred carvings" were used for monumental inscriptions, the prerogative of royalty and temples, and had to be pleasing to the eye.

DIGNITY IS EXPRESSED in every inch of this scribe, seated in the traditional posture with a papyrus on his lap (RIGHT). Wooden palettes (BELOW RIGHT) held ink, with a slot for pens made from reeds. The other is a stone model for use in the afterlife.

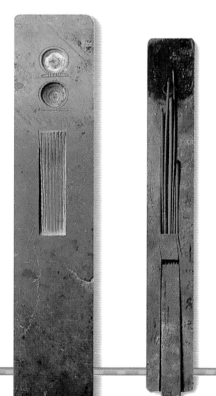

probably a sign of the growing complexity of administration. The state could never have been kept united without a writing system. Hieroglyphs provided a sophisticated if somewhat clumsy system of writing; they were too difficult to be used for ordinary communication. At their simplest, hieroglyphs were no more than pictures of objects, but they could also be used to represent a syllable of a longer word. A hieroglyph called a determinative could be added at the end of a word to clarify its meaning. The number of hieroglyphs expanded from about 1,000 in the New Kingdom to 6,000 by Roman times.

Hieroglyphs were used for formal inscriptions, usually on stone, on which they could be carved with absolute precision. Stonemasons added slight embellishments to each pictogram to make it a work of art in its own right. Hieroglyphs were visually tied in with other art so that a carving or painting was unified with the accompanying text. The word for writing was also used for drawing the outlines of pictures. Ordinary documents were normally written on papyrus with a reed pen. It was hard to create precise shapes this way, and shorthand versions of hieroglyphs appeared – two signs could be run together into one. This led to a second distinct way of writing, called hieratic or "priestly writing". Sacred or literary texts were carefully written in hieratic; administrative or legal documents were often less elegantly penned.

Despite the emergence of the hieratic script, hieroglyphs remained unchanged and continued to be used on formal inscriptions. Hieratic scripts, however, developed different forms and styles. At first they were written in columns, but by the 12th

THOTH
The God of Learning

THOTH, the god of writing, counting and knowledge, was said in legends to be the son of Horus. He was conceived in an extraordinary way: Horus concealed some of his semen in a lettuce and gave the lettuce to Seth to eat. Thoth then emerged from Seth's forehead. (To the modern reader, this might indicate a connection with the intellect, but the Egyptians thought that the mind resided in the heart.)

Thoth was among the most versatile of the Egyptian gods. He was originally associated with the moon, on whose waxing and waning the first measurement of time was based. In this aspect he became the god of time and counting. He was also credited with the invention of hieroglyphs, which he used to write 42 books containing all the wisdom in the world. They included the Egyptian laws, and Thoth became their guardian. His aspect of wisdom grew out of his role as scribe to the gods. When a human scribe settled down to write, he always began by pouring a libation to Thoth from the pot of water used for cleaning his brushes.

Thoth was shown in two physical forms. The earliest, known from the first dynasties, was a baboon, but by the end of the Old Kingdom he was also depicted as an ibis, whose curved beak echoed the crescent shape of the moon. Other gods traveled to the underworld on his wings, giving him yet another role: messenger of the gods. Thoth was also shown as a man with an ibis head carrying a palette and pen. Both the baboon and the ibis were often shown crowned with the crescent moon supporting a lunar disk. In the Late Period thousands of baboons and ibises were mummified near his cult center. The Greeks equated Thoth with Hermes, the Greek messenger-god, and so his cult center, Khemenu in the Egyptian language, became known to the classical world as Hermopolis.

THE TWO ASPECTS of Thoth. Ibis-headed (ABOVE) from the temple of Ramesses II at Abydos and as a baboon (BELOW) from the temple of Thoth at Hermopolis.

Dynasty they were written in horizontal lines, always from right to left. Business documents were written in a different style from literary texts. In the Late Period, business hieratic evolved into an even more cursive style known as demotic, which was used for daily and administrative purposes. Scribes were trained in hieratic and, later, in demotic. Even among their ranks, only specialists were able to read or write hieroglyphs.

Beyond recording official information, hieroglyphs had a sacred significance. (The modern word comes from the Greek meaning "sacred carvings".) Putting something in writing gave it a permanence which helped sustain the sense of order for which every Egyptian yearned. Names had a particular significance because their preservation was essential for the survival of an individual into the afterlife. Erasing a name was a momentous act – the equivalent of condemning a person to everlasting death.

Due to their conservative nature, the Egyptians retained the hieroglyphic system in spite of its limitations, but no other civilization adopted this method of writing. There is no record of any Greek or Roman learning how to read them. As a result, hieroglyphs soon acquired an aura of mystery among classical scholars, who speculated that they were the means by which the Egyptians had communicated directly with the gods. They were abandoned in the fourth century AD because the new Christian regime considered them idolatrous. For the next 1,500 years, until the first European scholars succeeded in deciphering them, the voice of ancient Egypt was silenced.

LIKE MOST ANCIENT PEOPLES, the Egyptians were enthralled by the stars, and they put them to

The Stars & the Calendar

practical use outside their mythology. The movement of the stars was used to define a calendar and thus to keep records. Each year on the same day – July 19 in the modern Western calendar – the Dog Star, Sirius, which had spent 70 days below the horizon, would rise above it simultaneously with the sun. The rising of Sirius coincided with the annual flooding of the Nile's waters, and so it was adopted as the start of a new calendar year. A calendar running on a yearly basis from each rising of Sirius corresponded well with the agricultural year based on the Nile's levels, and was used also to calculate the dates of religious festivals. This solar year was 365.25 days long.

CONSTELLATIONS from the ceiling of Sethos I's tomb in the Valley of the Kings (ABOVE) show a female hippopotamus with a crocodile on her back – one of the northern constellations. In the tomb, the deceased could use the realistic painting of the sky to tell the time and date. The Egyptians identified five planets: Mercury, Venus, Jupiter, Mars and Saturn (the last three associated with Horus). Many of their constellations differed from the ones familiar to us today, so they have proved difficult to identify.

Another way of measuring time was used. This was based on the movements of the night sky. As the year went by, the Egyptians noted which stars were on the horizon as night passed into day and saw that they moved according to a regular pattern. They divided the stars into 36 groups, or decans, which rose above the horizon for ten days before being supplanted by the next decan. These changes were used by the priests to determine the time of their evening ceremonies. Each lunar month, or full cycle of the moon, comprised three decans. The months in their turn were grouped into three seasons of four months: the season of the rising of the waters, the floods and cultivation. This made a total of 360 days. Added to these were five intercalary days which were the "birthdays" of the gods: one each for the children of Geb and Nut – Osiris, Isis, Seth and Nephthys – and one for Horus, the son of Isis and Osiris, to make a lunar calendar of 365 days. This calendar was used for administrative purposes. Unfortunately, the yearly length of this calendar was six hours less than the calendar based on the rising of Sirius, and the official "administrative" calendar fell behind the solar calendar by one day every four years.

Assuming the two calendars started together, it would have taken perhaps a hundred years for the discrepancy between them to have become obvious; by then it would have been some 25 days. However, the administrative lunar calendar appears to have been so well established already that it continued to run, even though it had become increasingly out of step with the solar and agricultural year. Thus, the two calendars coincided only once every 1,460 years.

This discrepancy in the calendars has proved useful for Egyptologists. A Roman writer, Censorinus, happened to record that the rising of Sirius and the start of the administrative year coincided in AD 139. By counting back and allowing for movement in the position of Sirius in the sky in that time, it is possible for modern historians to plot earlier coincidences. It has been calculated, for example, that the starting date for the two calendars must have been about 2773 BC. Occasionally, records have survived which mention the difference in number of days between the rising of Sirius and the administrative year for a particular event. The date for that event can then be calculated using the nearest coincidence as a base.

Time, Space & Technology

FOR MEASURING TIME within a day, the Egyptians appear to have used sun clocks. One surviving example is made in the shape of an L with a pillar standing on top of a base, forming an angle of 90 degrees. The device was pointed at the sun so that a shadow fell between the pillar and six marks on the base which indicated the hour; morning and afternoon were not distinguished by any special marks. So appeared the 12-hour day, although the length of the hours varied with the seasons. The night was also divided into 12 hours, as at any one time there were 12 decans visible, the one on the horizon at dawn and the 11 above it. This 24-hour day was later adopted by Greek astronomers, but the Greeks improved it by making the hours equal in length.

The stars were also used in the alignment of buildings. The southern constellation Orion, known to the Egyptians as the god Sah, and the northern Ursa Major were lined up through the *merkhet*, "the instrument of knowing". This was a primitive form of astrolabe used in conjunction with a sighting instrument in the form of the rib of a palm leaf. Using them both, the foundations of a temple or pyramid could be laid down to within half a degree of accuracy. Many gods were associated with a particular point of the compass – Horus with the East and Osiris with the West, the domain of the dead – and the orientation of

*B*ABOONS AND LOTUS *flowers decorate this bronze buckle* (ABOVE). *Bronze (an alloy of tin and copper) was made in the early dynastic period, but it was not used on a large scale until the Middle Kingdom. Before tin was imported from Syria, early bronze was hardened with arsenic.*

*A*N ANCIENT DEVICE *called a* Nilometer (BELOW) *was used to measure the rise and fall of the river. The "meters" (panels) are placed at several locations along the steps to allow for the variation in water level. Kings used the level to set annual taxes.*

buildings probably had a religious significance. Osiris was also associated with the constellation of Orion, and Isis with Sirius. Some scholars have suggested that the pyramids at Giza were laid out to reproduce the "belt of Orion" on the ground, but there is little evidence to support this claim.

The Egyptians were familiar with the basic mathematical functions and could perform practical calculations. However, they had no understanding of abstract mathematics and never developed formulae which could be adapted to practical problems. For whole numbers they used a decimal system, but when using fractions they were restricted by having no numerators higher than one (with the exception of 2/3), so that 7/8 had to be built up: 1/2 plus 1/4 plus 1/8. Arithmetic problems had to be solved by a series of small calculations. These calculations were made more manageable by prepared tables that showed how each problem could be broken down into smaller components. Similar tables were used for multiplication and division.

Geometry came more easily to the Egyptians. They had some understanding of its principles, though not as much as the Greeks later did. They appear to have understood that a right angle could be produced by making a triangle with sides in the ratio of 3:4:5, but they had no general statement of the proportions of the sides of a right-angled triangle such as Pythagoras devised. They could calculate the area of triangles and hence the volume of pyramids. They had a reasonably accurate method of measuring the circumference of a circle, which involved taking eight-ninths of its diameter and squaring the result.

These limitations seem insignificant compared with the achievements of Egyptian technology on both the largest and the smallest scale: the building of the pyramids and great temples, and the superiority of Egyptian craftsmanship (both of which required accurate measurement). These achievements are even more remarkable in light of the fact that Egyptian tools remained primitive. The pyramids were built using raw manpower, mallets, chisels, ramps and sleds. The wheel was known by the New Kingdom, but was impractical to use on sand. Stone knives continued to be used alongside copper and bronze even when these metals became available. Iron was the last metal to be developed; it was more scarce than gold. Iron tools existed in the New Kingdom but did not become common until the Greco-Roman period.

WEIGHTS
& Measures

Without the ability to weigh and measure accurately, the Egyptian bureaucracy could not have run smoothly. Grain had to be weighed, cattle counted, plans drawn up for building projects and huge slabs of stone sized, rations and materials issued to workmen, and all of these figures recorded by the royal scribes in their books. Measuring the level of the annual Nile flood was a matter of national importance, on which the levying of taxes depended. Weighing was prominent on the day of judgment itself, when the heart of the deceased was placed on the scales in the presence of Osiris.

For general measurements, the standard unit was the royal cubit – 52.4 centimeters (20.6 inches), about the same length as a man's forearm, on which the hieroglyph for "cubit" was based. The cubit could be divided into 28 digits of thumb width, each 4 digits making up a palm width. A "short cubit" was sometimes used, especially by artists when making up a grid; this was only 6 palms or 24 digits, or 44.9 centimeters (17.7 inches). Other measures based on the royal

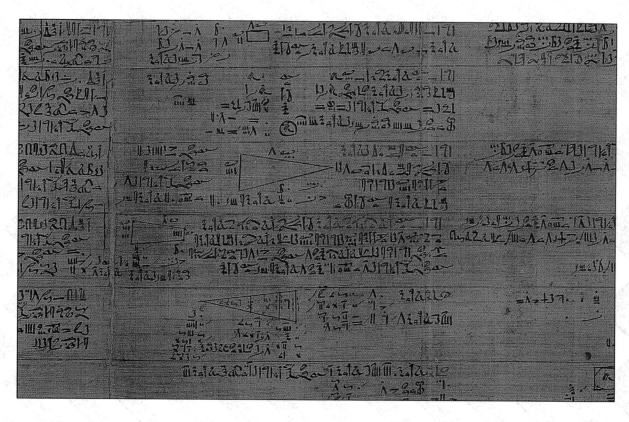

cubit were the *remen* (74.07 centimeters or 29.2 inches), the diagonal of a square with sides measuring one royal cubit; the double *remen*, divided into 40 equal units, and the *ta* (100 royal cubits), which were used to survey land. An area of 100 square cubits was called a *setjat*. Officials were sometimes buried with ceremonial measuring rods bearing inscriptions that gave useful facts such as the level of a flood or the statistics of a region or *nome* (province).

Stone weights were used at Naqada as early as 3500 BC. Later weights were made of

pottery and bronze and shaped as animals; bulls' heads were especially popular. The basic unit of weight was the *deben*, about 93.3 grams (3.3 ounces). The *kite* (pronounced "kitay"), weighing 9 to 10 grams (0.3 to 0.35 ounces), was added after the 12th Dynasty, and the *deben* was rounded off to 10 *kite*. The *kite* was used only to measure gold and silver, whereas the *deben* also measured copper. The value of other goods was often described in terms of so many *kite* or *debens* of a metal, in effect establishing a price guide, although there was no formal money system.

The metals themselves were valuable media of exchange. Workmen's metal tools were usually weighed before being issued to them from the royal store, and weighed again when returned to the overseer to ensure that no precious metal had been removed by devious means and sold for personal profit.

EGYPTIAN MATHEMATICS was concerned with practical problems such as calculating the volume of a pyramid. The Rhind Mathematical Papyrus (ABOVE) is one of four surviving papyri from which the rules of this system can be deduced. There was no zero. Counting was based on multiples of ten, from one to 1,000,000 – the latter often used loosely.

THE ROYAL CUBIT (BELOW) was graduated by fractions from the finger to the cubit. The finger and the palm (four fingers) were the main units. Made of stone or wood, the cubit was used by both architects and sculptors.

Finger⏌   Palm⏌   Cubit⏌   Royal cubit⏌

Sickness, Health & Healing

PAINTINGS ON TOMB WALLS always showed their subjects in the best of health, exactly as they hoped they would be in the afterlife. Any indication of deformity or disease was rare. In fact, the Egyptians were no more immune to illness than any other people, and the examination of mummies and skeletons shows how vulnerable they were. Many died in infancy, especially around the age of three, when a child transferred from its mother's milk to solid food. The average lifespan was only 29 years, but this reflected the high infant mortality. Those who did survive all the hazards of early life might expect to reach 50. Diseases of the lungs, caused by tuberculosis and the breathing of sand or dust, were common. So were parasites, absorbed from polluted water. The teeth of mummies appear worn down, probably as a result of chewing grit left in grain after it had been ground. Those who survived to 40 usually had worn and, doubtless, painful joints and showed evidence of strained spines.

Despite these telling signs, Egyptian doctors appear to have made the assumption that human beings were naturally healthy and that any illness was the result of the malevolence of the gods. Particularly to blame was Sekhmet, the lioness-goddess who had once been dispatched to earth by Ra to exterminate the human race. She could also be petitioned to restore health. Two other gods of healing were Horus, with his healing eye, and Isis, the restorer of the body of Osiris. For the cure to work, the sufferer needed to understand the rituals required, and so a visit to skilled priests of the temple was essential.

At some point these priests began to record on papyri the illnesses they saw. The observations were often carried out with meticulous care. In one papyrus the different kinds of snake bites were

*P*OLIO *may have been the cause of the condition of this man's leg* (ABOVE). *The Egyptians suffered from many diseases.*

*C*HILDBIRTH *was a dangerous time, and a woman and baby might be protected by a charm such as this one* (BELOW).

recorded; in another there are no less than 700 descriptions of internal symptoms. Other papyri concentrate on joints and swellings. A papyrus of around 1900 BC, which dealt largely with gynecological problems, shows that women were questioned closely about their past history and present feelings before their details were recorded. As a knowledge of the common symptoms of ill health was built up, the priest–doctors tried practical treatments along with traditional appeals to the gods. In fact, there does not seem to have been a clear distinction between the two – if the practical approach failed, physicians turned to magic. Direct treatment was most successful for external injuries, which could be seen. Fractures were mended and elementary surgery used to excise tumors. Some trepanned (drilled) skulls have been found healed over, showing that it was possible to survive intrusive surgery. The skill of the Egyptian doctors became a byword; analysis of the works of the later Greek physicians shows that the way they described and classified wounds and

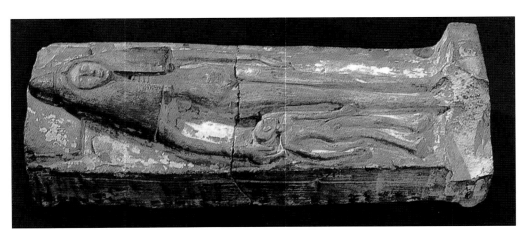

set out prescriptions for medicine was probably initially copied from the Egyptians. Homer wrote in the *Odyssey* about the superiority of their medicine to that anywhere else in the world.

However, the Egyptians knew very little about the internal workings of the body, despite observing the organs during embalming. They assumed that the heart was the center of the body and that all bodily fluids flowed through it. They did not understand the circulation of the blood. Ill health was thought to be the result of some obstruction. This was diagnosed by various tests, such as this one for infertility: a woman who was believed to be barren sat over a mixture of beer and dates. If she vomited, she could conceive. If she did not, it was clear that the aroma of the mixture had been held up somewhere inside her body. One possible cause of blockage was overeating, as it was thought that the body absorbed only the food it needed and the remainder might cause damage. The aim of medicine was to free the channels of the body. Depending on the symptoms, a wide variety of remedies could be prescribed, ranging from the raw liver of a donkey to fresh dew, mouse feces or the powdered root of the mandrake plant.

*H*EART AMULETS *in colored glass* (ABOVE) *were a crucial part of funerary equipment for the dead. The Egyptians knew the heart was important, though for the wrong reasons; they believed that it contained the mind.*

*P*RESSING FLOWERS *to make perfume or medicine* (BELOW) *on this limestone relief. Egyptian herbal medicine was well developed, and the Greeks sent their students to study it.*

Another weakness of Egyptian medicine was its reliance on the priests' texts. Although they scrupulously listed symptoms, a diagnosis and a prescription, the texts were copied and recopied without change over hundreds or even thousands of years. The Greek historian Diodorus recorded that a physician who treated a patient according to his own remedies might be held liable if the patient died, but one who simply followed the texts could not be faulted. Building on previous observations to experiment with new cures was discouraged. Such faith was placed in the medical texts that they were often worn as protective or healing amulets.

A more permanent legacy of Egyptian medicine was the bequest of its pharmacopeia. A large number of plants were used medicinally for the first time in Egypt and transmitted by the Greeks, Romans and Arabs into the herbal folklore of the Mediterranean. Among them were dill, onion, coriander, and pomegranate – the last used to deal with parasitic worms. The idea that undigested food was harmful is also found in Egyptian and Greek sources, and may have inspired the emetics and purgings which were so popular among the early physicians of Europe.

*C*HIEF OF DENTISTS *and
physicians to the 3rd
Dynasty king Djoser was Hesire
(ABOVE). His inkwells, palette and
pen case show him to be a scribe as
well as a physician. The staff and
scepter represent his authority.*

WRITTEN WORDS were not for all in ancient Egypt. The percentage of the population that was literate has been estimated by some scholars to have been as low as 0.4 percent, while others maintain it was closer to one percent. Even for those few who could read, there was no "literature" before the 12th Dynasty. Stories for entertainment were told orally. Fragments of pottery and papyrus illustrate animal fables in which the characters behave like humans. Late in the New Kingdom these fables developed into a distinct written genre. This period – most notably the 20th Dynasty – produced some of Egypt's finest writing, including love poetry which originated in banquet songs. By this time a complete break had occurred between official and literary form, reflecting the changes in the spoken language: official inscriptions were still written in hieroglyphs in the classical Middle Egyptian language, whereas purely literary works were written in hieratic Late Egyptian, possibly reflecting their source in oral tales and songs. By the Greco-Roman period, demotic was used for literary texts also.

The Wisdom Literature

Perhaps the most successful of the genres in which the Egyptians recorded their philosophy is the so-called wisdom literature. Much of it originated in the Old Kingdom, but the texts were copied and recopied – often as training exercises in the schools for scribes – over the centuries. There were two forms. One was a literature of pessimism, apparently written at times of national breakdown, when the writer bewailed all the horrors of disorder, famine and social disruption. Order was praised in this literature for providing the structure that allowed the social hierarchy to be maintained, the gods to be honored and rejoicing to be a part of everyday life.

The other kind of wisdom literature consisted of instructions on "the way of living truly", often passed on by a vizier or a king to his son. The earliest known example was traditionally credited to the 4th-Dynasty sage Hardjedef. In the First Intermediate Period, a Prince Merykare is given this advice: "Act justly, that you may endure on earth. Quieten him who weeps; do not dispossess the widow; do not deprive a man of his father's property." The emphasis was on maintaining good order but never at the expense of compassion for the weak. The good man showed sensitivity to the

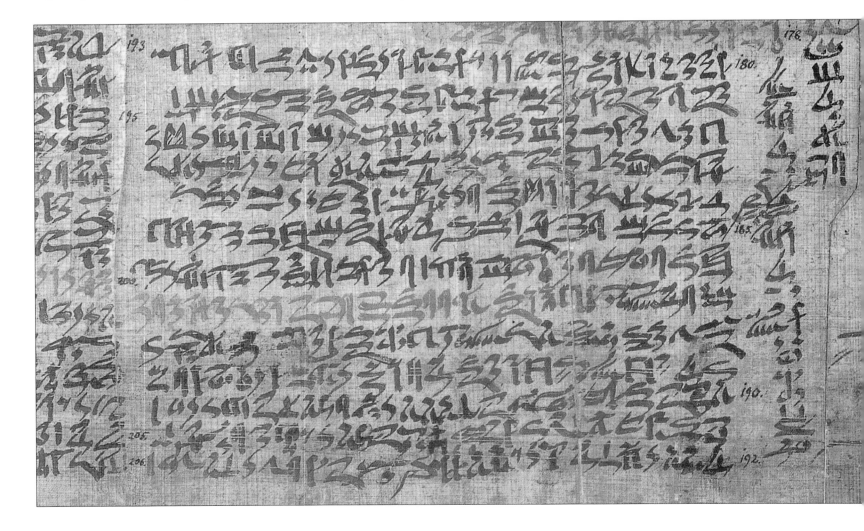

A PAINTED OSTRACON from Deir el-Medina (RIGHT) shows the playfulness that characterizes the Egyptians' animal fables. This is an illustration from the legend of Tefnut (shown here as a lion) in which she runs away to Nubia. She is escorted back to her father Amun-Ra by Thoth (shown in his baboon form). The bird above them is part of an inscription from a story which Thoth used to persuade Tefnut to return to Egypt and serve her father.

P APYRUS bearing part of the "Tale of Sinuhe", written in the hieratic script (BELOW), running from right to left. Hieratic was used for literary texts like this from the Middle Kingdom to the Ptolemaic period.

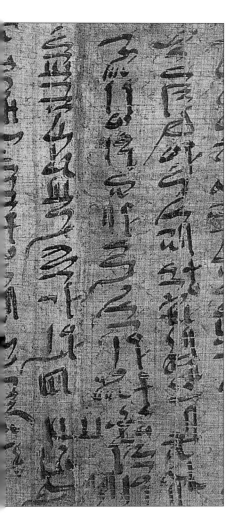

needs of others and respect to those in authority. He did not flaunt his knowledge and accepted that he could never achieve perfection. As the *Instruction of Ptah-hotep* put it, "Have no confidence that you are a learned man. Take counsel with the ignorant as with the wise, for the limits of excellence cannot be reached and no artist fully possesses his skill." This code of ethics stressed the individual's responsibility to the community – a subject that has not lost its relevance.

Traces of the influence of the Egyptian wisdom literature can be seen in other cultures. Perhaps the best known example is the *Instruction of Amenemope* dating from the 19th Dynasty, that of Ramesses II. One extract reads: "Do not exert yourself to seek gain, that your needs may be secure for you; if riches are brought to you by robbery, they will not spend the night with you; their places can be seen, but they are not there!... They have made themselves wings like geese, and have flown towards the sky." This reappears in the Hebrew scriptures in the Book of Proverbs, with eagles substituted for geese, which were unknown to Israelites: "Do not toil to become rich; cease from plundering! Do your eyes light upon it? It is gone! For riches make themselves wings, like an eagle which flies to the sky."

These lines summed up the Egyptian philosophy of life, easy-going and relaxed. There is no way of knowing, however, whether the poor as well as the rich were able to let go of material concerns and achieve contentment in their lives.

" *They appointed the book as the lector-priest, the writing board as beloved-son, the teachings as their pyramids, the pen as their baby, the stone surface as their wife... departing life has made their names forgotten; it is writings which make them remembered.* **"**

From a eulogy to dead authors, 19th-Dynasty papyrus

The Writing of the Gods

The earliest hieroglyphs were pictograms, pictures of what the writer wanted to represent. This approach was limited to physical objects – an eye, a hand, a falcon, perhaps, to mean the god Horus – and only the simplest of texts could be written.

Eventually each pictogram was also given the sound of the object that it represented and could be used whenever that sound was needed in another word. Some 24 hieroglyphs represented a single consonant; others expressed combinations of two or even three consonants. A mace was *h(e)dj*. Several other words, including "white", "silver" and "destroy", included the sounds *hdj*, and the mace hieroglyph was used in the appropriate place. There were no vowels in the script, so the single mace symbol represented several possible sounds: *hedj*, *ehdj*, *hdje* or *ehedj*. Each symbol could therefore be read either as a sound (phonogram), or for its meaning (ideogram). It was necessary to clarify how the symbol should be read on each occasion.

When a symbol was used to indicate a complete word (as a logogram, truly meaning "mace" in

this example), a vertical stroke was added after it. To indicate a plural, two such strokes were used. Longer words, made up of combinations of hieroglyphs, had an extra determinative symbol, which did not indicate a sound but clarified types of object. The word "silver" had a picture of a necklace added after it, whereas a strip of cloth with the same sound-symbols indicated "white cloth".

By the Middle Kingdom some 700 symbols were in use. It was easy to add more. When pyramids were first built, a pyramid hieroglyph appeared; it could be used to indicate the consonants making up the sound of "pyramid", *mr*, in other words. Similarly, the pictogram for a horse and a chariot was first used in the 18th Dynasty.

Each pictogram had associations that extended it beyond its literal meaning. A seated man could indicate "man" or "myself". Two arms – one carrying a shield, the other an ax – represented "fight". The word *hj*, "appear", was written with a sun appearing over the horizon, while a sail could also stand for "wind".

Background Hieratic, the cursive script of hieroglyphs, invented about 2600 BC

THE CONSONANTAL ALPHABET

SIGN	MEANING	SOUND
	Egyptian vulture	glottal stop (*a*)
	flowering reed	*i* or *y*
	lower arm	glottal stop (*a*)
	quail chick	*w* or *u*
	leg	*b*
	matting stool	*p*
	horned viper	*f*
	owl	*m*
	water	*n*
	mouth	*r*
	courtyard	*h*
	twisted flax wick	emphatic *h*
	placenta?	*kh* (soft)
	animal's belly	*kh* (hard)
	door bolt	*z*
	folded cloth	*s*
	pool	*sh*
	hill slope	*q (k)*
	basket	*k*
	jar stand	*g* (hard)
	bread loaf	*t*
	tethering rope	*tch*
	hand	*d*
	snake	*dj*

Far left "Serpent king" stela showing early use of hieroglyphs. They were used on early monuments to write titles and proper names; but some symbols already carried sound values (here the snake hieroglyph is used for the sound *dj*). This example is the funeral stela of the 1st-Dynasty king Djet . The "Horus-name" of the king (signifying his manifestation as a god) is written in a frame called a *serekh*. The lower part represents palace walls while Horus, as a falcon, sits on top.

Left The hieroglyphic "alphabet" of consonantal, uniliteral signs. These are classed as phonograms (sound-signs) but occasionally carry their original pictorial meaning (in which case they are used as pictograms). Although later writing systems came to rely exclusively on uniliteral characters like these, it is probable that the Egyptians developed them only slowly, when the more complex aspects of the hieroglyphic system were already in place. As a result, Egyptian can be very complex to read, especially as many words can be written several, very different, ways.

Right Some signs carried two or even three sounds, linked by vowels. Many of these signs are also used as independent words. *Center right* Some word-signs or logograms could stand for abstract concepts. *Far right* Another type of sense-sign or ideogram, the determinative was used to indicate the class of meaning to which a word belongs; it therefore distinguished between otherwise identical words. Hieroglyphs could be written from left to right or right to left: the animals and birds faced the beginning of the line.

TITULARY OF RAMESSES II

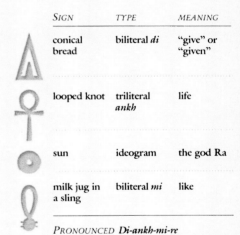

PRENOMEN
King of Upper and Lower Egypt
(*Nisut-bity*)

SIGN	TYPE	MEANING
sun	logogram	the god Ra
jackal head	triliteral *usr*	short form of "be strong"
goddess with a feather and *ankh* sign	logogram	goddess of justice Ma'at
adze on a block of wood	triliteral *setep*	short form of "choose"
water	alphabetic sign *n*	

PRONOUNCED *Userma'atre-setepenre*

TRANSLATION The *ma'at* of Ra is strong, one chosen for Ra

NOMEN
Son of Ra
(*Za-Ra*)

SIGN	TYPE	MEANING
god with falcon head, sun disk and *ankh* sign	ideogram	the god Ra
three fox pelts and folded cloth	biliteral *mes* and phonetic complement	
folded cloth	alphabetic sign *s*	abbreviation for pronoun "him"
god with two tall feathers and *was* septer	ideogram	the god Amun
canal	biliteral *mer*	verb "love"

PRONOUNCED *Ra-mes-es-mer-Amun*

TRANSLATION Ramesses (Ra has given him birth), beloved of Amun

SIGN	TYPE	MEANING
conical bread	biliteral *di*	"give" or "given"
looped knot	triliteral *ankh*	life
sun	ideogram	the god Ra
milk jug in a sling	biliteral *mi*	like

PRONOUNCED *Di-ankh-mi-re*

TRANSLATION Given life like Ra

BILITERAL & TRILITERAL SIGNS

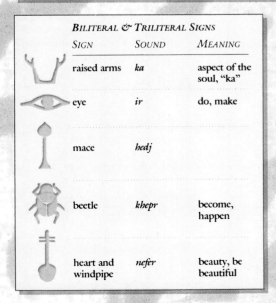

SIGN	SOUND	MEANING
raised arms	*ka*	aspect of the soul, "ka"
eye	*ir*	do, make
mace	*hedj*	
beetle	*khepr*	become, happen
heart and windpipe	*nefer*	beauty, be beautiful

IDEOGRAMS – LOGOGRAMS

SIGN	SOUND	MEANING
falcon	*hor*	the god Horus
foreparts of a lion	*hat*	front, foremost
star	*sba*	star
heart	*ib*	heart
bee	*bit*	bee
arm with stick	*nakht*	strong

IDEOGRAMS – DETERMINATIVES

SOUND	DET.	MEANING
wen	running legs	hurry
wen	sparrow, (used for bad and small things)	mistake
wen	hair	bald
wen	sun with rays	light
wen	city with crossroads	Hermopolis

EGYPT
IN THE
ANCIENT WORLD

As time passed, trade and conquest drew
Egypt into the evolving Middle East and
brought in waves of foreigners. Eventually
conquerors arrived. Egypt's civilization
was gradually transformed, and its ancient
treasures found their way to the newly
powerful cities of the region. In this way
Egypt's once unique culture became part of
developing Mediterranean civilization.

Main picture Greco-Roman temple of Sobek at Kom Ombo

Inset Zodiac ceiling from Dendara (19th-century copy).

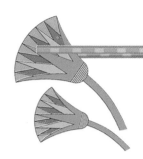

ALLIANCE & RIVALRY
Egypt & the Middle East

Its kings liked to portray Egypt as a land isolated from the rest of the ancient world, enjoying a unique and unchanging heritage for century after century. As living manifestations of the gods and guardians of the ancient traditions, it was their duty to keep the culture free of foreign influence. The great deserts to the east of the Nile valley formed a considerable natural barrier; the dense marshes of the Delta formed another. Home was heaven on earth, and the Egyptians only went forth in search of luxury materials, or to do battle. However, in reality Egypt was not so isolated. Its natural barriers were not impenetrable. Both traders and – with increasing frequency as the centuries passed – invaders made their way along the coast and over the Delta, across the corridor at top of the Sinai, or through the desert itself, guided by local tribes.

Egypt's prosperity always acted as a powerful magnet to its less affluent neighbors. Its records mention Libyans, Nubians and the numerous Middle Eastern tribes collectively called "Asiatics". These outsiders were mostly brought in as laborers – sometimes as prisoners of war, but often as willing immigrants who preferred the certainty of a good harvest in Egypt to the possibility of starvation at home. At the royal craftsmen's village of Deir el-Medina there were Syrians and Libyans among the Egyptian craftsmen, and the complex was guarded by Nubians. In the New Kingdom there were large crews of visiting workers, such as the Midians, who probably came from the Arabian

LOOSELY ORGANIZED nomadic tribes such as these Semitic peoples (ABOVE) formed a total contrast with stable, order-loving Egypt. It was this social difference that the Egyptians looked down on, and to which their favorite expression "vile Asiatic" referred, rather than racial differences.

TIMETABLE	
2040–1640	Middle Kingdom
1640–1532	Hyksos in Egypt
1600–1200	Mycenaean culture
1550–1300	Mitannian empire
1550–1070	New Kingdom
1450–1200	Hittite empire
c.1290–24	Exodus of the Israelites
c.1200	Sea Peoples invasions
c.1000	Kingdom of Israel founded
c.1000–612	Assyrian empire
c.945	Shoshenq I sacks Jerusalem
712–332	Late Period
671–651	Assyria rules Egypt
559–480	Persian empire
525	Cambyses conquers Egypt
525–404	27TH DYNASTY (Persian)
380–343	30TH DYNASTY (last)
332 BC–AD 395	Greco-Roman period
332–323	Reign of Alexander the Great

desert. Another group, known as the Apiru, may have been the early Hebrews; 800 of them worked in a single quarry. Mobile and considered lawless, they were the gypsies of their time.

The Egyptian sense of superiority to outsiders is clear from their art, in which other nationalities are typically shown unkempt and undifferentiated by origin or name. Disparaging references to "vile Asiatics" are plentiful: their body hair, their disorderly habits which made them unfit for society: "They live like wild game", in the Egyptian view. Yet in practice there was a level of toleration that most modern multi-ethnic societies would have cause to envy. Groups with a particular skill were marked out for favor, as with one invading clan that became the elite bodyguard of Ramesses II and was settled in a special area.

For the most part, new arrivals were assimilated into Egypt. A group of Syrian workers of the 18th century BC adopted Egyptian names within a generation. With the Nubians, the Egyptians enforced a policy of assimilation. The sons of local rulers were taken virtually as hostages and brought up as Egyptians at the capital. When they returned to Nubia, they took Egyptian ways with them.

The Hyksos, who infiltrated the Delta at the end of the Middle Kingdom, did not arrive as subordinate subjects, and their numbers came to rival that of the native population. They kept their own gods (though they adopted the Egyptian god Seth), and the Egyptians never ceased to regard them as outsiders, or to revile them as kings.

EGYPT'S LOCAL CONQUESTS, such as Nubia, were mostly inspired by the desire for luxury materials such as gold. Farther

Beyond the Borders of Egypt

beyond its borders Egypt's foreign policy was driven by the need for military security.

The early New Kingdom rulers were obsessed with the fear of new invasion by Asiatics and pursued an aggressive policy of expansion, turning much of Palestine and Syria into vassal states. Tuthmosis III reached as far into Asia as the banks of the Euphrates River, and the Egyptian army was the terror of the land. Whole populations were systematically deported to lessen local resistance. Garrison duty in these deserted places was dreaded by home-loving Egyptian soldiers. "I am living in Damnationville with no supplies. The heat here never lets up," opines an officer in one surviving papyrus.

This strategy was not appropriate everywhere. Some of Egypt's contacts were with cities even older than its own, and with military powers even more developed: the Hittites, the Mittanians and, later, the most formidable enemy of all, the Assyrians – all states that could meet Egypt on an equal footing. The best that Egypt could do was to negotiate stable boundaries with them. Compromises

AKKADIAN CUNEIFORM on one of the 382 surviving tablets (ABOVE) on which the Amarna diplomatic letters of the 18th Dynasty were written. Others of the tablets were written in the languages of the Assyrians, Hittites and Mittanians.

PRISONERS OF WAR from five different nations are shown on these faience tiles from the 20th Dynasty. Their distinctive clothes and hairstyles identify them as (from left to right) a Libyan, a Nubian, a Syrian prince, a Shasu (Bedu) and a Hittite.

can be seen in the great diplomatic archive found at el-Amarna, Akhenaten's capital. There are some 382 tablets dating from the period 1355–1335 BC. Most are written in Akkadian cuneiform, the language of Mesopotamia, which had become the standard language of diplomacy throughout the Middle East by the end of the Old Kingdom. The Egyptians could not impose their script on diplomatic equals, and among the finds at el-Amarna were texts to help scribes learn Akkadian.

The contrast between Egypt's control in the Levant and lands north and east is clear from these letters. The rulers of Syria and Palestine addressed the Egyptian king as "my lord"; they protested their loyalty while denouncing the activities of their neighbors. If they failed to show respect, they could expect an invasion, at least when Egypt's king was strong. Misbehavior by these Asiatics, described in Egyptian "lament literature", was a sure sign of the weakness or collapse of a dynasty.

The rulers of Babylonia, Assyria, Mitanni, and Alashiya (Cyprus), on the other hand, addressed the Egyptian king as "brother". They made marriage alliances and played diplomatic games. While the Egyptian kings were trumpeting themselves to their subjects as all-conquering warriors, their bureaucracy was corresponding with states that Egypt could never hope to defeat.

IN THE MIDDLE KINGDOM, the Egyptian empire had more contact with the Mediterranean world.

The Delta & the Great Sea

The Hyksos had maintained trade with the Aegean; Hyksos artifacts were found on Crete, and Minoan frescoes at the Hyksos capital of Avaris. Now Egypt's horizons opened further. The borders of the empire were confirmed by a treaty signed with the Mittanians in 1440 BC. Egypt's sphere was the whole of Palestine and Canaan, south and west of the Orontes river in Syria. This gave Egypt control of the eastern Mediterranean coast, giving control of land access to its northeastern borders and securing harbors as supply depots and bases for sea expeditions.

However, although their boats had long sailed the Mediterranean, the Egyptians were never a proper maritime power in the way that the Greeks and the Phoenicians were to become in later centuries. Their fleets had always been intended as a merchant service. A full-fledged navy was not set up until as late as the 26th Dynasty under Necho II, and it was staffed by Greeks, not Egyptians. Similarly, Egyptian goods were often carried by ships from neighboring kingdoms. The wreck of a fourteenth-century-BC trading vessel with Egyptian artifacts on board has been found in modern times at Kas off the coast of Turkey, suggesting that it had several ports of call in the eastern Mediterranean, including the Nile Delta.

Trade flourished, and tribute supplied Egypt with silver, copper, timber, iron, wine and spices. The Hittites, who ousted the Mittanians in the 1320s, dominated the market for iron, a new commodity that became crucial to the balance of power in the region. The movement of the Sea Peoples through the eastern Mediterranean and western Asia in the early twelfth century BC brought iron technology to many areas they invaded. Egypt – which alone remained relatively stable in the chaos – was left largely outside the range of the new technology. It was in this period, under the 20th-Dynasty kings, that Egypt's wealth and prestige suffered a dramatic decline. Iron-working was introduced in Egypt only in about 750 BC, and spread slowly.

One of Egypt's most important trading contacts was the port of Byblos (in modern Lebanon), which supplied timber to Egypt as early as 2900 BC and continued to do so

*C*EDAR LOGS *were transported throughout the Mediterranean in boats* (ABOVE) *from their origin in the Levant, as shown in this Assyrian relief of the island of Tyre.*

*E*GYPT'S INFLUENCE *on the Middle East can be seen in the spread of its gods, images and art styles during the Middle Kingdom. The sphinx and the winged sun-disk were widely adopted; so was the falcon collar* (RIGHT), *such as this one from Byblos, which had a particularly close relationship with Egypt.*

for 2,000 years. The Egyptians learned much about shipbuilding from Byblos, and one of their first words for a seagoing vessel was "Byblos ship". When a 21st-Dynasty king's request for timber was rudely rebuffed by the ruler of Byblos, it was a measure of how low Egypt's status had fallen.

One of Egypt's greatest contributions to the West came via the Mediterranean. From about 2000 BC, the rest of the region experimented with writing. Existing systems made words from syllables, using "letters" derived from cuneiform, hieroglyphs and other systems. A more flexible and concise method was needed. About 1500 BC an unknown scholar from Canaan began using hieroglyphs as consonants. Already many hieroglyphs represented a single consonant: a hand, *yad*, stood for a "d" sound. But no one had realized that relatively few consonants might be able to express the sound of virtually every word between them.

This was the achievement of the Canaanite, who took words from his own Semitic language. For instance, the word for "water" was *maym*, and the Egyptian hieroglyph for water is a wavy line. The Canaanite adopted the wavy line to represent

THE ANCIENT PORT and city of Byblos (ABOVE), about 40 kilometers (25 miles) north of modern Beirut, began trading with Egypt as early as the 1st Dynasty. Byblos was never a major power, but its strategic location and its access to the much-sought-after Lebanese cedar supply ensured its importance.

the "m" sound. Similarly, the Semitic word for house is *bet*; the Canaanite took a sign for "b" from the hieroglyph for house, a quadrilateral (this symbol could also signify "h" in spoken Egyptian).

Once it was grasped that words could be written phonetically with only a few of perhaps only 25 consonants, the alphabet was born. Each community could choose its own signs, hieroglyphic or cuneiform. The Phoenicians, who displaced the Canaanites during the first millennium BC, created an alphabet between 1300 and 1000 BC and transmitted it to the Greeks, who took the final step of adding vowels. The modern Western alphabet is derived from the Greeks'.

A VICTORY HYMN of the Egyptian king Merneptah of about 1200 BC lists his defeated enemies in Syria and Palestine.

Egypt & the Israelites

Among them are a people known as the Israelites, whose land is recorded as lying desolate. This is the earliest known historical reference to the Israelites, which is not surprising, as they were one small and relatively insignificant people among the many vassals of Egypt's New Kingdom empire. The Israelites have been traced by some scholars to the nomadic Shasu of Edom (south of the Dead Sea), who raided Egyptian territory frequently enough

MERNEPTAH of the 19th Dynasty trumpeted victory in the "Israel Stela" (ABOVE): *"Canaan is devastated, Ashkelon is vanquished, Gezer is taken, Yenoam annihilated, Israel is laid waste, its seed exists no more."*

EGYPT'S CULTURE depended on a huge workforce of laborers and craftsmen (BELOW), *many of them foreign. But not a single Egyptian source mentions the Israelites' period of slavery as recorded in the Old Testament.*

to draw repeated punitive expeditions by several kings before Merneptah. Their presence in large numbers in Egypt could be accounted for by the huge numbers of foreign captives forcibly resettled in Egypt after battles: Shasu made up 36 percent of the thousands of captives taken by Amenophis II in one campaign in the 18th Dynasty.

The Israelites almost certainly were still illiterate at the time of their defeat by Merneptah. Their earliest writings – stories of their origins, as told in parts of the Hebrew scriptures or Old Testament of the Christian Bible – were written much later, in the seventh and sixth centuries BC, though doubtless they drew on material from older oral tales. Historians are divided as to how much of the ancient Hebrew account is true or even plausible. Many scholars have turned to Egyptian history to crosscheck and date the biblical history of the Jewish people. They have dated the Exodus to the reign of Ramesses II (1290–1224 BC), and suggested that the raids of the Sea Peoples left eastern Canaan vacant for the Israelites to colonize. The Philistines, who became hostile neighbors to the Israelites in the coastal region around Gaza, were one of the Sea Peoples themselves.

The ancient Hebrew writings tell how, once they had been led out of slavery in Egypt by Moses and arrived in Canaan, the twelve tribes of Israel were united by a single king: first Saul, then David – who conquered Jerusalem, making it the sacred city of the Israelites – and Solomon (c.962–922 BC). Solomon's power and wealth were such that he married one of the daughters of the Egyptian king. The Bible describes the wisdom of Solomon as surpassing all the ancient wisdom of Egypt; this

▼ MOSES
and the Exodus

Moses holds a precious place in Jewish tradition as the leader of the persecuted Hebrews. According to the Bible, Moses was born into the community of Hebrews working in New Kingdom Egypt, but hidden by his parents to escape an Egyptian policy of killing newborn Hebrew males. Found floating in a basket by the Nile by the pharaoh's daughter, he was raised in the court. Moses became aware of his heritage and killed an Egyptian whom he saw beating a Hebrew. He fled to Midian, where he had a vision of God in a burning bush, telling him to return to Egypt to lead his people to freedom.

When the pharaoh refused to let the Hebrews go, plagues afflicted Egypt. The firstborn of every Egyptian family died. The pharaoh then begged the Hebrews to leave. As they made their way toward the Sinai, they were pursued by Egyptian chariots. These were lost in a marsh (the "sea of reeds", mistranslated as the Red Sea). The Hebrews wandered for 40 years before reaching the "promised land", Canaan.

MOTH . QVI GRELEDI
CITUR EXODUS :

qui ingreffi funt inegyptum cū iacob : finguli cū domib: fuif inttroierunt · Ruben · fymeon · leui · iuda ·

The Exodus is one of the Bible's most intriguing episodes. It is written as a factual account rather than a myth – but it is full of discrepancies. Although communities of foreigners existed, the Egyptians left no record of enslaving an entire tribe within

*T*HE WINCHESTER BIBLE *of the twelfth century contains this illustration (ABOVE) of a Hebrew being smitten by an Egyptian (upper panel) and Moses slaying the Egyptian (lower panel).*

Egypt for a long period – nor of the calamities that befell the land as a result of the captives' presence.

Although the pharaoh of the Exodus is generally thought to have been Ramesses II, some scholars argue that the Israelites may originally have been none other than the Hyksos. They came to Egypt about 1700 BC and settled in growing numbers, but were resented and expelled forcibly a century later – to the Levant. The memory of this event, with a slightly different interpretation, survived in a Phoenician legend of the fifth century BC; another version (including an army drowned in the sea) was written down by the classical author Strabo.

Moses himself can be linked to Egyptian traditions, beginning with his name: *mesu* was the Egyptian word for "child" and was a common suffix of Egyptian names (Ahmose, Tuthmosis). The story of the infant hidden in the rushes parallels the tale of the early life of Horus. Some early modern scholars tried to link him to Akhenaten, who also proclaimed a monotheistic religion, but the two have nothing else in common.

comparison was apt, since Solomon seems to have adopted many Egyptian customs. In addition to his main wife he had a large harem, as did the Egyptian kings, and the halls of his palace were graced with columns with flower-headed capitals, similar to those found in Egypt. The titles of his leading officials had some similarities with those of the Egyptian court. However, as king of Israel and servant of the Israelite god, Solomon neither wielded unlimited power nor claimed the personal godlike status of a king of Egypt.

After Solomon's reign his kingdom split apart. In the north ten tribes preserved the name Israel; in the south the remaining two formed the kingdom of Judah with Jerusalem as its capital. A powerful new Egyptian king – Shoshenq I, founder of the 22nd Dynasty – raided Judah and carried off the treasure of Solomon. His sacking of

David's capital city, Jerusalem, in about 925 BC, is one of the few historical events in the Bible that correspond to Egyptian records.

The true enemy of the Israelites was not Egypt but Assyria. In 722 BC the Assyrians annexed Israel and wiped out its identity. In the seventh century BC Egypt itself was invaded. A new phase now opened in Egypt's relationships with the outside world, with a tacit recognition that it could no longer pretend to retain its isolation.

The Assyrian conquests had left hordes of refugees in the Middle East. These were used as mercenaries and laborers. At Elephantine there was a Jewish community, probably placed there to protect the southern boundaries of Egypt. From Anatolia came the Carians, renowned as fighters; but perhaps most prominent of the newcomers were the restless, adventurous, versatile Greeks.

THE RELATIONSHIP between Egypt and the early Greeks – especially the Minoans and Mycenaeans –

Egypt & the Greeks

has fascinated historians since the fifth century BC. It has been claimed that at the height of the New Kingdom, Egypt's control over the Aegean influenced the development of Greek civilization. Although there is no doubt that the Egyptians had contact with the Aegean, the evidence of lasting influence is very limited. Only 21 pieces with an Egyptian royal cartouche have been found in the Aegean or the Mediterranean, mostly in Crete.

Greeks from the Mycenaean civilization (1550 –1200 BC) were present in Egypt. Mycenae was destroyed by raiders around 1200 BC, and trade and cultural contact were interrupted for hundreds of years. By 700 BC, contact had resumed enough to furnish 20 references to Egypt by Homer in his *Odyssey*. One episode describes a raid by Odysseus and his men on the Delta. The Egyptians used these adventurous people as mercenaries. A Greek force was stationed in the eastern Delta in the seventh century BC to buffer Egypt against Assyrian assaults. A haunting reminder of their presence in Egypt is the names of Greek mercenaries scrawled on a statue of Ramesses II at Abu Simbel in 593 BC. The graffiti identifies their home cities on the Ionian coast.

The more opulent Greek cities provided traders. Greece was always short of grain, and the Egyptians were more than willing to trade theirs

HERODOTUS
The World's First Travel Writer

In 449 BC the Greek historian Herodotus visited Egypt, which was then ruled by Persia and experiencing a period of relative calm between times of nationalist unrest. Herodotus was gathering material for his history of the Persian Wars, and he wished to have some understanding of the Persian empire, including its possessions. He had immense respect for the wisdom of Egypt and believed that Egyptian civilization had fostered that of the Greeks. The altars, processions and ceremonies of Greece all derived, he

believed, from Egypt, while each of the Greek gods had an Egyptian forebear. Ptah, the god of craftsmen, was the forerunner of the Greek god Hephaestus; Hathor, the goddess of sexuality, must surely be an early form of the Greek goddess of love, Aphrodite. Herodotus clinched his argument by claiming that the Greeks and the Egyptians were the only nations in the world who forbade priests to have sexual intercourse before temple ceremonies and banned sexual activity in the temples themselves.

It was soon clear to Herodotus, however, that the Egyptians did most things very differently from the Greeks. He struggled to understand how Egyptian society worked. This was a difficult task. Herodotus could not speak the language and had to rely on interpreters. As a result, his version of Egyptian history was frequently muddled, and he was sometimes fooled by his guides, one of whom claimed that an inscription on the pyramids recorded the number of radishes, onions and leeks eaten by the laborers! Herodotus

was also led to believe Egyptians had developed thick skulls because they shaved their heads and exposed them to the full heat of the sun.

But Herodotus was not always gullible, and much of his information was valuable. Observing the silt of the Delta, he guessed accurately that it must have built up over thousands of years. He visited Sais and Memphis, and probably went as far south as Thebes and Elephantine. Medicine, mummification, wildlife, religion and boatbuilding were all within the scope of his inquiries.

*D*ELPHI, *site of the most famous oracle in Greece* (LEFT), *enjoyed the patronage of late Egyptian kings. Amasis financed its rebuilding when it was destroyed by fire in 548 BC.*

*A*N EARLY *Greek papyrus found at Abusir* (BELOW, INSET) *speaks the language of Homer, copied by the later poet Timotheus of Miletus. The papyrus contains a lyric poem celebrating the Greek navy's victory over the Persians at Salamis in 480 BC.*

for Greek silver – used to pay the mercenaries. By the sixth century BC, Egypt was fully part of the trading networks of the Mediterranean. Greek traders from Chios, Aegina, Samos, Miletus, and later Corinth and Athens all settled at Naucratis in the Delta. A tourist service opened, complete with trained interpreters and souvenirs in the form of scarabs and faience – made in Greece.

Among Egyptians, however, Greeks and other foreigners were unpopular. A civil war broke out between the mercenary army and native soldiers in 570 BC. The king, Apries, was killed and the Egyptians' own choice, Amasis, was crowned in his place. Maintaining his throne required keeping his support balanced between native Egyptians and foreigners. He succeeded for 44 years.

Persia was now the rising power in Asia, and under Cyrus II (r.560–530 BC) it spread inexorably westward. Lydia was conquered in 546 BC, and Babylon fell in 539. Cyrus' son Cambyses struck Egypt in 526 BC. Their victory was swift, and Memphis was taken. For the first time Egypt was under direct foreign rule. The Greeks – also threatened by Persia – were Egypt's natural allies. During the 450s an Athenian force landed in the Delta to support the Egyptians, but it was eventually crushed by the Persians. When Alexander of Macedon arrived in 332 BC after defeating Persia, many Egyptians saw him as a liberator. He was proclaimed king of Upper and Lower Egypt, son of Ra. So began a new era, 300 years long, in which Egypt was ruled by Greeks.

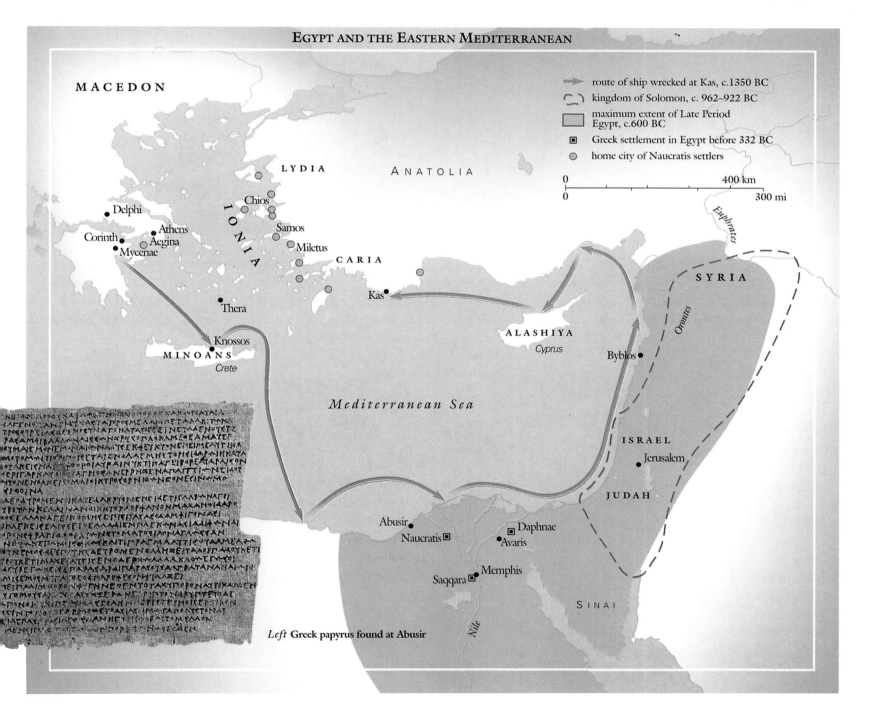

EGYPT AND THE EASTERN MEDITERRANEAN

→ route of ship wrecked at Kas, c.1350 BC
⌒ kingdom of Solomon, c. 962–922 BC
▢ maximum extent of Late Period Egypt, c.600 BC
▣ Greek settlement in Egypt before 332 BC
● home city of Naucratis settlers

MACEDON

LYDIA
ANATOLIA
Chios
Delphi
Athens
Samos
Corinth
Aegina
Miletus
Mycenae
CARIA
Kas
Thera
Knossos
ALASHIYA
Cyprus
MINOANS
Crete
SYRIA
Byblos
Mediterranean Sea
ISRAEL
Jerusalem
JUDAH
Abusir
Daphnae
Naucratis
Avaris
Memphis
Saqqara
SINAI
Nile

0   400 km
0   300 mi

Left Greek papyrus found at Abusir

CLASH OF CULTURES
Egypt under the Greeks & Romans

With the death of Alexander of Macedon in 323 BC, his empire fragmented as his succcessors, including his half-brother and son, contended for the spoils. A Macedonian noble named Ptolemy proclaimed himself governor of Egypt. He managed to grab the most sacred imperial relic, Alexander's body, which he installed in Memphis; he then successfully fought off his rivals. In 304 Ptolemy declared himself king and established a Greco-Macedonian dynasty that lasted almost 300 years. Rome's emperors then claimed Egypt for 300 more years.

The long period of Greek rule bequeathed many of the terms still used to describe ancient Egypt. The word "Egypt" itself comes from the Greek *Aigyptos*. Thebes is a Greek name for the city the Egyptians knew as Waset. The fullest account of the legend of Horus and Seth comes not from an Egyptian papyrus but from a Greek version by the Roman writer Plutarch. (It opens the question of how far he edited the story to appeal to a Greek audience.) The priest Manetho's list of kings, used by modern scholars to date Egyptian history, was drawn up at the request of a Ptolemaic king.

Facade of the temple at Dendara, painted in about 1820 (ABOVE). The main temple, dedicated to the goddess Hathor, was built by the Ptolemies and the Romans on a site dating back perhaps as far as the 6th Dynasty.

TIMETABLE

332 BC – AD 395	**Greco-Roman Period**
332–304	**MACEDONIAN DYNASTY**
332–323	**Reign of Alexander the Great**
323–316	**Reign of Philip Arrhidaeus**
304 –30 BC	**PTOLEMAIC DYNASTY**
304–284	**Reign of Ptolemy I**
51-30	**Reign of Cleopatra VII**
30 BC–AD 395	**ROMAN EMPERORS**
30 BC–AD 14	**Reign of Augustus**
14–37	**Reign of Tiberius**
54–68	**Reign of Nero**
117–138	**Reign of Hadrian**
284–305	**Reign of Diocletian**

The Ptolemaic Kingdom

PTOLEMAIC EGYPT stretched west into Libya, and north and east into Syria, Palestine and Cyprus. Its capital was Alexandria, the city founded by Alexander on the Mediterranean coast of the Delta. Its official name was Alexandria-by-Egypt and it was a Mediterranean city, bustling with commerce and intellectual activity. Its lighthouse on the offshore island of Pharos was one of the Seven Wonders of the World, first listed in the second century BC by Antipater of Sidon.

The palace of the extravagant Ptolemies covered a third of the city. Great patrons of culture, they founded a great library, with half a million books from across the Greek world, and a "museum" – a place for the Muses. Ptolemy II Philadelphos (r.285–246 BC) held sports competitions to rival the Greek Olympic games, and in 275 BC he held an ostentatious religious festival for the Greek god Dionysus. Whole pavilions were furnished in gold, and a vast procession complete with exotic animals paraded around the city.

GRECO-ROMAN EGYPT was a highly cosmopolitan place (RIGHT). The Delta was more settled than ever before, and was full of Greek immigrants, having both Naucratis (the old Greek trading city) and the new capital Alexandria, which was one of the most cosmopolitan cities in the world. The Greeks were also concentrated in Ptolemais and Antinoopolis, two newly founded Greco-Roman cities in the south.

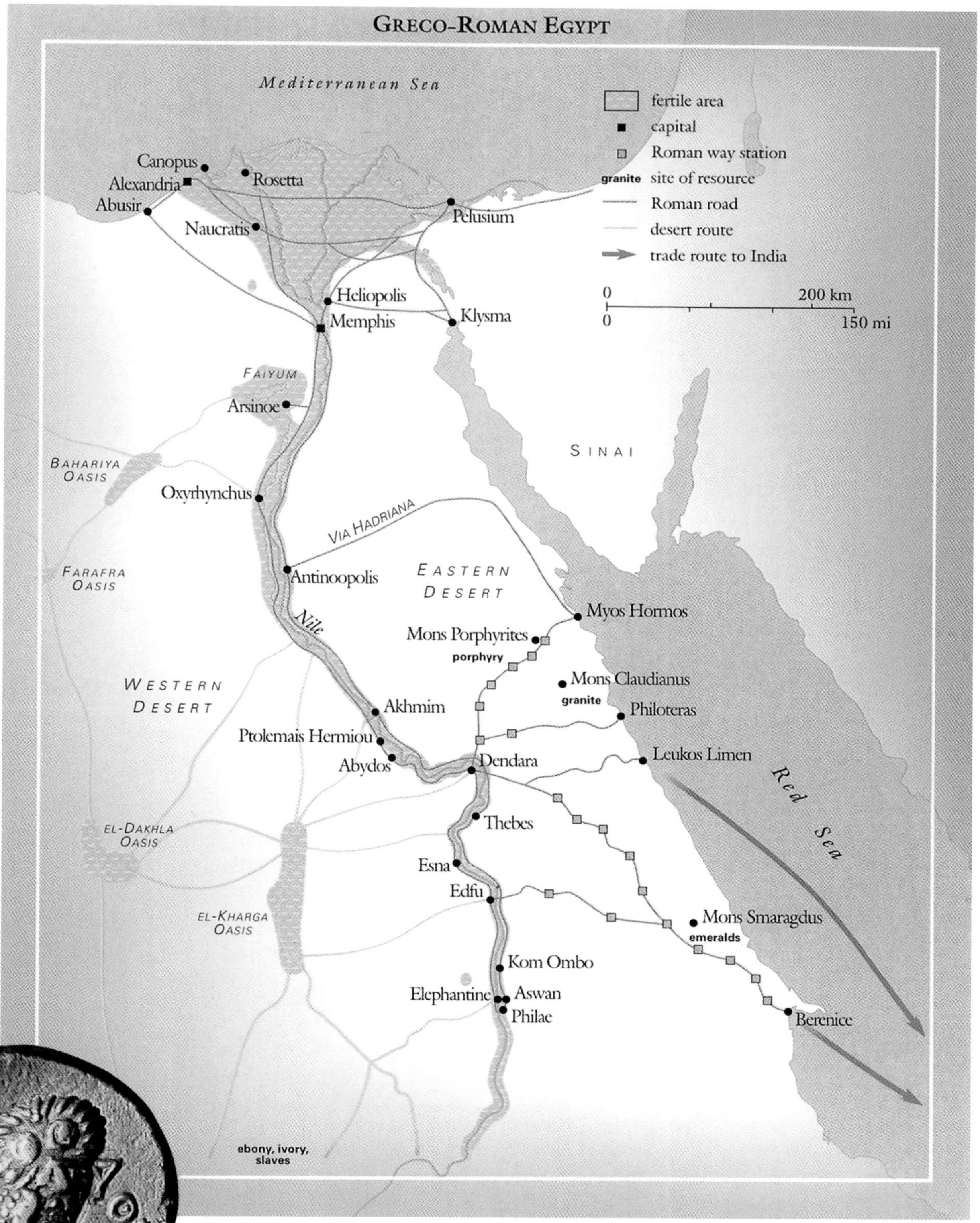

GOLD COINS, introduced under the Ptolemies, reflected the arrival of Greek influences in Egypt. The owl dedicated to Athena was used on coins (BELOW TOP and BELOW CENTER) found in both Athens and Memphis. Another Egyptian coin bore a portrait of Arsinoe I (BELOW RIGHT), wife of Ptolemy I Soter, the founder of the dynasty.

GRECO-ROMAN EGYPT

Map legend:
- fertile area
- ■ capital
- ▫ Roman way station
- granite — site of resource
- Roman road
- desert route
- → trade route to India

0 — 200 km
0 — 150 mi

Mediterranean Sea

Canopus • Rosetta
Alexandria ■
Abusir •
Naucratis •
Pelusium •
Heliopolis •
Memphis ■
Klysma •
FAIYUM
Arsinoe •
BAHARIYA OASIS
SINAI
Oxyrhynchus •
VIA HADRIANA
FARAFRA OASIS
Antinoopolis •
EASTERN DESERT
Myos Hormos •
Mons Porphyrites •
porphyry
WESTERN DESERT
Mons Claudianus •
granite
Philoteras •
Akhmim •
Ptolemais Hermiou •
Dendara •
Leukos Limen •
Abydos •
Red Sea
EL-DAKHLA OASIS
Thebes •
Esna •
Edfu •
EL-KHARGA OASIS
Mons Smaragdus •
emeralds
Kom Ombo •
Elephantine • Aswan •
Philae •
Berenice •
ebony, ivory, slaves

Nile

Native Egyptians were largely excluded from all this. They were expelled from Alexandria by royal decree, "with the exception of pig-dealers and riverboatmen and the men who bring down reeds for heating the baths". Outside the capital, they were second-class citizens in their own country, ruled in a foreign language, prevented from holding public office, burdened by heavy taxes and barred from owning property. Meanwhile, Greeks flocked to Egypt, attracted by its wealth and exoticism. "They have everything that exists or is made anywhere in the world", wrote one. "Wealth, sports, power, excellent climate, fame, sights, philosophers, gold, young men, a shrine of the sibling gods, an enlightened king, the Museum – everything that one might desire." The newcomers hailed from 200 places, as far north as the Black Sea. Immigration and natural increase raised the population from three or four million in the Late Period to seven and a half million by 100 BC.

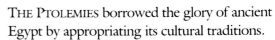

Once barely tolerated in Egypt, the Greeks were now the elite. They were the chief ministers of the king. The Ptolemies retained the centuries-old administrative districts, headed by stewards – usually Greeks. Greek farmers became subcontractors for local tax collectors. Greeks continued to serve as soldiers; they were also moneylenders and shopkeepers. Egyptians were relegated to the level of village clerk, and they had to learn Greek even for this work. Labor strikes broke out and were dealt with ruthlessly. Some Egyptians began to leave towns for the desert, establishing a tradition of hermitage that has lasted to modern times.

Ptolemy II Philadelphos ordered a thorough census from Elephantine to the Mediterranean coast, enumerating the temple lands, listing the crops, and giving details of the irrigation system. No final records survive, but it is clear the Ptolemies were determined to control Egypt's wealth totally. Most land was owned by the crown and rented out or awarded to favored courtiers. Soldiers were assigned their own estates and Greek settlers were given tax incentives to cultivate marginal land. Papyrus, beer and linen were all under a state monopoly.

Egypt was more open to Mediterranean trade than ever before. Grain was exported to the Aegean, as ever, while glass manufactured in Alexandria reached as far as China. Coinage – used by the Greeks for several centuries – was introduced. Money flowed into the royal coffers and into the accounts of Greek merchants.

A GLASS FRAGMENT of a theatrical half-mask (ABOVE) shows a "hetaira" – a Greek courtesan. Glass was an Egyptian specialty, and theater was first introduced to Egypt by the Greeks.

H ORUS AS A FALCON towers over the first court of the temple at Edfu (RIGHT). The Ptolemies were careful to placate the priesthood by obeying the conventions of Egyptian ritual.

C ATACOMBS were built under the city of Alexandria to use as tombs (BELOW). The catacomb of Kom es-Shuqafa was built in the first or second century AD; its burial chamber is shown here.

THE PTOLEMIES borrowed the glory of ancient Egypt by appropriating its cultural traditions.

New Kings & Old Cultures

In the temples and in sculpture they were represented within conventional forms. When Cleopatra was shown on reliefs, it was in a similar style to those of Hatshepsut 1,500 years earlier. The Ptolemies rebuilt temples at many traditional sites including Karnak. They also constructed new ones: the great temple of Horus at Edfu and the temple of Isis on the island of Philae were largely the creations of the period. Some Greek influences can be seen in the architectural detail but the buildings are essentially Egyptian. At Edfu the reliefs portrayed the oldest story of all, the overthrow of Seth by Horus, a myth rooted in predynastic Egypt 3,000 years before. Ptolemy V (r. 204–181 BC) declared to the priests of Memphis that he was the son of their local god, Ptah. Without completely accepting Egyptian religion, the Ptolemies adopted Isis and Serapis as royal gods, fostering cults that spread into the Mediterranean world. Religious practice at the local level was not affected. Villages kept their shrines to local gods; shrines to Isis, Thoth, Anubis and Bubastis have been found in one village alone.

In essence, however, Egypt was now a Greek colony, with the colonists priding themselves on their own heritage and actively protecting it from Egyptian influence. The long-standing Greek respect – even reverence – for Egyptian culture had vanished by the fifth century BC. In the course of a few hundred years, Egypt stagnated while Greece experienced a golden age – in philosophy, science, politics and art. The Greeks felt superior, and wished to maintain that superiority. One lasting indication of this was in their language: the few Egyptian words they adopted merely described Egyptian artifacts or flora and fauna.

This segregation of cultures was maintained through city life. Greek culture was urban, and the tradition was maintained in Egypt. In the south, Ptolemais was probably created as a counterweight to Thebes. Like Alexandria, it was a Greek enclave, with its own rules of citizenship, its own Greek-style temples and gymnasia – that mixture of bath-house, social club and sports arena which was the hallmark of Greek culture. The Greeks in Egypt continued to admire their own civilization. Modern archeologists digging in Egypt found some poems by the poet Sappho and a hitherto unknown play by the comedian Menander.

Outside these enclaves the barrier between Greek and Egyptian was not as rigid. One third of the farmers of a typical village might be Greek, and two-thirds Egyptian. Sometimes the Greeks bullied local Egyptians, but inevitably there were also marriages. The more remote the settlement, the more widespread the practice. By the third century BC many Greek men had Egyptian wives. Their children had both Greek and Egyptian names.

These bilingual offspring and their descendants provided the ideal village clerks. One whose name has survived was Menkhes, an Egyptian of the late second century BC who claimed Greek ancestors. He assessed the flood and the harvest, and reported unrest to the authorities. He was also responsible for unproductive land and was allowed to keep any produce above his tax quota. This was his pay.

NO DEGREE of ethnic segregation or integration, however, could ever be enough to wipe out more

Keeping Egypt Alive than 2,500 years of history and tradition. And no amount of discrimination could overcome the Egyptians' own sense of pride in their culture and identity. By the Greek period the use of demotic, a cursive script first invented in the Late Period, was widespread. It enabled Egyptian literature to

spread to a wider audience. There were strong nationalist overtones in much of the literature of this period. Some of the favorite themes of authors harked back to the days when Egypt was strong and independent, or portrayed the demise of Alexandria and the revival of Memphis.

But there was no strong leader or existing native dynasty to rally support against the well-entrenched Greek administration. The last Egyptian dynasty had survived a meager 37 years before a second conquest by the Persians. Now the Ptolemies also lost vigor. Administration in the south was

THE ROSETTA STONE, a black basalt slab (LEFT) inscribed in hieroglyphic, demotic and Greek, was discovered in 1799. The text is a decree dated March 27, 197 BC, the anniversary of the coronation of Ptolemy V, which concerns the re-establishment of Ptolemaic rule after a brief period of chaos. The inclusion of the names of Ptolemy, Cleopatra and Berenice (in cartouches) was crucial in deciphering the hieroglyphics.

LIFE-SIZED painted shrouds or hangings (LEFT) from the second century AD show further influence of Egypt on Rome. This type of funerary item has so far been found only at Saqqara and shows the deceased (dressed in white and standing in a pose invented by the Greeks) being taken under the protection of Anubis (in an Egyptian pose) and Osiris (in a frontal Eastern pose).

disintegrating by the second century BC. The level of nationalist unrest increased, and there were repeated revolts throughout the century, with a particularly serious one as late as 85 BC. The members of the Ptolemy family intrigued against each other and jockeyed for position, undermining their own dynasty. Between 170 and 160 BC, two Ptolemies (VI and VIII) were king simultaneously; a third, Ptolemy VII, reigned only in 145. Given this opening, a Macedonian Seleucid king actually conquered Egypt briefly in 168 BC.

These events bolstered the Egyptians' aspirations to renewed independence, but as a national group they had been too weak for too long. The wealth of the country, and its army, was in the hands of the Greeks. It is not likely that they could have produced any leader to throw off both the Ptolemies and the rising might of Rome.

The Rosetta stone, world-famous as the means by which hieroglyphs were eventually deciphered in the nineteenth century AD, is historically significant for another reason: it illustrates the tension of the relationship between Ptolemies and their subjects. The tablet's inscription is in Greek, demotic and hieroglyphic. It refers to the coronation of Ptolemy V (r.204-180) at Memphis and associates the king not only with Ptah but with Horus. Horus is specifically mentioned as an avenger of his father Osiris and a punisher of all those who cause disruption – a reference to yet another episode of nationalist unrest that swept Egypt at the end of the third century BC. By advertising the benefits he has brought to the kingdom, in particular its priests and temples, Ptolemy was belatedly seeking to reconcile himself with the national pride his family had trampled on.

❖ CLEOPATRA
Legendary Queen

Cleopatra – the last of the Ptolemies of Egypt and the seventh queen of that name – has survived in the popular imagination as a schemer and seductress, the ultimate *femme fatale*, but first and foremost she was a monarch and a politician. Her reign began in 51 BC, when at age 18 she succeeded to the throne with her younger brother Ptolemy XIII. Egypt was in decline but she was strong, pushing her brother aside and removing his image from the coinage. Such maneuvers were commonplace among the Ptolemies, but nevertheless it was too much for the court to swallow. Cleopatra was expelled from Egypt and the young Ptolemy re-installed.

Exiled to Syria, Cleopatra plotted to return. She saw her chance in the civil wars of the Roman Republic. Julius Caesar, the victor, had come to Egypt in pursuit of his defeated rival Pompey. He stopped in Alexandria. Rome had in effect been the protector of Egypt since 168 BC, when a Roman general repulsed a foreign invasion of Egypt; and Caesar was now the dictator of

Rome. Maintaining good relations was a matter of politics. Cleopatra was perhaps not as beautiful as her legend claims, but she was charming and very intelligent. Furthermore, Egypt was rich, and Caesar needed money. They enjoyed a brief liaison, and her son Caesarion may have been Caesar's, but their dalliance was fundamentally pragmatic.

In 47 BC Cleopatra's throne was restored. She followed Caesar to Rome and lived quietly. When he was assassinated three years later, she returned to Egypt to wait out the power struggle for Rome. Mark Antony emerged the winner and sent for her to discuss an invasion of Persia. She met him in Asia Minor, sailing up the Cydnus river in a

CLEOPATRA VII wearing a Hathor headdress (LEFT), from the temple at Dendara.

barge of breathtaking opulence. Mark Antony was overwhelmed. He followed her to Egypt to live in Alexandrian splendor, causing criticism in Rome. Their subsequent marriage offended Caesar's nephew and heir, Octavian, whose sister was Antony's Roman wife. Even worse, Antony took it upon himself to assign Roman territory to his and Cleopatra's children. Meanwhile, Cleopatra had alienated her powerful neighbor, King Herod of Judea, an old friend of Antony's.

They were doomed. When Octavian declared war, Egypt could not look to Judea for help. At the naval battle of Actium in 31 BC Cleopatra's fleet suddenly sailed for home. Mark Antony had become a liability, and she probably tricked him into suicide, leaving her free to negotiate with Octavian. Mark Antony obligingly fell on his sword in true Roman style. But Octavian was intractable, and Cleopatra herself preferred suicide to defeat.

The most powerful threat to the Ptolemies came from outsiders. By the early second century BC the Romans were expanding into the eastern Mediterranean, attempting to ensure that no power rivalled their own influence within the area. After the corrupt king Ptolemy Auletes was forced to flee in 58 BC, he had to call on the Romans to help restore him. The Ptolemies now depended on Rome's goodwill for their survival. Romans came to Egypt as tourists. Arrangements were made for the visit of one Lucius Memmius: "Receive him with special magnificence and take care that the customary tidbits for Petsuchos (the Greek for Sobek the crocodile god) and the crocodiles, the necessities for the view of the Labyrinth, and offerings and sacrifices be provided."

Cleopatra VII, the final Ptolemaic ruler, succeeded in 51 BC. She saw clearly that the only way to keep her kingdom intact was to ally herself personally to the Roman supreme commanders, first Julius Caesar and then Mark Antony. Although she bore the child of Caesar and then married Mark Antony, her efforts to keep the dynasty alive failed. Caesar's nephew Octavian, later the emperor Augustus, brought Egypt into the Roman empire on her death in 30 BC.

AUGUSTUS AND HIS SUCCESSORS were well aware of Egypt's enormous potential as a source of wealth. Its annual revenue was said to be 12 times that of neighboring Judea. Rome itself, now with a population of a million, controlled its unruly residents with free handouts of grain supplied by Egypt. Every year a fleet of ships laden with grain set out from Alexandria to Italy. The largest, the *Isis*, reputedly displaced 1,200 tonnes – a size not equalled in the Mediterranean until the sixteenth century. In the civil war of AD 69, Vespasian, on his way to power as emperor, entered Egypt to take control of the corn supply and thus ensure his success.

Egypt in the Roman Empire

The Roman emperors, like the Ptolemies, were soon integrated into the traditional pharaonic cults. On the wall of the temple to Khnum at Esna the emperor Titus (r. 79–81) is shown with a mace in his hand, in a pose much like that of king Narmer over 3,000 years before. The Romans built more temples, and decreed that the priests keep their old practices, refraining from sexual intercourse during their time of office, washing themselves three times a day, shaving their heads and wearing only linen

THE VICTORIAN VIEW of the Roman period in Egypt, represented on the canvas entitled "The Juggler" by the British painter Sir Lawrence Alma-Tadema (LEFT). The juggler, an Egyptian, performs for wealthy Romans in a lavish setting. He was probably a slave – slave labor was now widespread – but there were many public theaters and actors were well paid, as were athletes. Roman culture fostered ever more entertainment, which the wealthy empire supported.

AN EMPEROR, probably Nero, wears the Egyptian king's headdress with the "uraeus" (ABOVE). Not content with outer trappings, the emperors claimed Egypt as their personal property; its wealth underpinned their power. Not even senators could visit Egypt without permission.

clothes. However, the status of the temples was now under threat. Their estates had shrunk, and some only survived through direct help from the state. The emperor Hadrian (r.117–138) placed all temples under the supervision of the high priest of Alexandria, a civil bureaucrat.

Roman exploitation proceeded with typical efficiency. A census was held every 14 years. Most state revenue came from a land tax, probably of some ten percent of total produce but lower when the floods failed. The Romans preferred to rule through local elites rather than through an army of administrators. To achieve this, most land reverted to private ownership. Greeks were the main beneficiaries, but in return they were expected to take on local responsibilities: maintaining order locally, embellishing cities and supervising tax collection. This gave the Greeks a chance to build up their own status, but over time the demands on them proved too great. In the town of Oxyrhynchus, the property of 120 citizens was confiscated when it was discovered that they had fled the city rather than fulfill their expensive duties.

The wealth of papyri surviving from this as from earlier periods shows that underneath the formal administrative structure everyday life continued to center on the family. The stories told in these fragments of history make clear the difficulties of the daily lives of ordinary people in the empire. A wife wrote to her soldier husband that she was so consumed with anxiety while he was away that she stayed awake all night and could not eat. Lack of money is a common complaint: a son wrote to beg forgiveness from his estranged mother, saying that his debts had reduced him to nakedness and living in filth. There is also an account of a Roman centurion who had a chamber pot emptied on him from an upstairs window.

In the third century there was unrest in Egypt, as in other parts of the empire, when Rome reeled under the blows of invasion from both north and east. For a brief time Egypt was even incorporated into the "empire" of the Syrian trading city Palmyra. The reforms of the emperor Diocletian (r.284–305) bound Egypt more tightly into the empire and imposed one system of coinage. Under Diocletian's successor Constantine, even more important changes were underway. Constantine set up a new capital for the eastern empire at Constantinople. The grain of Egypt was diverted here instead of to Rome, tying Egypt more firmly into the eastern Mediterranean. It was also under Constantine that Christianity was first tolerated.

▼ THE FAIYUM PORTRAITS
Capturing Life

Egypt during the Greco-Roman period was a multi-ethnic society, but it was still influenced by ancient Egyptian customs, above all those of burial. All those wealthy enough to do so – which mostly meant foreign immigrants – mummified their dead. However, instead of funerary masks, the mummies were finished with individual portraits.

The gradual discovery throughout the nineteenth century of more than a thousand of these portraits from the Faiyum region, south of Cairo and west of the Nile, perfectly represents the blending of cultures in the Greco-Roman period. The subjects lived in Egypt and were buried as Egyptians. They had Greek faces and wore Roman clothes. Yet they are neither Greek nor Egyptian or Roman.

The quality of the portraits is not uniform. The finest portraits are marked by the distinctive naturalism of classical Greece. Some of them

are masterworks, painted from life by gifted individuals trained in the Greek style. Some resemble Byzantine icons (whose forebears they were); some look modern; still others most closely resemble later Asian art. They also vary in technique, painted on wood or linen, in tempera (similar to oil painting but using a colloid or albumen instead of oil) or encaustic (wax-based paint). Many of them also have gilding. They are not signed, but the names of some artists are known from papyri, including some of the painters' own notes on color and the features of the subject. Some of the artists were itinerant, as in classical Greece, but others lived and worked in the Faiyum and were buried near their own works.

*T*HE PAINTING of "Aline" *(ABOVE) has the naturalism, immediacy and close observation typical of the Greek tradition.*

*S*TYLIZATION *and a frontal perspective give this portrait in tempera on linen (LEFT) a closer kinship with Asian art.*

CHRISTIANS HAD PRACTICED in Egypt well before there was official toleration by Constantine. There

The Christians in Egypt

was a large Jewish population at Alexandria (where the first translation of the Hebrew texts into Greek had taken place), and early Christianity had its roots in the Jewish community. Two of the most celebrated early Christian theologians, Clement and Origen, were from Alexandria. In the rest of the country Christianity spread more slowly, and, as elsewhere, Christians were persecuted at times of political tension. The first record of Egyptian Christianity is a set of extracts from the *Book of Isaiah* of the early third century.

The steady spread of Christian belief can be seen in burial customs. Mummification had lasted all through the Greek and Roman era. Bodies were still preserved and even the poorest Egyptian was closely wrapped in bandages. In the third century AD the texts on coffins still contained 2,000-year-old prayers to Osiris-Sokar, "the great lord of Abydos". Even in Alexandria there are tombs, such as the Tegran tomb from the second century AD, in which a mummy is shown attended by Isis and Nephthys with a winged sun disc hovering above. These ancient customs vanished as Christianity spread. Perhaps 80 to 90 percent of the native population was Christian by the end of the fourth century AD, and the prayer to Osiris disappeared as bodies were wrapped in ordinary clothes.

As Egypt was now simply a province of a huge empire, with all important political activity occurring far away at the imperial capital, religious leaders achieved great prominence. The patriarch of Alexandria, responsible for the bishops of Egypt and Libya, was the most important figure in the land. Through him the emperor in Constantinople negotiated the continued supply of Egyptian grain to Rome. At the same time, local bishops took on roles that were as much political as spiritual. The best known of these was the fifth-century bishop Shenoute, later canonized. When refugees fled north as a result of Nubian raids, he fed them. Another bishop, Apion of Syene – whose diocese was right on the border between Egypt and Nubia – took the initiative and ordered more troops to defend his churches and congregations.

With the majority of the population converted, the fourth century saw a hardening of attitudes against non-Christians. This was the final blow to traditional Egyptian religion and culture. As the church historian Eusebius wrote, "See what blessings God's Christ came to bestow on us, since through His teachings in the Gospels he has redeemed even the souls of the Egyptians from such a disease of lasting and continued blindness, so that most of the people of Egypt have been freed from this insanity." The use of hieroglyphs had survived centuries of Greek and Roman rule, even though not a single outsider is known ever to have learned to understand them, but now they were eradicated. The last example dates from AD 394. The Serapeum, the great cult center of Serapis in Alexandria, was sacked by monks in 391. Christian vigilantes made their way through the towns of Upper Egypt, burning temples and destroying traditional cult statues. The temple of Isis at Philae was closed down by Justinian in 536. Karnak itself was converted to a church, its temple walls plastered over to hide the idolatrous images.

The separate identity of Christian Egypt was consolidated by the doctrinal disputes of the fifth century. There were major conflicts over the nature of Christ in his earthly existence: was he

THE TEMPLE of Kom Ombo north of Aswan (BELOW) combined two existing cult temples, one of the crocodile-god Sobek and Haroeris (an aspect of Horus). This relief from about 220 BC shows Ptolemy VII on a boat in a marsh approaching Min, the god of fertility (whose characteristic erect phallus was effaced by later Christians). At the upper right Sobek receives offerings from the king.

predominantly human, predominantly divine or with two natures in one? While the official line was that he had two natures coexisting with each other, the Egyptian Christians tended to favor Monophysitism, a doctrine that Christ had a single, divine nature. By the sixth century the emperors in Constantinople were persecuting Monophysites and the church in Egypt became increasingly isolated. It eventually went its own way as the Coptic church – which, ironically, is one of the few relics of ancient Egypt to have lasted to the present.

This schism may have been one of the reasons why the Egyptians made little protest when the country came under the sway of Islam in the 640s. The conquest was not harsh in its immediate effects. The invading troops were forbidden to take land for themselves, and they were at first prepared to tolerate Christianity. A new capital, Cairo, was founded, leaving the old towns intact. Egypt had entered a new era. Once again it was to prove long-lasting, and to this day Egypt remains one of the cultural centers of the Arab world.

> **"** *As the boat glides between glistening boulders, those sculptured towers rise even higher against the sky* **"**
> Amelia Edwards 1873

PHILAE
Cult Center of the Goddess Isis

The island of Philae, in the First Cataract above Elephantine, is unlike any other site in Egypt. It was small, which restricted what could be built there, and it was right on the traditional southern border of the kingdom. Rich in silt, it was a fertile island in an otherwise barren region: the ancient Egyptians considered it an epitome of the mound of creation rising from the primeval waters.

Yet it was not until the 6th century BC that it was first built upon, and only a century later was the great temple to the goddess Isis built. On the nearby island of Biga there was a shrine to her husband, the god Osiris, and in the Ptolemaic and Roman periods Philae became one of the most important cult centers in the land.

The Romans, who found Isis much the most attractive of the Egyptian deities, contributed a great deal to the splendors of the island: Augustus, Trajan, Hadrian and Diocletian all built there, and the colonnades of the southern part of the island (where pilgrims once arrived) are more reminiscent of the public spaces of the Classical world than of ancient Egyptian temples.

For two hundred years a Christian community shared the island with the priests of the traditional religion, who enjoyed special protection because the worship of Isis was so popular the authorities feared a revolt if they closed it down. The walls were covered in Egyptian, Greek, Roman, even Meroitic graffiti and inscriptions – some official, others highly informal – relating to the flourishing business of receiving visitors to the shrine of the goddess. The latest known hieroglyphs were carved here in AD 394; when the emperor Justinian finally closed the temple down in the 6th century AD, the last memories of the old faith went with it.

In the 19th century, Philae was seen as the "pearl of Egypt", a romantic reward for travelers who ventured as far south as Aswan. When the first Aswan Dam was built in the early 20th century, Philae was submerged for part of each year and plans were discussed for moving the shrine to Biga. But it was not until 1960, with the High Dam under way, that a scheme was fully developed. The nearby island of Agilkia – some 13 meters (40 feet) higher than Philae – was remodelled to resemble the original island as closely as possible, and the monuments were moved in a complex international operation.

1	Hall of Nectanebo I	7	Kiosk of Trajan
2	Colonnade	8	Temple of Hathor
3	Temple of Imhotep	9	Church
4	First pylon	10	Temple of Augustus
5	Temple of Isis	11	Gate of Diocletian
6	Birth-house	12	Gate of Hadrian

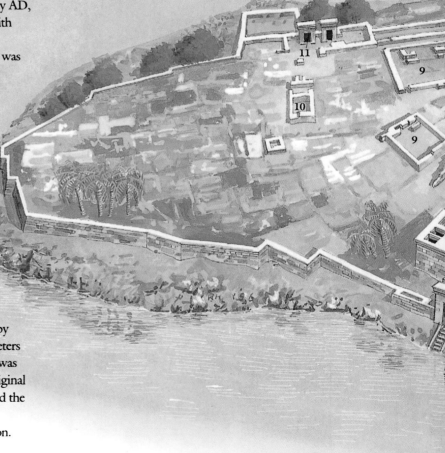

Left This painting of 1873, by Carl Werner, shows the kiosk of Trajan, seen through a doorway by the gateway of the temple of Isis. The painted decoration was then still visible, but it did not survive its annual submersion in the early 20th century.

Philae ■

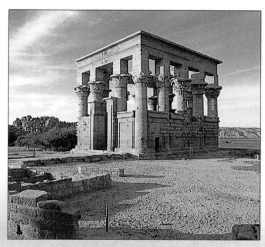

Above The kiosk of Trajan (c.AD 96), built in a fusion of Egyptian and Roman style. It is sometimes known as "the bed of the pharaohs".

Above The entrance court of the temple of Isis, seen from the Roman-era porticoes. To the right is a small temple to Imhotep, the Old Kingdom architect and god of healing. Beyond the pylon is the *mammisi* or birth-house, a common feature of Ptolemaic temples, where the goddess was supposed to have given birth to her child, Horus.

Left This colossal statue of Isis was made in Italy and found at Hadrian's villa in Tivoli. Though not obviously Egyptian, the frontal pose and the hairstyle mark her out as exotic. Some later writers claimed to have found evidence of a cult of Isis in India, China and – even more unlikely – ancient America. Her attributes were perhaps also trans-ferred to the Virgin Mary and, like those of Osiris, to pagan fertility deities.

AN IMAGE OF EGYPT
The Impact of Egyptian Art & Architecture

When Greek soldiers, traders and tourists began to arrive in the seventh and sixth centuries BC, Egypt was already deep in decline, but it had not lost its power to awe and astonish outsiders, especially those from younger civilizations. The 2,000-year-old pyramids at Giza were only 120 kilometers (75 miles) from the Greek enclave of Naucratis, and many Greeks doubtless journeyed up the Nile to see them. By 590 BC some mercenaries had even penetrated as far south as Abu Simbel. At this time Psamtek I and his successors of the Saite Dynasty were engaged in great building projects in the north, drawing on Old Kingdom models in an attempt to distance themselves from the foreigners on whom they depended for trade and defense.

THE GREEKS were inspired by the experience of watching Egyptian stonemasons at work. They

Greek Building & Egypt

could see that the pyramids and other great stone monuments of Egypt were not the work of a vanished tribe of legendary masters but of ordinary humans whose skills might be copied. In the process they learned from the Egyptians and

INSPIRED BY rows of sphinxes at Egyptian temples, a row of lions (ABOVE) guards the temple of Apollo on the island of Delos – the most important Aegean shrine.

built on the Egyptian achievement. In giving it their own stamp, they shaped it further to form one of the classical traditions of the Western world.

Greeks had begun to work in stone long before they went to Egypt. The Mycenaeans (1550–1200 BC) had built great domed "beehive" tombs at their capital, and many Mycenaean cities were protected by well-fashioned stone walls. Much skill in stone masonry was forgotten with the collapse of Mycenaean civilization, but in the eighth and seventh centuries BC stone was being used again, alongside mud-brick and wood, for the temples of the newly emerging Greek cities. What the Greeks needed, however, was confidence and, possibly, some direct models to follow for their building projects. Egypt provided them with both.

Prominent among the early Greek traders in Egypt were the Ionians from the opulent cities of the Asian coast. The Ionians developed a form of architecture that had as its essential ingredient a decorated form of column known as the Ionic order. Some scholars have linked the volutes or scrolls on the capitals of its fluted columns to the lotus-flower design used on Egyptian columns.

The Ionians appear to have been inspired also by the great hypostyle halls of Egyptian temples.

By the sixth century BC the main temples of Ionian cities were built with a double row of columns surrounding the entire temple, echoing the halls of Egypt. Intriguingly, a cup inscribed with the name Rhoikos – the architect of a massive sixth-century temple on the island of Samos – has been found in a sanctuary at Naucratis on the Delta. Access to the inner temples of Egypt was restricted to priests, so the interiors could not be copied even if outsiders had wished to do so, but outside the walls the Ionians could admire the great processional rows of sphinxes joining the temples. These inspired a row of lions built in the sixth century BC in front of the sanctuary of a Greek temple on the island of Delos, which had a shrine particularly sacred to the Ionians.

In the seventh century BC the city of Corinth, in the northeast of the Peloponnese (the southern peninsula of mainland Greece), emerged as the most prominent city of the Greek world. Its colonies spread far, and it dominated trade in the eastern Mediterranean. Corinthians were among the first Greeks in Egypt in the Late Period, and a sixth-century BC Corinthian ruler was even given the name Psammetichus, after Psamtek of the 26th Dynasty. After Corinth's first contact with Egypt in the seventh century BC, the so-called Doric order of architecture appeared – shorter, thicker and with a plainer capital than the Ionic. Architectural historians have often speculated whether its form

was derived from Egyptian design. The columns of the Doric order resemble those found in the shrine of Anubis in Hatshepsut's temple at Deir el-Bahri; and there are tombs from the Middle Kingdom at Beni Hasan in Middle Egypt that have the same flat square abacus, but at the top of a 16-sided column. The fluted columns of the hall adjoining the Step Pyramid at Saqqara, a site much visited by Greeks, may have been another influence.

HUMAN FIGURES were represented completely and flatteringly in Egyptian art to ensure that the person depicted was provided with a fully intact, functioning body for the afterlife. The Greeks observed this careful representation and

The Perfect Human Form

transformed it into a love of physical beauty for its own sake. The earliest examples are the large free-standing marble male figures, the *kouroi* (singular *kouros*), found in Greece from about 650 BC. *Kouroi* were placed by wealthy patrons as markers over a grave or as dedications in a sanctuary. Although some *kouroi* were representations of the god Apollo, most were unnamed, simply figures of ideal young manhood. Their pose was stylized and they always stood nude, with their left foot in front of their right and their arms clenched by their sides. They were carved according to set proportions.

*P*APYRUS SHEAVES *decorate the capital of a column* (ABOVE) *from the kiosk of Qirtasi near Aswan, part of a temple built in the reign of Augustus (30 BC–AD 14). Reed bundles, papyri, palms and lotuses were the most common motifs on columns on the earliest Egyptian buildings. They were intended to evoke the original "Island of Creation".*

*S*EVEN DORIC *columns of limestone, fluted in a way that suggests the reed-bundle column of Egypt, are all that remain at the temple of Apollo in Corinth* (LEFT). *There were originally 38 columns surrounding the sides of the temple. Built in the mid-sixth century BC on a site dating back to the seventh century, it is one of the oldest temples in Greece.*

*T*HE ATHLETIC FORM *of a "kouros"* (FAR LEFT), *a life-sized naked young man, carved in 530 BC – about 200 years after the Greeks adopted the style from the Egyptians. Its significance was not in the person represented but the beauty of his body (or hers – there were also female "korai").*

It was the Greek historian Diodorus Siculus, writing in the first century BC, who grasped where the origin of the *kouroi* lay. "This type of workmanship," he wrote, "is not (now) practiced among the Greeks, but among the Egyptians it is especially common. Dividing up the layout of the body into twenty-one parts, plus an additional one-quarter, they produce all the proportions of the living figure." The proportions of the parts of the body of the *kouroi* are almost identical with those of Egyptian figures, and they appear to have been carved in the same way, with the outlines drawn out on each side of a marble block and then the figure gradually chiseled into life. The Greeks can only have learned the technique at first hand.

The *kouroi* are not, however, slavish copies of Egyptian originals. The Egyptian examples are clothed, and are rarely free-standing. The balance of their legs is different, and the pose is much less stiff in the Greek figures. Once the Greeks had borrowed the idea of carving large statues and mastered the art, they set off on their own path,

showing that they could outdo the Egyptians at the forms the Egyptians had invented. *Kouroi* became ever more relaxed and natural. They were the forerunners of the Greeks' immortal sculptures in marble and bronze of the fifth century BC.

UNDER THE PTOLEMIES, Mediterranean access to Egypt was unprecedented, and Egyptian influence spread far and wide. The cults of Isis and Serapis (a fusion of Osiris and Apis with several Greek gods, who appeared early in the Ptolemaic kingdom) introduced a whole array of new images into both the Greek and Roman worlds. There was also a growing fascination with the sheer exoticism of Egypt. Although the Romans were not interested in Egypt in such a detailed, almost scientific manner as the Alexandrian Greeks, they could not fail to be impressed by what they found there, and they introduced the images into their own land.

Egypt Comes to Rome

A famous example of this fascination with Egypt is a mosaic that graced a grotto in the important religious and commercial center of Praeneste (modern Palestrina) near Rome. Known as the Nile mosaic for the river scene it depicts, it is dated to the early first century BC. Praeneste had trading links with Alexandria, and the mosaic was probably copied from an Alexandrian picture. In the next 200 years pictures of Nile landscapes became particularly popular in Italy. Many of them have been found in Pompeii, near the port of Puteoli which serviced ships from Alexandria.

The Romans were attracted to the portrayal of fertility and abundance in the paintings. Gardens and summer rooms were common settings, and the water of the Nile suggested coolness. The Nile mosaic itself was probably designed for the bottom of a shallow pool. Another theme was the exotic. Some paintings showed Egyptian animals; others focused on the Egyptians themselves, who were sometimes even shown as pygmies. These images presented Egypt as a land mysterious, different, otherworldly and, above all, fashionable. Romans enjoyed the pictures as art, but they did not fully adopt Egyptian culture, such as all its gods.

The Romans also liked to portray Egypt in sculpture, and drew on similar themes, such as the Nile river personified as a male figure looking much like the Roman Neptune or the Greek Poseidon. There is such a statue in the Vatican collection today. Though a Roman work, probably of the second century AD, it almost certainly draws on a Hellenistic original. By the elbow of the god sits a sphinx, against his feet a crocodile. Behind him, a cornucopia overflows with fruit symbolizing the abundance of the Nile. This impressive statue was probably placed in the Iseum Campense, the major temple to Isis in Rome.

Egyptian plunder flooded Rome after Octavian's victory over Antony and Cleopatra at Actium, which gave Rome direct control of Egypt. Octavian needed Egypt's wealth to pay

TAPERING SKYWARD, a lone Egyptian obelisk (LEFT) stands in the Piazza del Populo in Rome. The shape of the obelisk was derived from the "benben" stone of Egyptian myth, and obelisks were copied by Canaanites and Assyrians long before they became curiosities in Europe. In Egypt they were set up in pairs outside temples, but foreign importers chose to use one per site. Rome had more obelisks than any other city.

off his disbanded troops, and he took Egyptian art and objects as personal trophies. The prows of captured Egyptian ships were cut off and displayed in triumph in the Roman Forum, and obelisks were transported to Rome. The Romans understood that obelisks had a sacred significance related to the worship of the sun. One obelisk, originally from Heliopolis, was used as the pointer of a great sundial set out on the Campus Martius. It was positioned so that on Octavian's birthday the shadow of the obelisk fell on the monumental altar, the Ara Pacis,

SIXTEEN SMALL BOYS gambol over a Roman statue personifying the Nile (BELOW). The number 16 had come to represent the number of Egyptian royal cubits which the Nile was believed to rise in the annual flood. On the base of the statue are waves.

THE PYRAMID-TOMB of Gaius Cestius (RIGHT) is the only one of Rome's several pyramids to have survived to the present. It now looks very oddly placed next to the Aurelian wall, which was built some 250 years later. Only 37 meters (120 feet) high, its sides have much steeper angles than those of the Egyptian pyramids. But it passed as an accurate model for 19 centuries of visitors who never saw the originals.

ONE OF EGYPT'S most venerable images, the sphinx, was copied throughout the ancient Middle East. A winged sphinx (BELOW) was popular in Rome. The half-man, half-animal hybrid lent itself particularly well to imaginative reinterpretations. In ancient Egypt the sphinx sometimes had the head of a ram or a hawk instead of a man; or even a crocodile's tail.

which had been erected by the Senate to Octavian the emperor, now styled Augustus. He also placed an obelisk in the Circus Maximus, the hippodrome where the chariot races took place. It formed the turning mark, or *spina*, and established a new use, far removed from the original intentions of the men who first erected the obelisk.

The emperor Caligula (r.AD 37–41) had an obelisk brought from Egypt to set up in a new hippodrome. This hippodrome was said to be the site of the apostle Peter's martyrdom, and in 1587 the same obelisk was hauled off to be set up in front of his church on the Vatican hill. As late as AD 357 yet another obelisk was brought to Rome for the emperor Constantius. It came on a barge with 300 rowers and became a second *spina*

in the Circus Maximus. With obelisks came Egyptian statues. A fine example is a pair of lions from the 30th Dynasty which may have come from Memphis. In Rome they formed part of the Iseum Campense.

TRANSPORTING OBELISKS and other statues to Rome was difficult, and before long Egyptian styles were being copied in Rome itself. Often the work was done by Egyptian craftsmen who had settled in the city. One magistrate, Gaius Cestius, chose to be buried in a pyramid which still survives close to where the road from the port of Ostia entered the city. It is much more steeply pitched than Egyptian pyramids, but credulous visitors to Rome over the centuries assumed it was a copy of the real thing.

In the Egyptian Style

Perhaps the most important setting for Egyptian sculpture was the Iseum Campense, which was rebuilt on the Campus Martius in Rome by the emperor Domitian (r. 81–96). It was distinctly Egyptian in style. Enclosed within great walls, as Egyptian temples normally were, it had two temples inside, one to Isis and one to Serapis, joined by a processional route of sphinxes, lions and small obelisks. Some fragments of surviving columns show that there was an attempt to copy the lotus buds of true Egyptian columns.

Much of the statuary in the Iseum and in other shrines to Isis and Serapis was created locally, sometimes from imported Egyptian marble such as porphyry or from pastiche (fabricated stone) which was mixed to resemble Egyptian granite. There are statues from various centuries of a wide range of subjects, from Apis bulls to baboons and sphinxes, from statues of pharaohs and priests to those of the gods Bes, Isis and Horus. As well as originals and direct copies from originals, shrines contained imaginative attempts to create something with Egyptian spirit as it was interpreted at the time. This style is described today as "Egyptianizing".

Some pieces of Roman Egyptianization were highly mistaken in their borrowings from the original. One of the strangest examples is a bronze table inlaid in silver, the Mensa Isiaca. It was a Roman creation from the time of the emperor Claudius (r.41–54) and was certainly intended for a sanctuary. It shows divine figures surrounded by friezes of "hieroglyphs" which, with the sole exception of the name of the emperor, are completely meaningless.

Outside the temples the fascination with Egyptian landscape paintings and mosaics led to attempts to create Egyptian gardens. These were often centered on an artificial river or lake, surrounded by statuettes of pharaohs or Egyptian gods. The first examples come from around Pompeii, reflecting its close links with Alexandria. These creations were mocked by sophisticated Romans such as Cicero, the orator and statesman of the first century BC, but they spread north to Rome nonetheless. The gardens of Sallust on the Pincio Hill of Rome had an Egyptian pavilion, an obelisk and statues of pharaohs.

Under the emperor Hadrian (r. 117–138), Rome was in the grip of full-fledged Egyptomania. Hadrian paid two visits to Egypt in person and became an enthusiast. In his magnificent villa at Tivoli outside Rome he set about recreating buildings he had admired in his travels, among them the Serapeum, the temple to Isis and Serapis, at Canopus near Alexandria. The original Serapeum had a canal with the temple at one end (depicted on the Nile mosaic from Palestrina), and this is what Hadrian reproduced. Building was started in the 130s after his return from his second

IMAGES OF Egyptian divinity are presented in stately fashion across the surface of the Mensa Isiaca (BELOW), a bronze plaque of Roman workmanship from the first century AD reproduced in this 17th-century engraving. The rendering of the figures provides a clue that this is a painstakingly executed but far from accurate copy of Egyptian art: not all figures stand in the classic Egyptian pose.

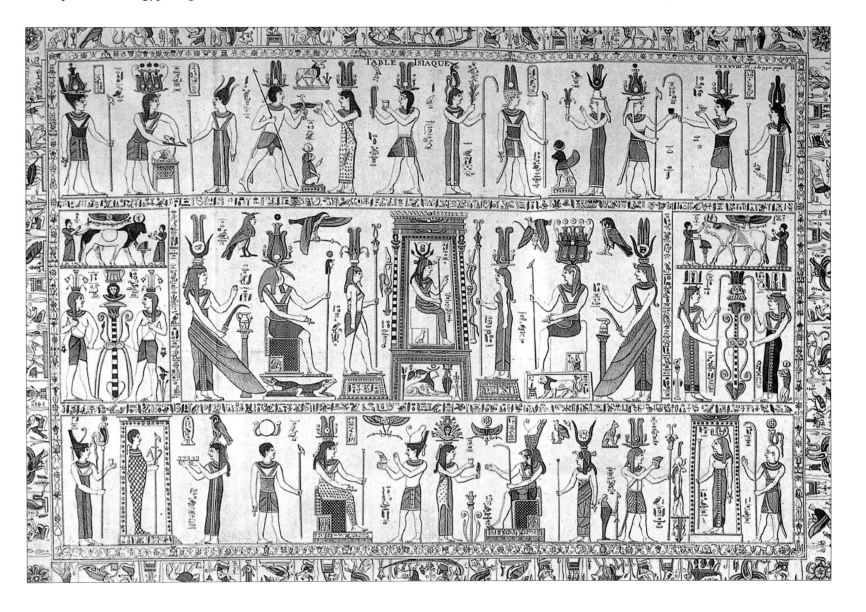

ANTINOUS
The Emperor's Favorite

One day in late October in the year AD 130 a man's body was hauled out of the floodwaters of the Nile in Middle Egypt. He was soon identified as Antinous, an 18-year-old Greek from Bithynia. Antinous was no mere tourist visiting Egypt. He was the companion of the 54-year-old emperor Hadrian, who was on a grand tour of the country. The exact nature of the relationship between the two men can only be speculated upon, but Hadrian was a devotee of all things Greek, and in Greece sexual relationships between men and teenage boys were accepted.

The grief-stricken emperor reacted almost hysterically to the loss of his companion. Hadrian declared that Antinous was to be worshiped as a god and that a city was to be founded in his memory on the site of his drowning. Work soon began on the construction of Antinoopolis. No expense was spared. It was designed as a Greek city and laid out on a grid-iron plan. (Not far away was a much earlier city planned in the wilderness, Akhenaten's capital el-Amarna.) Its walls ran for five kilometres and enclosed one great avenue 1,300 meters (4,160 feet) long, running parallel with the Nile, and another at right angles to it, 950 meters (3,116 feet) long, which ran up from the Nile. These were graced with columned arcades.

Everywhere there were statues of the dead youth – over 1,300 in the two main avenues alone – and there were at least two temples dedicated to him. Every four years there were Greek-style games in his honor, with chariot races and rowing races on the Nile. To ensure that this mausoleum came alive, Hadrian

ANTINOUS *carved in red marble (RIGHT), a statue from Hadrian's villa at Tivoli.*

granted its citizens special privileges. Antinoopolis flourished, and by the late Roman empire it was an important seat of administration.

From the start Antinous was adopted as a manifestation of Osiris, perhaps in hope that he would be reborn, and he was worshiped at several sites in Egypt. His cult spread into Greece and even Italy, linked to other gods such as the messenger-god Hermes. Nine cities in the east held games to him and many issued coins portraying him. Statues of him were found at the oracle in Delphi and in Egyptian temples in Rome. The cult lasted 200 years, until the Christian era, when Antinous was denounced as the slave of the unlawful pleasures of Hadrian and his worship was suppressed.

Egyptian tour. To make the canal more realistic, stone crocodiles were placed in it and an elephant by its banks. Along the sides there was a mass of statues: Egyptian gods such as Ptah, Isis and Osiris; priests and pharaohs; and animals such as falcons, baboons and sphinxes.

Among this collection of traditional Egyptian images there were also many statues of Antinous, Hadrian's lost companion and lover. One of these was rediscovered in 1740, with Antinous modeled in classical form but wearing an Egyptian kilt and headdress. Like the pyramid of Cestius, it was later mistaken for an original Egyptian piece and provided an important model for Neoclassical sculptors of the late eighteenth century in their own attempt to revive the Egyptian style.

Egypt became almost totally cut off from the European world after the Arab invasions in the mid-seventh century AD. Except for the tales of a few intrepid travelers, there was no information available by which to judge true Egyptian art or architecture – much of which had been defaced, destroyed or concealed during the later Roman empire by local Christians, who did not approve of the idolatrous images of their country's past.

Rome itself had never contained much genuine Egyptian architecture, and even many of the "Egyptianized" monuments disappeared with time. Cestius' pyramid of 12 BC survived, but the Iseum Campense, itself only an artificial recreation of a true Egyptian temple, was destroyed, possibly when Rome was sacked by the Normans in 1084.

WELL TRAVELED and curious about the world, Hadrian built a sumptuous villa (ABOVE) outside Rome at Tivoli. It consisted of a series of pavilions influenced by architecture in different parts of the empire, somehow combined into a more or less harmonious grouping. The enclosure of the pool shown here duplicated the series of arches and pillars seen by the emperor at the Egyptian city of Canopus.

It was in Rome, however, that most of the surviving fragments of Egyptian art remained. Some Egyptian objects, like the lions of Nectanebo (which were eventually placed in front of the Pantheon), were never lost from view. They were used by Roman sculptors as models for lions in the thirteenth century. From the sixteenth century onward, the revived interest in ancient Rome meant that many more sculptures – including a liberal supply of Egyptianized examples among the genuine Egyptian – were dug up among the ancient ruins. One was the Mensa Isiaca, which was rediscovered in the early sixteenth century. Its design was soon copied and it was acclaimed as a masterpiece of Egyptian art. Not until the nineteenth century was its Roman origin realized.

> **"** *What is it that walks on four legs in the morning, on two at noon, and on three in the evening? If you cannot tell me I will carry you off and devour you.* **"**
>
> Answer: a man
> Greek riddle of the sphinx, 5th century BC

Left The story of Oedipus and the sphinx was depicted on this Greek vase of the 5th century BC. After solving the sphinx's riddle, Oedipus speared the sphinx to death, and was acclaimed king of Thebes. In this myth, the sphinx was an angel of death who escorted young men killed in combat to the underworld, and who was sent to Thebes as a curse by the goddess Hera.

The Evolution of the Sphinx

The Great Sphinx, a recumbent lion with a human head carved from an outcrop of rock on the edge of the Giza plateau and battered by centuries of wind-driven sand, is one of the most distinctive symbols of ancient Egypt. Despite a recent claim that it dates back even earlier than the unification of the kingdom, most scholars accept that it was built by Khephren, whose pyramid it appears to guard, and whose features it carries. The Egyptians believed that a lion watched over the gates of the underworld, and so it is appropriate that Khephren, in the form of a lion, should be placed before his own tomb.

For much of its history the Sphinx has been buried in sand. Before his accession in 1401 BC, the future Tuthmosis IV, out hunting one day, rested in the shadow of the half-covered Sphinx. He had a dream which promised that if he cleared away the sand, the crown of Egypt would be his. His efforts to keep the Sphinx clear did not last and it vanished once more, though the Romans are known to have found it and cleared it again. There have been no fewer than four new clearings in the last century and a half, and it is probably thanks to the sand that the Sphinx has survived at all. It is now suffering from modern air pollution.

Left This Assyrian sphinx of the early 8th century BC is displayed with eagles' wings and an Egyptian crown. The oriental sphinx usually acted as a guardian of the sacred ruler, or of the tree of life. Similar creatures, such as the winged bull with the head of a man, are found throughout the Middle East, as on the doorways at the Assyrian capital, Nimrud (Kahlu).

The sphinx – the word appears to derives from a Greek word meaning "bind together", or possibly from the Egyptian *shesep-ankh* "living image" – was a common symbol in ancient Egypt. A king is shown as a sphinx, defeating his enemies; avenues of sphinxes, some with human heads, others with rams' heads, line the processional routes to temples. Sphinxes in Egypt were always associated with the theme of protection.

The sphinx was known in the Middle East and Minoan Crete by 1500 BC. Then, in the centuries when Egypt dominated the Near East, the sphinx traveled more widely. From the 8th century

Right The seated sphinx of the temple of Apollo at Delphi was made in Naxos in the 5th century and was placed on a nine-meter (30 ft) column. In style resembling the winged oriental sphinxes, it is a symbol of Apollo's wisdom and justice. The sphinx was only one of several Greek hybrid monsters: the Centaurs were half-human, half-horse, and the Chimera has the head of a man, the body of a goat and the tail of a serpent.

Left The Great Sphinx of Giza dates from about 2500 BC, with the head of the king and the body of a lion, a creature associated with the sun-god Ra. He thus links the king with the god, as well as guarding his own entrance to the under-world. Avenues of sphinxes *(below)* at Karnak guarded the routes along which the statue of the god Amun was carried during the annual *opet* festival.

Right The emperor Augustus adopted the sphinx as his personal seal. Despite the key role Egypt played in the Roman empire under Augustus, this sphinx is Greek in style; its links with Apollo embody hope and oracular powers.

BC they were found in Palestine and Syria, sporting wings close to their bodies and displaying the Egyptian crown on their heads. Often standing figures, they were guardians of the sacred: even the Israelites' Ark of the Covenant in Solomon's Temple was flanked by winged cherubs like sphinxes.

When the early Greeks began to trade with the east, the sphinx was among the mythical beasts that they imported. In Greek art and legend, however, the sphinx was always female; she still usually maintained the role of protectress, and was sometimes carried on shields.

Perhaps the most famous Greek sphinx had a very different character. She was the ghostlike monster who carried off those killed in fatal combats; and, famously, she stood outside the gates of Thebes and devoured those who could not answer her riddle. It was Oedipus who outsmarted her and won the crown of the city. Later versions of this story imbued her with qualities of inscrutability and cunning. In classical Greece, however, the sphinx reverted to a benign creature, often displayed with a serene human face, and associated with Apollo, the sun-god. In this incarnation she was a symbol of justice and a singing messenger of divine justice.

Later, the sphinx traveled to Italy, turning up in the sculpture and paintings of the Etruscans. It was also adopted by the Romans, who found it a striking and exotic motif for domestic furnishings as well as for religious settings such as the temple of Isis at Pompeii.

EXOTIC TRADITIONS
The Influence of Egyptian Gods & Learning

Psalm 104 in the Bible is a great hymn of praise to Yahweh, the source of all fertility and abundance. "From your palace," the psalmist sings, "You water the uplands until the ground has had all that your heavens have to offer; You make fresh grass grow for cattle and those plants made use of by man, for them to get food from the soil. . . . The trees of Yahweh get rain enough, the cedars of Lebanon he planted; here the the little birds build their nest; and, on the highest branches, the stork has its home."

When a hymn in praise of the Aten, the sun-god promoted by Akhenaten, was discovered on the wall of a tomb at his capital el-Amarna, its similarities to Psalm 104 were soon noticed. "The entire land sets out to work," runs the hymn. "All beasts browse on their herbs; trees, herbs are sprouting, birds fly from their nests, their wings greeting your *ka*. All flocks frisk on their feet, all that fly up and alight, they live when you dawn for them." Yahweh and the Aten are both seen as creator-gods whose presence allows life to flourish.

The study of ancient Egypt has frequently paralleled biblical studies, and similarities in outlook and phrasing such as these have been

IN A ROMAN ceremony in honor of Isis (ABOVE), one of the participants carries a water jug, one a rattle, and another a snake.

THE ATEN, its rays adored by Akhenaten (BELOW), was never embraced by the polytheistic Egyptians and was forgotten.

seized on by scholars eager to point out significant connections between the two cultures. Some enthusiasts even argued that the Aten, worshiped in Egypt some 500 years before the Psalms were written, was the forerunner of the single god of Judaism, Christianity and Islam. Akhenaten has sometimes been claimed not simply as a revolutionary in the context of Egyptian religion but as a key figure in the development of monotheism.

Such claims are easily overstated. The two creeds had little in common apart from their universal scope and the emphasis on a sole deity. In the case of the Aten, this emphasis was insisted on by the king, whereas Yahweh himself presented this demand to his followers. After the death of Akhenaten Egypt quickly reverted to polytheism and any closer links between the two gods are extremely unlikely. Nevertheless, the hymn to the Aten and a mass of other Egyptian literature may have passed down the generations and fed into the rich cultural mix of the ancient Middle East when Egypt dominated Syria and Palestine.

There are other hints of Egyptian influence in the Hebrew scriptures. One of the most noticeable is the reappearance of meditations on the

▼ THE PHAROS OF ALEXANDRIA
Wonder of the Ancient World

Alexandria, the capital of the Ptolemies, had one of the finest natural harbors in the Mediterranean, two basins divided by an island; but the coastline was flat and treacherous. Some marker to the harbor entrance was essential to guide in the merchant ships from the Ptolemies' trading partners. This was the incentive for a famous lighthouse that was built at the tip of the island, Pharos, probably in the early third century BC. The lighthouse itself became known as the Pharos.

The Pharos lighthouse had a three-storey structure rising from a massive stone base; the second storey was octagonal and the third cylindrical. The height of the tower may have been 120 meters (394 feet). At the top stood a gigantic statue of Zeus Soter – Zeus the Savior – who appears to have held a rudder under his arm. Isis was also linked to the Pharos in her role as the patron of sailors. A temple to her may have been built close by the tower; her statue, worn by centuries spent in the sea, has been dredged up from beside the causeway.

Few ancient sailors chose to be on the sea at night, and the early Pharos may not have had a light. However, the Roman writer Pliny the Elder mentioned a light in his *Natural History* of the first century AD. The light seems to have been a beacon of burning oil reflected towards the sea by mirrors of polished iron or brass. Pliny reported that sailors could mistake it for a star close to the horizon.

The Pharos was legendary, and it was listed as one of the Seven Wonders of the ancient world. An Arab story claimed that the streets of Byzantium were reflected in its mirrors, and that it could be used to set fire to foreign fleets.

An earthquake toppled the 1,700-year-old Pharos in 1375, but its name survived in the word for "lighthouse" in several European languages, recalling the great beacon that guided visitors to Egypt.

THE PHAROS was destroyed in 1375, but observations were left to inspire fanciful pictures like this one (BELOW) from 1817.

unimportance of wealth from the 19th-Dynasty *Wisdom of Amenemope* in the Hebrew *Book of Proverbs*. Similarly, there are Egyptian texts that describe humans as made in the image of Ra, just as later Judeo-Christian sources talk of men made in the image of God. In another text, from Egypt's First Intermediate Period, Ra is described as "the good shepherd of the people...He is the shepherd of everyone in whose mind there is no evil". This theme reappears throughout the scriptures.

A SIMILAR PROCESS of assimilation of Egyptian ideas may have provided an inspiration for early Greek philosophers.

The Roots of Greek Philosophy

Most of the early philosophers came from the cities of Ionian coast around the sixth century BC, a time when these cities were busily trading with Egypt – and when Greeks were traveling to Egypt not as common tourists but as serious students in pursuit of wisdom in Egyptian temples. Thales of Miletus, a wealthy trading city, is generally considered to be the father of Greek philosophy. Legend has it that Thales was taught by Egyptian priests, and his idea about the nature of matter certainly echoes the Egyptian creation myths in which the earth was originally covered with water: Thales claimed that water was the origin of all matter, which eventually returned to this liquid primeval state.

The principle of the unity of opposites was also clearly derived from Egyptian mythology. Stories of the Egyptian gods repeatedly show this theme, with the goddess of humidity, Tefnut, and the god of dryness, Shu; the earth-god Geb and the sky-goddess Nut; and the conflict of Horus and Seth, good and evil, order and chaos, light and dark. Intrinsic to these stories is the possibility of reconciling the opposites. Similar ideas surface in the philosophy of another Ionian Greek, Heraclitus from Ephesus (c.540–c.480 BC). He argued that the idea of a day could not be understood without that of its opposite, night, and that both were inextricably linked to each other. Heraclitus used the Greek word *harmonie*, the creation of something greater by bringing opposites together: again, surely an echo of Egyptian belief.

The Roman historian Ammianus Marcellinus, writing in the fourth century AD, recorded other Greeks who were actively drawn to Egyptian wisdom. He reported that the philosophers Plato and Pythagoras visited Egypt personally, while the sixth-century BC Greek statesman Solon consulted

Egyptian priests in drawing up a law code for Athens. These literary and historical anecdotes reinforce the tradition that the Greeks accorded special reverence to the ancient learning of Egypt, as their "pilgrimages" suggest.

LIKE OTHER FOREIGNERS who attempted to establish themselves as Egyptian rulers,

Gods in Many Guises

the Ptolemies quickly aped the pharaohs and associated themselves with Egyptian gods. This may have impressed their Greek subjects as much as it did the conquered Egyptians, who had even more substantial reasons than tradition to dislike the Ptolemies. In any case, the Ptolemies' adoption of tradition was not undiluted. Their chosen god was Serapis, an amalgamation of Osiris and the sacred bull Apis with several Greek gods, among them Zeus, Dionysus and Helios. A great cult center to Serapis, known as the Serapeum, was set up at Alexandria. Other centers appeared at Memphis, Ptolemais and on the Aegean island of Delos. When Isis (sister-wife of Osiris) became the favored goddess of Queen Arsinoe II, the wife of Ptolemy II, she was, predictably, cast as the wife of Serapis. By the time of Ptolemy III (r.246–221) the kings included Serapis and Isis in their royal oaths and worshiped them as a pair. A proclamation of the second century AD declared, "Give special consideration to the ancestral gods and revere Isis and Serapis, the greatest of the gods, saviors, good, kindly benefactors."

This official cult caught the popular imagination. Between them Serapis and Isis catered for the deepest spiritual needs of ordinary worshipers: one was a god who offered abundance and rebirth after death, the other a goddess who represented many aspects of femininity, from fertility to healing and motherhood. With true Egyptian flexibility, Serapis and Isis could take on additional attributes as needed. Serapis, for instance, was revered as a healer (an attribute from the Greek god Asklepios), and his cult at Canopus in the Delta attracted distinguished patients. The Roman emperor Hadrian copied this Serapeum in his villa at Tivoli.

The cult of Isis was an even more spectacular success. It had been spread to the Aegean by Egyptian sailors to whom she always remained a patron. A shrine to her at Piraeus, the port of Athens, had been set up as early as 333 BC, even before the Ptolemies had come to Egypt. One of the ceremonies associated with Isis was the

DRESSED IN a Roman toga, the dog-headed Egyptian god Anubis (ABOVE) nevertheless did not appeal to most Romans, who considered the worship of animals unnatural. This statue was originally created for the emperor Hadrian's villa at Tivoli, where representative objects and styles from all over the empire were collected. Although Anubis had a place in the popular cult of Isis and Serapis, this statue may have been simply a curio.

dedication of a ship to the sea at the beginning of each new sailing year. Her cult seems to have spread to Italy in the second century BC, probably via the Serapeum at Delos where she was worshiped alongside Serapis, and it was along the south coast that her cult was first accepted. This area of Italy, the natural stopping place of the ships from the east, had always been more receptive to outside influences than the inland city of Rome. The cities of Herculaneum and Pompeii had temples to Isis as early as 105 BC.

The government of Rome was suspicious of foreign cults and viewed the sweeping popular enthusiasm for Isis with some hostility – which was often the flip side of one culture's fascination with the exotic qualities of another. In the first century BC there were frequent attempts by the senators to destroy the temples to Isis which her devotees were building in the city. In 50 BC, when workers were ordered to demolish a temple, they refused on the grounds that it would be sacrilegious to do so. A few years later the fears of the more conservative senators were confirmed by scandal. A young noblewoman undergoing the rites of initiation into the mysteries of the goddess was seduced by a man at the temple who convinced her that he was an Egyptian god and her submission was part of the required ritual.

By the first century AD, however, Isis had become accepted within the Roman pantheon. The emperors Vespasian and Titus visited the Serapeums of Egypt. In Rome itself, Caligula (r.AD 37–41) rebuilt the temple to Isis on the Campus Martius, and after it was destroyed by fire in AD 80, Domitian (r.81–96) rebuilt it yet again. Isis came to be identified with many of the goddesses of Rome: Ceres, the goddess of corn and abundance; Artemis, the goddess of hunting, who also protected women during childbirth; and Venus, the goddess of love.

By the second century AD she had acquired yet more attributes. As she proclaimed to one believer in an apparition, "I am Nature, the universal mother, mistress of all the elements, primordial child of time, sovereign of all things spiritual, queen of the dead, queen also of the immortals, the single manifestation of all gods and goddesses that are. My nod governs the shining heights of Heaven, the wholesome sea breezes, the lamentable silences of the world below."

THE CULT OF ISIS
A Religion for All

The cult of Isis – the one Egyptian god who was adopted wholeheartedly by the Romans – catered to so many different spiritual needs that it spread to every corner of the empire. Cult statues, altars, and other symbols of her worship have been found as far west as Britain and Spain and as far east as the borders of the Persian empire. Roman soldiers and merchants took her cult to settlements along the Rhine and Danube. Isis could be associated with Aphrodite, the goddess of love, as she was in Cyprus, or Athena as she was in Athens. In Thrace she was identified with "the Mother of the Gods"; in the Hellespont she was the "Lady of the Mysteries".

Isis-worship involved a complex initiation ceremony which was described in one of the few surviving Roman novels, *The Golden Ass*, written by Apuleius in the second

O*NE OF Isis' ceremonies was water purification* (LEFT), *as practiced at Herculaneum.*

century AD. Its hero, Lucius, was transformed into a donkey and could only be restored to human shape by eating roses, which he was unable to obtain. After much suffering on his part, Isis appeared to him near Corinth and told him to go the next day to the dedication of a boat in her honor to usher in the new sailing year. A great procession assembled, with shaven priests, pipers, and cult statues including Hathor and Anubis. (Clearly Isis had not lost her Egyptian heritage.) Lucius the donkey nosed his way forward among the devotees until he could take a mouthful from a garland of roses for the goddess. He was instantly transformed back into a man, and the worshipers praised the goddess more fervently for the miracles she produced. Lucius was initiated into the cult of Isis and eventually became a counselor in her great temple in Rome.

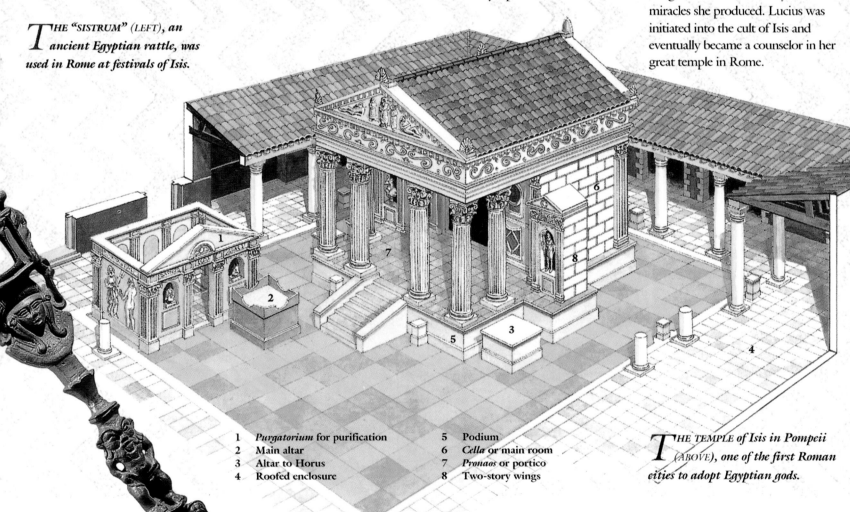

1   *Purgatorium* for purification
2   Main altar
3   Altar to Horus
4   Roofed enclosure
5   Podium
6   *Cella* or main room
7   *Pronaos* or portico
8   Two-story wings

T*HE TEMPLE of Isis in Pompeii* (ABOVE), *one of the first Roman cities to adopt Egyptian gods.*

It is unlikely that Isis would have achieved so much popular appeal in Rome if she had not usually been represented, in Egypt as well as in the wider Mediterranean world, in human form. If she had only been known as a cow-goddess, her successful transition to the Roman pantheon would never have been made. The evidence that Egyptians worshiped animals was received with some disgust by traditional Romans. The poet Virgil played on their prejudices when he described the battle of Actium, at which Octavian had

An image of the Madonna and Child (ABOVE) echoes the theme of the protective mother and hunted child in the story of Isis and Horus, who appear on a statue beyond the crowd. This 1883 canvas by the British painter Edwin Long contrasts the sober simplicity of Christian tradition with the perceived excesses of ancient Egypt.

defeated Antony and Cleopatra, as a clash between two irreconcilable cultures in which "monster forms of gods of every race, and the dog-god Anubis barking, held their weapons up against our Neptune, Venus and Minerva." In the early second century AD the Roman poet Juvenal complained, "Who knows not what monsters demented Egypt worships? One district adores the crocodile, another venerates the ibis that gorges itself with snakes." In Thebes the long-tailed ape was worshiped; elsewhere it was fish, cats and dogs.

Not all Roman writers were so dismissive of Egypt. Lucian, also of the second century AD, wrote a dialog in which Zeus was berated for allowing heaven to be crammed with ibises, apes and goats. Zeus replied that indeed the worship of animals was shocking but the animals represented some deeper wisdom provided by Egypt.

PAGAN AND CHRISTIAN beliefs fought for ascendancy in the Roman empire for 300 years.

Egypt & Christian Belief

Christianity finally won, with the decree in AD 313 by the emperor Constantine which made it tolerated throughout the empire, including Egypt. Up to this point in history, Christians had often been persecuted by the traditionalists. According to the Bible, while St Mark was celebrating Easter with his followers in AD 68, he was attacked and murdered by Alexandrians celebrating a festival of Serapis. By the end of the century the Christians had gained the upper hand. "Idolatrous" images were defaced; temples were destroyed, or rebuilt as churches. A mob in Alexandria destroyed the Serapeum in AD 391, egged on by the city's Christian bishop and monks; and worship of the Egyptian gods was finally banned outright in Egypt in 553 by the emperor Justinian.

But the ancient non-Christian beliefs could not be easily eradicated, and many maintained their influence. Some of them may have persevered through being absorbed into the new Christian traditions – though scholars are by no means in agreement as to what extent this occurred. There are, however, obvious examples of Christianity borrowing from the rich cultural heritage of the classical world. For instance, many of the titles given to Isis reappear in the Mediterranean in those used of the Virgin Mary. Mary was praised for her fruitfulness and as *medicina mundi*, "the power that heals the world". As "Queen of the Sea" she became associated with the care of sailors. Her special flower, like that of Isis, was the rose. There is even evidence that Serapis was identified with Joseph while Horus, the son of Isis and Serapis, has been directly linked to Christ. On an early Egyptian church at Abydos, Christ is shown on a throne with the horned disc of Horus. Mary, like Isis, is a protective mother, and the similarity between portrayals of Isis with Horus and Mary with Jesus in Egypt is obvious.

Borrowing these traditions made the new Christian religion more familiar and helped it to gain a foothold in the culture. There were already many Jews in Alexandria and elsewhere in Egypt, practicing their earlier brand of monotheism; and it was among them that Christianity first took hold.

The great fourth-century Christian writer Augustine considered that Rome had been converted "extremely fast", considering the amount and force of opposition the new religion initially met from Rome's government and aristocracy, and the time it takes to establish new traditions.

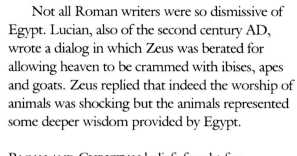

*H*ORUS *on horseback prefigures Christ, Bellerophon and St George, triumphing over the forces of evil* (TOP RIGHT).

*A*N ANKH-CROSS *on a shroud from about 200* (RIGHT) *now resembles the "chi-rho" monogram of Christ.*

The Egyptian habit of syncretism – the merging of gods, such as that of Amun with Ra – may also have left traces in Christianity. Some scholars have seen the doctrine of the Trinity – God the Father, Jesus the Son and the Holy Spirit as three in one – as having its origins in Egyptian syncretism. (Interestingly, the Egyptians themselves could not accept the idea of Jesus as being partly human.) In the same way, the doctrine of the resurrection of Jesus must have been more acceptable to those already familiar with the legend of Osiris, who was killed, restored to life and eventually presided over the Underworld.

The idea of judgment in the next world may also have owed something to Egyptian mythology. In some later Jewish writings there are references to the scales on which the good and evil deeds of men are weighed at a judgment, harking back to the weighing of the deceased's heart against the feather of *ma'at* in Egyptian tradition.

*C*HRIST is shown as the "good shepherd" in a Coptic sculpture (ABOVE). **The pharaoh was often described in a similar way in Egyptian writing.**

Retreat, Community & Prayer

ALTHOUGH ROME was the capital of the empire and the seat of the Christian church, Alexandria was second only to it in importance as a stronghold of Christianity in the Roman world. Its intellectual traditions and institutions made it a center of debate in the ongoing internal and external struggles of the early Church – but the steadfastness of Egyptian Christians also secured for Alexandria the role of the preeminent defender of the faith in these struggles. A college of catechism was founded here in the second century BC, probably in response to the flourishing of unorthodox creeds. In its first 150 years it trained a half-dozen distinguished Christian teachers including Clement and Origen; another, Heraclas, was the first Christian patriarch to be addressed as Papa, or Pope.

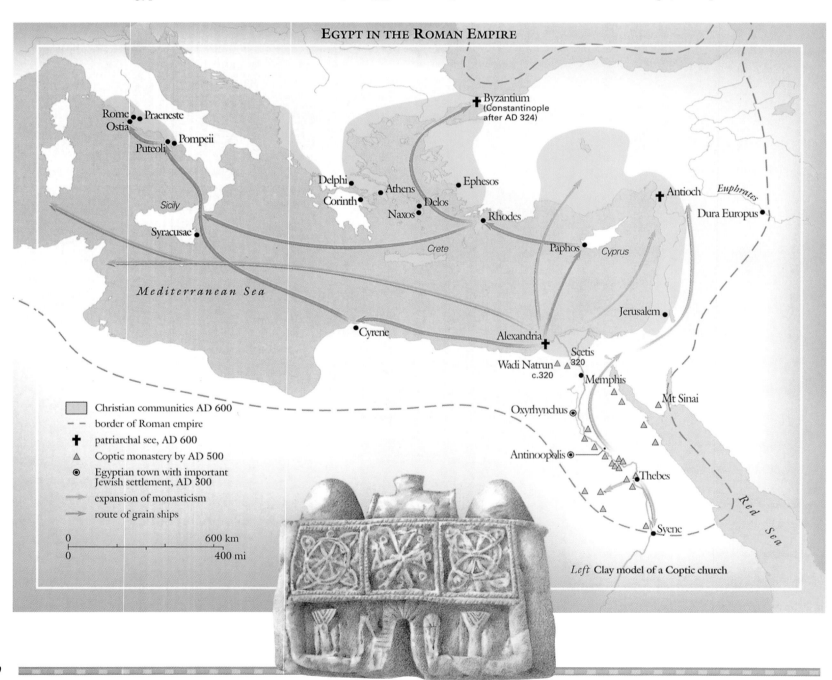

EGYPT IN THE ROMAN EMPIRE

Rome
Praeneste
Ostia
Puteoli
Pompeii
Sicily
Syracusae
Byzantium (Constantinople after AD 324)
Delphi
Corinth
Athens
Delos
Naxos
Ephesos
Rhodes
Crete
Paphos
Cyprus
Antioch
Euphrates
Dura Europus
Mediterranean Sea
Cyrene
Jerusalem
Alexandria
Scetis 320
Wadi Natrun c.320
Memphis
Mt Sinai
Oxyrhynchus
Antinoopolis
Thebes
Red Sea
Svene

Christian communities AD 600
border of Roman empire
patriarchal see, AD 600
Coptic monastery by AD 500
Egyptian town with important Jewish settlement, AD 300
expansion of monasticism
route of grain ships

0   600 km
0   400 mi

Left Clay model of a Coptic church

A COPTIC EMBROIDERY *from the sixth century with a nativity scene* (BELOW). *Although the Copts preserved Egypt's ancient spoken language, they did not add to the glory of its art. Coptic art was only distinguished for its weaving (mostly using silk and wool). The colors are notably bright.*

An ascetic and contemplative tradition had been present from the earliest days of Christianity in Egypt. In about 270 – not quite 100 years after the emperor Septimus Severus began the first organized largescale persecution of Christians – an Egyptian Christian nobleman named Anthony sold his land and retreated into the desert. Without any intention of setting up a community, he attracted disciples, who pursued him even across the Sinai. They formed the first Christian monastic community, and their leader was canonized. St Anthony's monastery at the edge of the Red Sea exists to this day.

Persecution of Christians continued, becoming especially severe under Diocletian, who became emperor in 284 and encountered resistance to his claims to association with divinity. It began with orders to the Roman army to worship the Roman gods. Church closures and book burning were followed by vicious blinding, crippling, torturing and burning of believers. Egyptians were killed by the tens of thousands, among them many of their holy men. The Egyptians preserved the memory of these atrocities in the Martyrs' Calendar, which they dated from the start of Diocletian's reign.

These conditions encouraged more Christian hermits to take to the desert. The monastery of St

Anthony was soon followed by a half-dozen others, collectively known as the communities of the Desert Fathers. The monastery of St Makarius the Great, directly inspired by that of St Anthony, was considered the most important of the retreats, and many of the leaders of the Coptic church came from its ranks. In the seventh century it had as many as a thousand monks. Another famous monastery, that of St Catherine in the southern Sinai, was supposed to have been visited in 337 by the empress Helena, mother of the emperor Constantine, who was visiting the Holy Land.

The retreats were made up of hermits who met once a week to hold mass or celebrate other church festivals. The monastery of St Palemon developed an offshoot community under the founder's disciple St Pachomius, a former soldier who set up his organization on a military model. It proved particularly popular in spite of its severity, and was even extended to communities for women.

The monasteries emphasized celibacy, prayer, manual work and education. They set the pattern for religious communities today. The monastic

T RADITIONAL TEMPLES *were modified by the Copts and used as churches* (FAR LEFT). *They used adobe and made use of the dome, which was copied by the Muslims. Carved reliefs and plant motifs were also used in addition to Christian symbols.*

tradition spread to western Asia, Africa and Europe, aided by Egyptian missionaries, who traveled to India and as far north as Britain. Monasticism became an essential part of Western Christianity.

The Christians became the persecutors of the pagans late in the fourth century. Tragically, Alexandria's magnificent library – the legacy of the Ptolemies, 600 years earlier – was burned by a rampaging Christian mob in the name of defending their faith against heathens. With it went an irreplaceable collection of classical writings.

THE ALIEN CULTURE of Egypt gave the Greeks and the Romans much to admire and imitate. One

Wisdom, Real & Imputed

major import was the calendar. The Greeks learned of the 365-day lunar calendar from the Egyptians and spotted a discrepancy between it and the solar calendar, which was six hours longer. In the Ptolemaic period an extra day was added to the lunar year every four years (the leap year) to reconcile the two. This system was adopted by Julius Caesar in 45 BC on the advice of Sosigenes, an Alexandrian astronomer. The Roman lunar calendar had become unwieldy, with extra days added to keep the months in line with the seasons. The new Julian calendar, with its leap year, proved accurate to seven days every thousand years and lasted in Europe until further modification by Pope Gregory XIII in the sixteenth century. The Greeks also adopted the 24-hour day from the Egyptians.

Sometimes the Egyptians were credited with accomplishments that were not their own, such as the invention of writing. The Roman historian Tacitus wrote, "The Egyptians, in their animal pictures, were the first people to represent thought by symbols." Plato passed on the Egyptian myth crediting writing to the god Thoth, who had also divided sounds into vowels and consonants (really a Greek achievement). The Roman statesman and writer Cicero repeated the story 300 years later. In the Greek world Thoth became associated with the messenger-god Hermes, who gave his name to the Hermetic tradition: the belief that Egypt had been a repository of mysterious ancient knowledge.

One source of this knowledge was hieroglyphs. In his account of initiation into the cult of Isis, Lucius related that a priest brought out books written with unknown characters which were

impossible to read; these must have been hieroglyphs. Some of them were obviously pictures of things, but no Greek or Roman ever learned to read them. A few writers understood that a hieroglyph might represent an abstract idea. Fragments of a first-century AD treatise on hieroglyphs show that the writer, Chairemon of Alexandria, appears to have learned the correct meanings of some signs. But most Greek and Roman interpretations were little more than guesses: one Roman scholar suggested that a hieroglyphic figure of a bee making honey stood for "king", on the grounds that a ruler should combine sweetness with having a sting in the tail. The *Hieroglyphica* of Horapollo (fourth or fifth century

EGYPTIAN HERBALISM was highly developed – they knew the properties of chamomile, among many plants – and it was particularly admired by the early Greeks. This illuminated twelfth-century copy of a Greek herbal (ABOVE) was copied by one Pseudo-Apuleius. Fragments from ancient Egypt survived into medieval Europe in this way and were picked up by later Renaissance scholars, fueling the rediscovery of Egyptian wisdom as filtered through classical sources.

CELESTIAL MAP of the planets according to Ptolemy (RIGHT). An Alexandrian Greek, he won much of the Egyptians' reputation for astronomy, though he worked almost entirely on observations from Mesopotamia. The zodiac was introduced to Egypt by the Greeks and became associated with decans (10-day-long star patterns through the year). The decans lost significance except as pertaining to the zodiac; in this form they became known to Europe as "Egyptian astronomy".

AD), which claimed to be a Greek translation of an Egyptian original, interpreted 200 individual hieroglyphs. A few were correct, but the accompanying explanations were mostly nonsense.

Hieroglyphs were seen as symbols with power beyond their linguistic meaning. The Egyptians had usually defaced negative symbols (as of harmful animals) to neutralize their threat. The Greek Egyptian-born philosopher Plotinus (AD 205–270) argued the converse: that a hieroglyph representing "goodness" might lead the way to understanding the essence of goodness. Hieroglyphs, therefore, contained the eternal truths. This gave them a mystique that lingered over centuries and extended to other branches of Egyptian learning. In the Renaissance, for instance, astrology was credited to the Egyptians, but in fact it was much more developed in other eastern cultures such as Mesopotamia and China.

Christianity appropriated the Hermetic tradition and assigned the role of chief wisdom-giver to Moses, but Egypt's part was not completely forgotten. The revival of classical scholarship in the Renaissance gave Europeans access to Greek and Roman texts in which Egyptian culture was described. Plutarch's account of Osiris and Isis brought these gods to life again, and Horapollo's *Hieroglyphica* caused a sensation when it was rediscovered in the fifteenth century. It was one of the first manuscripts to be printed as a book. Like the many "Egyptianized" Roman artifacts, it had no value as an authentic guide to Egyptian culture, but it was some time before anybody realized this; in the meantime, the *Hieroglyphica* helped to generate interest. There were many attempts to link the West to Egyptian wisdom. The Italian scholar Giovanni Nanni (1432–1502), a secretary to Pope Alexander VI, concocted the idea that Osiris himself had taken Egyptian learning directly to Italy. The fact that the Pope had a bull on his coat of arms was used by Nanni to claim that his family was descended from a divine Apis bull. The Pope was so impressed that he commissioned paintings of the legend on the walls of his private apartments. They are still there.

THOTH AS HERMES, wearing Oriental dress, gives a book of ancient wisdom to the Greeks and Egyptians (ABOVE), represented by the two men. This pavement in the cathedral of Siena, Italy, was inspired by the work of the Florentine scholar Marcilio Ficino (1433–99), who was fascinated by the problem of finding a place for Egyptian learning in the Christian world. His idea was that Thoth, as Hermes, represented the first attempt to find divine truth.

The REDISCOVERY OF EGYPT

WHILE ISLAMIC EGYPT IGNORED ITS PAGAN PAST,
CHRISTENDOM PAINTED AN IMAGE OF ANCIENT
EGYPT THAT WAS BOTH PARTIAL AND FANTASTICAL.
ONLY IN THE 19TH CENTURY WAS THE TRUE
EXTENT OF THE LEGACY OF THE NILE VALLEY
APPRECIATED. EGYPTOMANIA SWEPT THE WEST.
THE FASCINATION ENDURES, AND EGYPT ITSELF
HAS RECLAIMED ITS PAST AND OFFERED IT TO THE
WORLD AS A PRECIOUS COMMON HERITAGE.

Main picture The plain of Thebes, painted in the 19th century by Jean Gerôme

Inset "Pharaoh's Daughter" brooch c.1935

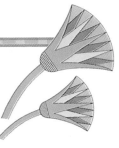

REVEALING THE PAST
Egypt & Scholarship

By the time the Muslim Arabs conquered Egypt in AD 642 – only 22 years after Muhammad's flight from Mecca to Medina marked the beginning of Islam – the Egyptians' own awareness of their past had been erased by Christian belief. The Arabs had little reverence for ancient Egypt. They were proud of their own culture, and they had no means of discovering what lay behind the ruins along the Nile. Often, though, these ruins were looted. The mosques and citadel of Cairo were graced with limestone from the outer cases of the Giza pyramids. Europeans were banned from traveling in the Islamic empire, and few had the nerve or wherewithal to attempt it.

In 1517 Egypt became part of the Ottoman empire, ruled from Constantinople, and Europeans were allowed to trade with its provinces. A few travelers now made their way up the Nile. Some got no farther than Giza; others, though, reached Aswan. James Bruce, who arrived in Cairo in 1768, even got as far as Meroë in modern Sudan. The sight of the Egyptian ruins was overwhelming.

Early Travelers to Egypt

THE RUINS of Karnak (ABOVE), painted by David Roberts in the 1840s, inspired many wealthy Victorian tourists to travel to Egypt to experience the romance of the ancient past in person.

TIMETABLE

449 BC **Herodotus visits Egypt**

AD 395–642 **Egypt ruled by Eastern Roman empire**

642 **Islamic Arab conquest of Egypt**

1798 **Napoleon in Egypt**

1799 **Rosetta Stone discovered**

1801 **French army defeated in Egypt**

1801 **Vivant Denon publishes** *Voyage in Lower and Upper Egypt*

1817 **Belzoni uncovers Abu Simbel**

1822 **Champollion deciphers hieroglyphs using Rosetta Stone**

1842 **Prussian expedition by Lepsius**

1858 **Mariette appointed Director of Antiquities in Egypt**

1882 **Egypt Exploration Fund established in London**

1922 **Tutankhamun's tomb found**

"Let them talk to me no more of Rome; let Greece be silent. What magnificence! What mechanics," enthused the Danish explorer Frederick Norden in 1737. "What other nation ever had the courage to undertake works so surprising?" Some of these visitors were no more than treasure hunters sent by kings to bring back curiosities for the royal collections of Europe. Others did try to conduct serious investigations. In the 1640s John Greaves, professor of anatomy at Oxford, published a survey of the pyramids; Claude Sicard, a French Jesuit who had been sent to Egypt to survey the Coptic communities in the early eighteenth century, confirmed the site of Thebes, Luxor and Karnak.

By the late eighteenth century many more sites had been identified and the first rudimentary excavations had taken place. But no one could read any of the hieroglyphic inscriptions, and scholars relied heavily on surviving Roman and Greek descriptions of Egypt to make sense of what they found. More ominously, a mass of Egyptian antiquities were shipped to Europe for the first time since the Roman conquest some 1,800 years before. While this gave European scholars something to study, it also encouraged the destruction of tombs and the dismantling of monuments. It was a foretaste of what was to come.

POWER POLITICS finally brought Egypt to the attention of the European public. In the 1790s Britain was at war with

Napoleon & his Expedition

France. The young Napoleon Bonaparte had been ordered by the French government to break Britain's line of communication with India and the east. To do this he had to take Egypt, through which ran the land route from Alexandria to Suez; it provided swifter access to India than the sea route around the Cape of Good Hope. The French also had hopes of being the first Europeans to exploit what appeared to be a fertile but undeveloped country. There seemed little danger of effective resistance from the Egyptians themselves. The country was weak, locked into struggles with its Ottoman rulers and ravaged by plagues and famines.

*V**ICTORIOUS GAUL** uncovers the female personification of Egypt in this medal (ABOVE), minted in 1826 for the ongoing publication of the French expedition's "Description de l'Egypte". (BELOW) Napoleon winning the Battle of the Pyramids, by the French painter François Louis Joseph Watteau.*

The French expedition landed in July 1798. As a military expedition it proved a disaster. Despite defeating the Egyptian army in a battle at the foot of the pyramids, the French were forced to retreat after their fleet was destroyed by the British admiral, Nelson, at Aboukir Bay in August 1798. A combined force of British and Ottomans finally drove the French out of Egypt completely in 1801. Yet the three years of occupation had profound effects on Egypt's past and present. Napoleon had taken with him a remarkable collection of experts – historians, astronomers, engineers, artists, botanists and mineralogists, 167 of them in all – to carry out the first truly scientific survey of Egypt, both ancient and modern. As soon as he landed, Napoleon set up an Egyptian Institute in Cairo, and attended many of its meetings himself. While the French forces disintegrated, these experts were exploring the resources of the country and

measuring, drawing and surveying the ruins they found along the Nile. The magnitude of what they achieved was first revealed in 1802 when one of the accompanying scholars, the diplomat and artist Dominique-Vivant Denon, published his own account of the expedition, *Voyage in Lower and Upper Egypt*. Denon was a gifted publicist and his book was written in a vibrant style that caught the imagination of all Europe. Egypt became the rage, and Denon was appointed the first director of the Louvre museum in Paris. The ground was laid for the publication of the account compiled by the expedition itself, the 12-volume *Description de l'Egypte*, which appeared between 1809 and 1828. It was the first work to do justice to the magnificence of the ruins of ancient Egypt. There was a rush to acquire original Egyptian objects. Europe's scholars were not too scrupulous to join in.

WHEN THE FRENCH army of soldiers and scholars withdrew from Egypt, they were intended to hand

Scholars Reveal the Past

over their data and various collections to the victorious British army. However, realizing the historical importance of their work – and asserting their own unique ability to interpret it properly – the French experts threatened to throw their collections into the sea rather than to allow them to be scattered and passed on to ignorant buyers of novelties. The French zoologist Geoffrey Saint-Hilare warned the British that

they would be guilty of committing a crime equivalent to the Christian mob's burning the library at Alexandria 1,500 years earlier. With one notable exception, the English commander, General Hutchinson, agreed to let Napoleon's experts ship their work back to France.

While digging defenses near the coastal town of Rosetta, the French had found a large stone with three identical inscriptions: one in Greek; one in what proved to be demotic Egyptian; and one in hieroglyphs. Scholars instantly saw that its text might hold the key to the decipherment of hieroglyphs; plenty of scholars read classical Greek, and by understanding the meaning of the Greek, they might be able to construct a plausible key for decoding the Egyptian. Copies of the three texts were soon circulated to scholars throughout Europe. The French commander wished to keep the Rosetta stone, but the English commander, General Hutchinson, was adamant that it should be sent to England. So it was that the stone was taken to Britain and placed in the British Museum by the order of King George III himself.

The problem of decipherment lay in understanding how hieroglyphs actually conveyed language. Most scholars assumed, as the Greeks and Romans had done, that hieroglyphs were a series of symbols, each conveying the name of an object or an idea – a bee for kingship, for instance.

The fact that a hieroglyph stood for a sound as well, and that the combined sounds of a row of hieroglyphs could make up a word, was

ILLUSTRATIONS from the 12-volume "Description de l'Egypte" included the grand gallery of the Great Pyramid (ABOVE) and a study of ibises with the white or sacred ibis (LEFT). The "Description" was the most complete account ever of Egyptian art, architecture, history, society, natural history and geology.

Although the expedition did not discover any new sites and could not translate any of the inscriptions in hieroglyphs, its revelations about Egypt still had a huge impact on the public.

CHAMPOLLION
and the Decipherment of Hieroglyphics

Hieroglyphs came early to Jean-François Champollion. At the age of 11 he was introduced by his older brother to Jean-Baptiste Joseph Fourier, one of the members of Napoleon's great expedition to Egypt. Fourier showed the boy his collection and a passion was born. By the age of 17 Champollion had drawn up plans for an encyclopedia of ancient Egypt, and he had learned Coptic, Hebrew and Arabic in the hope of finding the key to hieroglyphs. But, like virtually every scholar before him, Champollion failed to grasp that hieroglyphs represented sounds as well as pictures of objects.

His early career was complicated by post-Revolution politics, and he was dismissed from a teaching post. Meanwhile, he labored over hieratic and demotic texts looking for a link. Eventually he guessed at the hieroglyphic script for "Ptolemaios" and checked it against the Rosetta stone. It fit. (He may have borrowed this idea from the work of the English scholar Thomas Young.) This confirmed the links between the three scripts and showed that the signs had a phonetic element, at least when used for foreign names. Soon Champollion was able to identify the names of all the Ptolemies and the Roman emperors. He made a list of 79 of them with suggested readings for some 20 hieroglyphic signs. He went on to suggest that hieroglyphs might be used phonetically in writing Egyptian names.

Champollion soon found confirmation of this crucial insight. He had been sent, from Abu Simbel, a royal name beginning with the hieroglyphic sign for "sun" and ending in two signs for "s". Champollion knew that the Coptic for sun was *Ra* and suddenly realized that the name must be that of the great king Ramesses. It followed that the central hieroglyph after the "Ra"

CHAMPOLLION (ABOVE) read Sanskrit and Persian as well as Arabic, Hebrew and Coptic.

A PAGE from Champollion's grammar (RIGHT) with royal names in hieroglyphic, hieratic, Greek and French. The name of Psamtek is written entirely alphabetically.

must have the sound equivalent to "m". Another royal name began with a hieroglyph of an ibis. Champollion knew that this was the sign of the god Thoth, and so the name Tuthmosis was revealed.

By 1824 Champollion had published his work and won fame. In 1828 he led an expedition to Egypt in search of inscriptions. His travels led to more discoveries and by 1830 Champollion had completed an Egyptian grammar. He did not solve every problem. He fell back on Coptic too quickly when he was puzzled, and he believed that all hieroglyphs had a single sound, not realizing that many represented two or even three consonants. It was the Prussian scholar Karl Lepsius who finally solved these problems.

especially difficult to grasp. The only person who is known to have guessed this before the nineteenth century was the English scholar William Warburton (1698–1779), but no one had followed up his early lead.

The Rosetta stone allowed a fresh start. An important breakthrough was made by Thomas Young, an English physicist (1773–1824). He discovered from research on the stone and other papyri that demotic Egyptian was not a totally different script from hieroglyphs as many had assumed, but a script derived from it. Young also took some well-known Greek names from the Greek text on the Rosetta Stone: Ptolemy, Cleopatra and Berenice. He managed to identify these names in the hieroglyphic text, where they had been enclosed in cartouches as all royal names were. He then grasped that the names had been made up of hieroglyphs which represented the sounds of the Greek words. Unfortunately, Young assumed that this method was only used for foreign names; he did not guess that all Egyptian words were written in this way, and so he never deciphered a single word of the Egyptian language.

It was left to the French scholar Jean-François Champollion (1790–1832) to make the discovery that Egyptian royal names were written in the same way as Greek ones. Tuthmosis and Ramesses were the first he deciphered. Once he had a few sounds to work with, Champollion worked quickly to unravel a whole array of other sounds and words. He was helped by another discovery, made in the seventeenth century by a Jesuit scholar, Athanasius Kircher (1602–80). Kircher had found that Coptic, which was still spoken by Copts, was the living link to the ancient Egyptian tongue. Comparing Coptic with hieroglyphic texts allowed more Egyptian vocabulary and some rules of grammar to be understood. For the first time in 1,500 years, ancient Egypt could tell its own story.

As new discoveries were announced, treasure-hunters descended on Egypt. Some were simply tomb-robbers aiming to make an immediate profit. Others justified their plundering by claiming that the antiquities would be safer in the care of European museums, and it was their duty to sell what they found to their national institutions.

Henry Salt, the British consul-general in Egypt between 1815 and 1827, was one of the most notable of these "collectors". Like his rival, the French consul-general Bernardino Drovetti, he often acquired choice pieces by less than honorable means, and then attempted to bully his national museum into buying them. Salt's chief agent was Giovanni Belzoni, a former weightlifter from Italy. Belzoni, known during his theatrical days as the "Patagonian Samson", may not have been the most destructive of these early "collectors", but he was one of the most adventurous. He was the first European known to enter both the Great Pyramid and the temple of Abu Simbel. In his bestselling memoirs, published in 1820, he described walking on the frail remains of mummies, which crumbled under his feet – a vivid and unrivaled picture of the ramshackle way in which the exploration and exploitation of Egypt was taking place. Many of his activities were pure showmanship. Belzoni prided himself on moving statues whose size and weight made them apparently immovable. One of his acquisitions for Salt was a colossal head of Ramesses II found buried on the West Bank at Thebes. It was discovered, Belzoni later wrote, "with its face upwards, and apparently smiling at the thought of being taken to England". It was laboriously floated

GIOVANNI BELZONI in Arab dress (ABOVE). Bold, quick-thinking and powerfully built, Belzoni was responsible for many of the Egyptian acquisitions of the British Museum. He left Egypt in 1819 after his rivalry with the French consul Drovetti led to an expensive unresolved lawsuit.

up the Nile and shipped to England, where Salt presented it to the British Museum. This was probably the only instance of Salt's making a gift rather than a sale. His most impressive piece was the magnificent alabaster sarcophagus of Sethos I, father of Ramesses II, found by Belzoni in the Valley of the Kings. It was sold by Salt to the architect John Soane, and remains in Soane's house (now a museum) in London to this day.

In May 1821 Belzoni opened an exhibition of models of his discoveries in London, in the Egyptian Hall in Piccadilly. It was the talk of the town. His rivals had their successes too. One of Drovetti's finds was a "Royal Canon" papyrus from the reign of Ramesses II in which the names of 300 kings were noted, together with the number of years they reigned. It proved essential in helping reconstruct Egyptian chronology and eventually became part of the Egyptian collection in Turin, Italy. Other parts of Drovetti's collections ended up in the Louvre in Paris and in Berlin.

From this time on, great European collections of Egyptiana were on display. Public interest developed in the preservation, interpretation and assimilation of this material. Throughout Europe, writers, artists, architects and designers began incorporating Egyptian motifs into their work.

*T*HE HEAD OF *Ramesses II was
dug out of the sand by
Belzoni (ABOVE), who did not
realize its identity and called it
by its classical name, Memnon.*

SALT AND DROVETTI were able to extract such major antiquities because they had permission to excavate. The British had

The End of Pillage by Permit

chosen not to annex Egypt after defeating Napoleon. Egypt's ruler from 1805 was an Albanian general, Mehmet Ali, officially a subject of Constantinople, who treated Egypt as his personal fief. Initially he cooperated with the looting for political reasons, but pillaging became so widespread that in 1835 he issued a law forbidding the export of Egyptian antiquities and ordering all new finds to be kept in Cairo, where a national museum was established.

Although the law was seldom observed, these same years saw a new emphasis on recording rather than removing monuments. One of the most dedicated scholars was an Englishman, John Gardner Wilkinson (1797–1875), who virtually single-handedly made a vast compilation of inscriptions, texts and tomb paintings, each one meticulously copied from the original. They included the names of many hitherto unknown kings. Wilkinson's work proved all the more valuable as so many original paintings later disappeared or became inaccessible. Wilkinson also produced a factual account of daily life in ancient Egypt. This added a new realistic dimension to Egyptian studies, though it remained neglected by those addicted to monuments and treasures.

France and Britain now had competition for rediscovering Egypt. In the 1840s King Frederick William IV of Prussia, determined that his country should be at the forefront of academic endeavor, organized a major expedition and survey. It was probably the most sophisticated and best planned ever sent from Europe. Under the direction of the Prussian scholar Karl Lepsius, it spent three years recording at sites from the Delta to Meroë. So much material was assembled that the project was not complete until early in the twentieth century, and its 12 illustrated volumes (1849–59) remain the largest work on ancient Egypt ever published. Napoleon's experts, unable to read hieroglyphs, had often copied them hurriedly and inaccurately. Lepsius, whose understanding of hieroglyphs was good, ensured his copies were exact.

Lepsius used a personal meeting with Mehmet Ali to get permission to take antiquities from Egypt. To the fury of less favored excavators, no less than 15,000 objects and plaster casts were shipped to Berlin. This was not the only instance when Mehmet Ali's 1835 ban on exporting antiquities was circumvented. A small museum had been set up in Cairo but its contents were given away by Mehmet Ali's successor, Said Pasha, to Archduke Maximilian of Austria when he visited Egypt in 1855. (They remain in Vienna.) A much more determined effort was needed to provide a center in Egypt where antiquities could be preserved and restored. Otherwise the European

*T*HE BRITISH *negotiate with
the Egyptian viceroy, Mehmet
Ali, 1839 (LEFT). The British
had been politically the most
prominent Europeans in Egypt
since defeating Napoleon in 1801,
but the viceroy kept on good terms
with all Western powers by
endlessly awarding "special"
concessions. Perhaps surprisingly,
given Europe's long tradition of
warfare, feuds between rivals
(such as Salt and Drovetti)
engaged in the antiquities trade
remained primarily personal;
the viceroy avoided upsetting the
European powers by refusing to
get involved in their disputes.*

collectors could justly claim that they could preserve monuments and papyri better than the Egyptians themselves. It was a Frenchman, Auguste Mariette (1821–81), who finally set up a permanent national museum. It survives today as the Cairo Museum, the foremost collection of Egyptian antiquities in the world.

Mariette had first been sent to Egypt to collect Coptic manuscripts, but he had studied hieroglyphs and his interest in ancient Egypt was profound. Having found few manuscripts, he diverted himself to Saqqara after reading a passage from the classical Greek traveler Strabo which suggested that sphinxes found on the site were part of a processional route to a temple. Though his funds were limited, Mariette not only found the temple with a collection of bronze statues of the gods but unexpectedly broke into the galleries of the Serapeum where the sacred Apis bulls had been buried in giant sarcophagi. Fearing that Said Pasha would claim the Serapeum's treasures and then give them to some European ruler or other,

COPYING became important as more sites were looted and defaced. (ABOVE) This example is from a French book of 1879 on the history of Egyptian art.

Mariette smuggled many of them back to France, where the grateful government rewarded him with a post at the Louvre. However, life as an official in France provided little satisfaction for one of the most energetic figures in the history of Egyptology. Mariette returned to Egypt. In 1858, through the help of Ferdinand de Lesseps (later builder of the Suez Canal and a close friend of Said Pasha), he was appointed Director of Ancient Monuments in Egypt, with responsibility for creating a new museum of antiquities. The poacher of Saqqara had become the gamekeeper of Egypt.

Said Pasha had little real interest in Egypt's past, and Mariette's position was often precarious. But as an official he could call on native labor, and he now unleashed a mass of excavations. The great temples of Horus at Edfu and Amun at Karnak were cleared and the imposing mortuary temple of Hatshepsut at Deir el-Bahri was uncovered. At one point some 37 sites were being excavated under Mariette's direction, while other excavators were refused permission to dig at all. This aroused great

◼ CLEOPATRA'S NEEDLE
An Unwanted Oddity from Egypt

On September 12, 1878, London became the latest European city to set up an ancient Egyptian obelisk as a curio. The massive red granite stone had been found buried near Alexandria by British troops fighting Napoleon. Legend said that it had been intended for Cleopatra's palace, and so it was dubbed Cleopatra's Needle. In fact the obelisk was one of a pair erected at Heliopolis by the great king Tuthmosis III about 1468 BC. The Roman emperor Augustus later transported the two 180-tonne obelisks to Alexandria.

In 1820, the Egyptian viceroy Mehmet Ali presented this obelisk to Britain as a memorial to Admiral Nelson, who had saved Egypt from French domination. Although the British troops in Egypt were enthusiastic about the gift, it did not generate equal interest in London – which seems odd, as Egyptomania had already begun. The obelisk remained in Alexandria until 1877,

when a British businessman raised £10,000 to pay for transport by paddle steamer. The obelisk, in a specially built barge, went adrift off the coast of Spain, and was only recovered with difficulty.

In London at last, the obelisk was put up on the Embankment outside the heart of the city. Despite its pedestal with four great bronze sphinxes surrounding it, people complained at this obscure position. "It is deplorable," wrote a fastidious Victorian, Augustus Hare, in his *Walks in London*, "adorning nothing, emphasizing nothing, and by nothing emphasized." However, Cleopatra's Needle has remained in its position to the present day. The other Heliopolis obelisk was presented by the Khedive Ismael to the United States in 1869 and is now in Central Park, New York.

THE NEEDLE is positioned on the Embankment of the Thames River in London (LEFT).

resentment, as did Mariette's ruthless treatment of anyone caught looting – or trying to purchase. When Mariette discovered the jewelry of Queen Ahhotep, the French empress Eugénie attempted to acquire it for herself. Mariette firmly told her no.

Mariette did not have the meticulous approach of the modern archeologist. He recorded little and used explosives to blast his way into sealed tombs. His aim seems to have been to expose the most magnificent sites and to collect treasures which he could use to maintain the support of the Pasha. Nevertheless, his "reign" marked a turning point. Antiquities were now collected for Egypt, and the Cairo Museum, despite a disastrous flood in its early years, was established. For the first time some attention was given to the conservation of monuments. When Mariette died in 1881 he was buried in a sarcophagus in the museum's grounds.

Mariette's successor was another energetic Frenchman, Gaston Maspero (1846–1916). He continued to stamp out illicit trade in antiquities. In 1881, tracking down a stream of fine objects onto the black market, he discovered an enormous cache of mummies hidden in a hillside near Deir el-Bahri. These turned out to be some of the greatest kings of ancient Egypt, including Ahmose, Tuthmosis III, Sethos I and Ramesses II – some 40 in all, reburied in the tenth century BC to hide them from tomb robbers. All the mummies were sent to the Cairo Museum. Their barge sailed down the Nile past crowds of watching Egyptians. Whether they were honoring their ancient kings or mourning the loss of a profitable trade, no one can say.

Maspero was a gifted and prolific writer. In addition to producing the first full edition of the Pyramid Texts in translation, he wrote many

*B*Y THE 1850s, no respectable European museum was without an Egyptian collection (ABOVE); some cities, such as London, had more than one. So well stocked were the European institutions that the sites where Egyptian objects were discovered were often left merely with copies, as was the case with an enormous zodiac relief taken by the French in 1820 from the ceiling of the temple at Dendara.

THE EGYPT EXPLORATION FUND gave crucial support to the man who finally established a secure tradition of scientific archeology. William Flinders Petrie (1853–1942) was the son of a Christian fundamentalist who believed that the Great Pyramid was built with divine guidance and held God's message to humanity. It was to confirm his father's beliefs that Petrie was first sent to Egypt, in 1880. He carried out one of the most accurate surveys of the pyramid but rejected the theories of his father. This gained him the respect of scholars, and with the support of the Fund he was able to return to Egypt in 1883 to excavate at Tanis, an important site in the Delta.

Modern Archeology is Born

Flinders Petrie became a legend. Visitors often found him living in squalor, subsisting on cans of food sent out from London, sleeping in tents or sheds crammed with his finds. Irascible and autocratic, scornful of pedantic scholars who destroyed sites, and a meticulous excavator who regarded even the smallest find as worthy of study, Petrie set Egyptology in a new direction. By painstakingly recording everything and piecing together fragments, he made startling new discoveries.

Before his time, nothing had been known of Egyptian history before King Snefru of the 4th Dynasty (2575 BC). Petrie uncovered the tombs of the first kings of Egypt at Abydos and laid down the outlines of early dynastic history. An equally important achievement was to establish, through excavations at Naqada, that Egypt had been settled long before unification in 3100 BC. This exploded the theory that Egyptian civilization was founded by a migratory race. Radiocarbon dating was still far in the future, but Petrie arranged the pottery he found by style and eventually established a chronological sequence into which similar pots found at other sites could be fitted. The sequence has been accepted in its essentials to the present day.

From the Middle Kingdom came a study of the pyramid-builders of the 12th Dynasty from their village at Kahun. This provided a mass of material on daily life in Egypt. At the same site Petrie found pottery imported from the Aegean. By dating this in its Egyptian context, Petrie gave the first secure dates for the Mycenaean civilization in Greece as well as providing evidence that Egypt was not totally isolated from the Aegean world. The existence of more sustained contact with the Aegean in the Late Period was also confirmed by his discovery of the Greek trading city of Naucratis.

popular works which gave the public a balanced account of what was now known about ancient Egypt. This kept European enthusiasm for Egypt at a high pitch. Maspero was also prepared to allow other nations to excavate in Egypt and even to take selected antiquities back to Europe. The English, who had been left out of the most recent discoveries, were eager to seize an opportunity but lacked funds to mount a major expedition of their own. Now that the export of antiquities for sale was effectively banned, excavations could no longer finance themselves by selling booty.

From 1869, when the opening of the Suez Canal linked the Mediterranean with the Red Sea, British civil servants and their families could visit northern Egypt on their way to or from India, the "jewel in the crown" of the British empire. Organized tours allowed inexperienced travelers to venture up the Nile in safety. On one such tour went a well-known British romantic novelist, Amelia Edwards, in 1873. She was shocked by the relentless destruction of sites and became passionately concerned with raising money for proper scientific excavation. Returning to England, she wrote a stream of newspaper articles and published a best-selling travelogue, *A Thousand Miles Up the Nile*. With the help of powerful backers, she set up the Egypt Exploration Fund in 1882 to appeal to the public for donations to pay for an expedition. Today the Egypt Exploration Society has an international reputation for excavation and surveying in Egypt and Nubia.

THE LOUVRE in Paris had one of the largest and earliest collections of Egyptian artifacts (ABOVE) – the legacy of Napoleon's great scientific expedition in 1798. The French painter Guillaume Larrue (1851-1925) painted these exhibition-goers.

ONE OF Flinders Petrie's many excavations took place at the seventh-century BC Greek settlement of Daphnae (ABOVE RIGHT), south of Port Said along the Suez Canal. This engraving from the "Illustrated London News" in 1886 shows the west wall of the fort, which was destroyed by the Persians in 525 BC. Petrie's excavations revealed that the fort had been 450 meters by 200 meters (500 yards by 220 yards).

FLINDERS PETRIE in 1923 (RIGHT). He helped shift the emphasis in Egyptology from mystique to improved general knowledge of all aspects of ancient Egyptian life. He was pleased to see people from all social backgrounds poring over his discoveries of predynastic pottery at exhibitions.

His achievements at el-Amarna were no less remarkable and included the Amarna diplomatic letters (some of which had already been sold by looters) as well as reliefs from Akhenaten's palace. It was Petrie who first recognized the importance of the painted mummy portraits of the Roman period from the Faiyum.

Petrie later became the first professor of Egyptology in London, a post created by the bequest of Amelia Edwards. He not only set new directions and standards for archeology; he personally trained or inspired a generation of Egyptologists. The impact of his work spread far beyond Egypt. Many of his followers, such as the German–American George Reisner (1867–1942), developed his techniques to even greater degrees of precision. Reisner took Petrie's passion for recording a stage further, carrying out the first land surveys of areas threatened by development or flooding. Others, more scholarly than the modestly educated Petrie, were encouraged to study hieroglyphs and modern Arabic.

Among Petrie's protégés was a young man named Howard Carter. He was to make the Valley of the Kings near Thebes the most celebrated site in archeological history. "The Valley of the Tombs of the Kings," Carter wrote later, "the very name is romance, and of all of Egypt's wonders there is none, I suppose, that makes a more instant appeal to the imagination. Here in this lonely valley-head, remote from every sound of life, with the highest peak in the Theban hills standing sentinel like a natural pyramid above them, lay thirty or more kings, among them the greatest Egypt ever knew." Although some of the royal tombs had been explored earlier, it was not until the 1890s and 1900s that systematic excavation of the valley was undertaken, notably under the patronage of Theodore Davis, a retired American lawyer. Davis uncovered some 30 tombs but all had been robbed in antiquity. Surviving artifacts were poorly recorded by Davis and he never followed up clues that might have taken him to the door of the one tomb which lay virtually intact. By the time of Davis' death in 1915, many felt that the valley had

retained Maspero's good opinion, and when Carnarvon inquired after a suitable excavator, Maspero recommended Carter.

Despite enormous differences in background and temperament, the two men were to become close friends. In 1915 they took on the concession to excavate in the Valley of the Kings. The site was well known to Carter, and he was convinced that Tutankhamun's tomb would be discovered there. After five years of unrewarding work (1917–21), Carnarvon's patience was wearing thin. He only retained his concession for the 1922 season to allow Carter to excavate at his own expense. In November of that year, Carter uncovered Tutankhamun's tomb – the most impressive discovery in Egyptian archeology, and possibly in world archeology as well. Public interest in Egypt had begun to wane; now it was riveted.

The impact on Egyptology was less profound. Although the tomb's contents were magnificent, they contributed little new information and reinforced the popular image of ancient Egypt as a mysterious land of unimaginable opulence. By this time most Egyptologists were more concerned with everyday life in ancient Egypt, which owed less to dramatic discoveries of gold than to dirty, plodding, meticulous excavation and recording.

DESPITE THE DEPREDATIONS of the early treasure-hunters, there still remains a mass of material, thanks to Egypt's climate and the custom of burying so much with the dead. Archeologists continue to piece together the story of

Modern Egyptian Studies

Egypt, which is still far from complete. Their task has become increasingly urgent as pollution, exposure to the elements and heavy tourist traffic have taken their toll on even the most durable of the great monuments. One, the tomb of Queen Nefertari, favorite wife of Ramesses II, was closed to the public for 50 years because the beautiful painted walls were being corroded by damp. They have now been magnificently restored thanks to generous sponsorship by the J. Paul Getty Foundation of the United States.

Improved technology has led to increased technical specialization and expertise. Remote sensing and aerial surveys help locate new sites. Computers assist with studying texts, and graphics programs helped to match paintings from Akhenaten's temples which had been scrambled when the walls were pulled down and used as landfill.

yielded all its secrets, although it was known that Tutankhamun had been buried there and no tomb attributed to him had yet been found.

On Davis' death the concession in the Valley of the Kings was taken on by a rich English earl, Lord Carnarvon, an enthusiastic amateur. He needed a skilled archeologist to direct the excavations, and he had been introduced some years before to Howard Carter. Carter, the youngest of the eleven children of an illustrator, had first gone to Egypt in 1891 and made a reputation as a draftsman. In 1900 Maspero appointed Carter to be Inspector-General of Monuments of Upper Egypt. By this time Carter had undertaken several excavations of his own. In 1905, however, he had been forced to resign after refusing to apologize over an incident involving a fistfight between his officials and some inebriated French tourists. Nevertheless, Carter

HOWARD CARTER opens the doors of the gilded shrine containing the sarcophagus of Tutankhamun (ABOVE). Carter, a veteran of tomb clearing, took great care when opening the tomb so as not to destroy a single artifact. Preserving the treasures was even more important than displaying them to the world. Carter's team spent two years just working through the jumble of goods found in the antechamber which preceded the shrine.

AN EGYPTIAN MUMMY inside its painted cartonnage coffin is undergoing computer tomography (CT) scanning (RIGHT). CT was used on several mummies from the Boston Museum of Fine Arts without disturbing the coffins or their contents. The examination was intended to reveal details of the medical condition of the bodies at the time of death as well as their present condition. The 3-D image (BELOW) was compiled from CT data. It is the head of Ta-bes, a woman who lived about 900 BC and was a singer in the temple of Amun at Karnak.

Investigating mummies has produced a totally new field, paleopathology – studying diseases in ancient people whose bodies have been preserved. Radiosterilization was used to destroy parasites that were attacking the body of Ramesses II. (The team also established that he had a fair complexion and reddish hair.) Scientists on the Manchester Mummy Project in Britain have used DNA from a collection of 21 human and 34 animal mummies to pinpoint everything from the relationships between members of the ancient Egyptian royal families to the appearance of new viruses among monkeys. In 1984 the 2,400-year-old DNA from a child's mummy was cloned in Sweden, opening the door to study the genetic descent of Egyptians. Other archeologists have teamed up with brewers to recreate beer, the everyday beverage of ancient Egypt, by analyzing dregs from Tutankhamun's tomb and sweepings from the floor of breweries in el-Amarna.

The knowledge of ancient Egypt accumulated by archeologists, geologists, surveyors, geneticists, doctors, botanists, historians and linguists is gradually being integrated to create a coherent picture of ancient Egypt – which was not only a unique civilization but also a part of the common heritage of humankind. All history is provisional, but it is possible that we will eventually come closer to knowing the essence of what it was like to live in ancient Egypt than in any other society in the world.

" *At first I could see nothing, the hot air escaping from the chamber causing the candle flame to flicker, but presently, as my eyes grew accustomed to the light, details of the room emerged slowly from the mist, strange animals, statues and gold – everywhere the glint of gold* "

Howard Carter

The Tomb of Tutankhamun

When, on November 2, 1922, Howard Carter uncovered the first steps leading down to what turned out to be the greatest moment in Egyptology, he had little idea that this might be the tomb of the king for which he had been searching for six years. Close to the entrance to the tomb of Ramesses VI, and with narrow steps, it seemed to be the tomb of a noble or perhaps the hiding place for treasures and mummies from other royal tombs. Yet the name of Tutankhamun on the door raised hopes that this was what Carter and his patron, Lord Caernarvon, had long hoped to find: a royal burial place with most of its treasures intact. The steps led down to an antechamber. Carter and Caernarvon had their first glimpse of the tomb's contents on November 25. "A sight I have never dreamed of seeing," wrote the archeologist James Henry Breasted, "The antechamber of a pharaoh's tomb still filled with magnificent equipment... still standing as it was placed there when the tomb was last closed in antiquity."

Despite minor plundering in antiquity, an extraordinary array of treasures remained. They showed evidence of having been assembled in a hurry but in their opulence and variety they are unequaled. The gold coffins and statues, the sumptuous throne, the state chariot, all tell of a monarch close to the gods; on the other hand the body itself, the mummies of two premature girl fetuses (presumably daughters of the king) and so many personal belongings, including "a reed which His Majesty cut with his own hand" and a lock of his grandmother's hair, show that this was a human being no different from any other.

The discoveries were headline news, and while Carter undertook more than a decade of painstaking work to record and protect what he had found, the beauty and richness of the grave goods caused a craze for all things Egyptian: "Tutmania" pervaded the 1920s. They have continued to exert a fascination, and an exhibition toured the world in the 1960s and 1970s, its profits helping to pay for restoration work at Abu Simbel and Philae.

Background The treasures are removed.

Left The throne of Tutankhamun covered in gold leaf – an example of the "wonderful things" that Carter saw as he first peered into the tomb. The composition on the back of the chair, which shows the king with his wife Ankhsenamun, shows the legacy of the informal style of el-Amarna, where Tutankhamun grew up. The small room off the main antechamber, where this was discovered, was piled high with furniture and other objects.

Far left The exquisite gold mask that protected the mummified head was a fair, though idealized, likeness of the king. It is made of gold inlaid with lapis lazuli and turquoise, with eyes of obsidian and quartz, and has come to epitomize the glories of Carter's discoveries.

Left Anubis, wrapped in a fringed linen cloth, lay on a wooden box in the small chamber known as the Treasury. Behind him was the canopic ensemble, a wooden shrine containing the canopic jars. It was covered in gold leaf, and topped by a *uraeus* frieze, with each side protected by a golden statue of a goddess. To the side was a jumble of chests and a fleet of boats.

Above It was many months before the coffin itself could be opened and the mummy revealed. Here Carter and others watch an autopsy being performed. *Right* The mummified and shaved skull wore a bead *uraeus*. It showed signs of damage, possibly caused by a blow from an ax.

Below The treasures of the tomb, chief among them two of the three nested coffins (the solid gold coffin is seen here), are the primary attractions of the Cairo Museum. The tomb itself has been closed to visitors to prevent deterioration, and conservation of the objects in the museum is a paramount concern.

> **"** *The youthful pharaoh was before us at last: an obscure and ephemeral ruler, ceasing to be the mere shadow of a name, had re-entered, after more than three thousand years, the world of reality and history* **"**
>
> Howard Carter

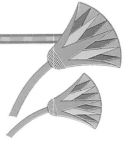

ANCIENT MYSTERIES
Egypt & the Western Imagination

There is almost no limit to the occult power with which later societies have credited ancient Egypt and its artifacts. "Mummy hath great force in staunching blood," wrote the English scholar and early scientist Francis Bacon (1568–1626). Mummies were among the many bizarre concoctions which doctors recommended for their patients in Bacon's time. Perhaps as early as the thirteenth century, mummies were smuggled out of Egypt to supply European apothecaries. No less a figure than King François I of France was said to carry a packet of "mummy" mixed with pulverized rhubarb around with him. To this day, it is rumored that mummy dust can be found for sale in New York.

This belief in the special qualities of mummy dust is just one example of how ancient Egypt has kept a hold on the Western imagination since the days of the Greeks and Romans. Unable to read hieroglyphs, both conquering groups endowed the foreign symbols with a mystic significance, forever enshrining Egypt as a place of wisdom, mysterious forces and strange, often sinister powers. The Greeks and Romans bequeathed to Western culture a tradition of fascination leading to efforts to revive and harness such powers. This tradition was fiercely opposed by the Christian church; later, it has drawn the ridicule of scientists. But each generation seems to find new inspiration in ancient Egypt: the Romans "Egyptianized" their sculpture; medieval Europeans created "Egyptian" alchemy; the nineteenth-century Romantics were entranced by ruins; modern occultists have elaborate theories about the origin and purpose of the pyramids.

THE MURDERED Osiris – forerunner of the Christian death and resurrection theme – from a detail of a fifteenth-century ceiling (ABOVE) in the Vatican in Rome, painted by Pinturicchio (1454–1513).

A FRENCH tarot card from 1889 (BELOW), with the "Wheel of Fortune" typically illustrated with a sphinx and an Egyptian figure. There is no real connection between Egypt and the tarot, which may have been invented by Arabs. The idea that the tarot was Egyptian in origin was invented in fashionable circles in the 1870s in France.

la Roue de Fortune

DURING THE RENAISSANCE a renewed interest in the distant past led to a search for prophecies of Christ's coming in ancient Egyptian texts. Faked "Egyptian" documents from Alexandria were said to date from the time of Moses and to contain a prophecy of the Second Coming of Christ. The writings were known as the Hermetic writings for the Greek messenger-god Hermes, who was associated with Thoth, the Egyptian god of wisdom. Their supposed age made the writings respectable, and their theme allowed Egypt's glorious ancient past to be incorporated into a Christian vision of the world.

In Search of Deeper Truths

The Catholic Church frowned upon excessive enthusiasm for pagan writings. The Dominican friar and astronomer Giordano Bruno (1548–1600) not only argued that Christianity was strongly influenced by Egyptian religion (especially by the cults of Isis and Osiris), but also that ancient Egypt offered a model of spiritual harmony superior to that of contemporary strife-ridden Christianity. Bruno was condemned as a heretic and burned at the stake. A few years later, in 1614, the Hermetic texts were shown to be fakes, dating from no earlier than the first century AD.

However, Bruno had established a legend that the civilization of Egypt contained some kind of universal wisdom which those in authority wished to suppress. Many groups seeking deeper "truths" than those enshrined in traditional Christianity were now attracted to the Egyptian past. One was the Freemasons. Their origins lay with the stone-masons who worked on large medieval buildings such as cathedrals. They shared a workshop, their "lodge". The masons took pride in their work and held particular reverence for the art of geometry, on which the accuracy of their work depended. Classical sources attributed the invention of geometry to Egypt, where it was assumed to have been used in designing and building the great monuments and temples. By the seventeenth century, scholars with a strong interest in architecture were welcome among the Freemasons, and the lodge developed as a center of ritual. Masons shrouded themselves in mystery, controlling admission through sacred rites, offering reverence to ancient symbols and fostering a sense of seclusion. The influence of Egypt pervaded the movement, especially after 1750. The initiation rites of the goddess Isis, known through classical sources such as the Roman writer Apuleius' novel *The Golden Ass*, were drawn on as models.

Napoleon's expedition to Egypt strengthened the hold of Egyptian influences on Freemasonry. A new lodge in Toulouse, France, was named " the Sovereign Pyramid"; its altar was flanked by statues of Isis and Osiris and the entrance guarded by sphinxes. Freemasonry was even more popular in Scotland, where dour Calvinist Christianity was offset by the exotic rituals of the Masons. The Chapter Room of the Supreme Grand Royal Arch Chapter of Scotland (1900–01) in Edinburgh is a large hall graced with Egyptian columns and with illustrations of the story of Isis and Osiris told in the frieze around its upper walls.

Another sect which drew on Egypt was the Rosicrucians, whose name derives from their symbol – a rose combined with a cross. The Rosicrucians date from the early seventeenth century and tell of a legendary founder, Christian Rosenkreutz, who traveled to many countries including Egypt in search of wisdom. Some Rosicrucians date their movement back even further to take in two great thinkers of Alexandria, Philo and Plotinus, and even Jesus. All three were associated with Egypt and its secret wisdom, which the Rosicrucians enshrined in their own rituals. Their central belief is that the mysteries of existence have been handed down from ancient times and can only be revealed to the initiated. Like the Halls of the Freemasons, the temples of the Rosicrucians are decorated with Egyptian interiors. The Rosicrucian headquarters in San José, California, built in the 1980s is one of the finest reconstructions of an Egyptian temple ever built.

Others chose to see the Egyptian gods and goddesses as precursors of the deities familiar in Europe. The Jesuit Athanasius Kircher, one of the first men to study hieroglyphs in the 17th century, saw Isis as a seminal figure not just in the development of Christianity but in Indian, Chinese and even Aztec religion as well. Kircher mentioned a belief that Isis was the protective goddess of Paris (and that the city, indeed, incorporated the goddess within its very name); he argued that her cult endured in that of the Virgin Mary, in the Cathedral of Nôtre Dame on the Ile de la Cité. Kircher's theory was to prove influential in the early years of the French Revolution (1789–93), when the worship of Isis was revived by some revolutionaries who had rejected Christianity.

Masonic images seen here (BELOW) in the frontispiece of a French volume of 1844, tie together Egyptian and Judeo-Christian history. Anubis helps to draw back the curtain on a scene of the murder of Hiram, king of Byblos, at the hands of apprentices who are attempting to acquire the secrets of masonry from him. The pillars are those of Solomon's temple of Jerusalem, which Hiram helped to build; at the foot of the steps sits Isis with the child Horus.

Egypt struck an equally resonant chord with the Romantic painters. The Scottish-born David Roberts, who went to Egypt in 1838 – the first trained artist who went there solely in order to paint monuments – produced a series of canvases which won him instant renown and inspired several generations of tourists. His themes echoed not the scientifically-based *Description de l'Egypte* – which Roberts felt did not do justice to Egypt – but the Romantic themes which appealed to early Victorian Britain: lavish scenes from the Bible, gorgeous artifacts, and Egypt's Arab conquerors, who were still widely regarded as outlandish, heathen Turks by the average European audience. The tale of Egypt's "fleshpots" as described in the Old Testament sold very well in Roberts' time. The chief difference between Roberts and other contemporary painters of Egyptian scenes was in the superior accuracy and detail of his work.

*S*ET DESIGN *of 1816 from Act II (the Garden of Sarastro) of Mozart's "Magic Flute", by Karl Friedrich Schinkel* (ABOVE). *The garden has a lake with a sphinx-shaped mausoleum on a small island with palm trees. Before Schinkel, the sets for this opera had been straightforward archeological reconstructions or fairytale scenes. Schinkel created a sumptuous, mysterious and powerful illusion which inspired theatrical spectacle from then on.*

*T*HE SEVENTH PLAGUE *of Egypt* (RIGHT), *attributed to the English painter John Martin (1789–1854). Temples, pyramids and colonnades serve as a magnificent backdrop for the coming of the plague (hailstones), from a darkened storm-ridden sky. Martin was known as "the poet's painter" for his sense of drama. His choice of visionary and apocalyptic subjects appealed to the Romantic audience of Europe. The effect he produced has been described as "sublime terror".*

THE COMPOSER MOZART was a Freemason and his opera *The Magic Flute*, first performed in Vienna in 1791, drew on a typical Masonic theme in the journey of Pamina and Tamino towards truth after they have defeated the dark forces of the night. The atmosphere of ancient Egypt pervades the opera. An Egyptian priest, Sarastro, acts as a personification of Good, and Pamina and Tamino are led towards their goal by Isis and Osiris. Stage designers responded with enthusiasm to the challenge of creating a mystical world characterized by Egyptian motifs. The sets of Karl Friedrich Schinkel for the Berlin Opera production of 1816 were particularly evocative. Here was Egypt as the home of mysterious and exotic grandeur. Schinkel's sets were a forerunner of the epic stage and film sets of 150 years later.

The Romantic Vision

In the nineteenth century, the exoticism of Egypt appealed to the Romantic movement – an intellectual reaction to the Enlightenment, with its emphasis on logic and science. Splendid ruins, crumbling mummies, ancient curses and princesses buried with their jewelry were just the sorts of things the Romantics drew their inspiration from. Following the example of Shakespeare, who had written so movingly of Cleopatra, the Romantic poets produced some of the finest English (and French and German) verse ever written. The giants of late eighteenth- to mid-nineteenth-century European literature all drew on Egypt as a symbol of the desolation caused by the passing of history.

Europe Acquires Egypt

THE BIRTH OF THE ROMANTIC movement followed Napoleon's expedition, which opened up the remains of Egypt to the European public. This was the first confirmation that ancient Egypt had been a great civilization – one which lent itself to the disciplined scientific study advocated by Enlightenment thinkers. The problem now was how to fit Egypt into European history so that it might be treated as something other than an unrelated oddity. The solution was to appropriate ancient Egypt for the West. The enthusiastic Dominique-Vivant Denon, writing soon after the expedition returned, gave Napoleon the role of heir to the greatness of ancient Egypt, linking him in his glory as conqueror and public benefactor with great Egyptian kings such as Senwosret and Menes

LONDON'S PICCADILLY district was the location of the Egyptian Hall, built by an entrepreneur in 1811–12. Ten years later it housed the great Egyptian exhibition brought to London by Giovanni Belzoni, the Italian strongman turned treasure-hunter. It later became a hall for popular entertainment. The figures at the hall's entrance (as shown on this poster, RIGHT) look distinctly Native American rather than Egyptian.

(Narmer). The historical preface to the *Description de l'Egypte*, the 12-volume published account of the expedition's findings, took the story further. It tied Egypt tightly into European history by citing the pilgrimages of Homer, Lycurgus, Solon, Pythagoras and Plato to Egypt to study its sciences, religion and laws – even though most of these visits only occurred in legend. The importance of Egypt in the Roman world was also emphasized as the place where Pompey, Caesar, Mark Antony and Augustus battled for control of the empire, especially its rich grain supply. Egypt was thus placed in the center stage of classical history. When the Egyptian rooms in the Paris museum of the Louvre were first decorated in the 1830s, one of the ceilings showed Egypt, in the shape of a woman on a throne guarded by sphinxes, being revealed to Athens, the embodiment of Greek civilization. Likewise, Christians could point out the great importance of ancient Egypt for the formation of Old Testament Jewish history, and as a place of refuge for the infant Jesus and his family. The wish to validate history as presented in the Bible was behind many of the semi-scientific expeditions to Egypt in the nineteenth century. "Won't the reverends be pleased," remarked one archeologist when the Israel Stela, the first evidence of Israel's ancient existence, was found.

What had happened to Egypt since the Greeks and Romans had shown it such respect? The accepted story was one of decline under the Arabs, with Napoleon credited – by the French at least – with the restoration of the benefits of "civilization" to the land that had once been its cradle. The painter David Roberts, while visiting Egypt, summed up the prevailing belief: "These splendid cities, once the wonder of the world, are now deserted and lonely or reduced by mismanagement

and the barbarism of the Muslim creed to a state as savage as the wild animals by which they are surrounded." Europe need have no inhibitions about taking Egyptian antiquities home where they would be safe, and where they would help towards an understanding of the roots of European history. In this way Egypt acquired a place in the ideology of European imperialism. The finest modern brains, from France, Britain, Germany and the United States, would unlock the secrets of this civilization, stifled by a less advanced culture.

In fact, ancient Egyptian civilization had been stifled not by Arabs, but long before the Arab conquest by Egyptian Christians, who forbade the writing of hieroglyphs, banned the old gods and did their best to Christianize the remaining temples. However, this inconvenient fact was overlooked by a Christian Europe admiring its own roots.

VERDI'S OPERA "Aida" was closely supervised by the French Egyptologist Mariette, who provided the story line to which Verdi wrote the score (ABOVE). Mariette also visualized the costumes (RIGHT) for the première of the opera in Cairo's new opera house in 1871.

A Celebration of Egypt

NO EVENT was more symbolic of Europe's new dominant role in Egypt than the building and opening of the Suez Canal, which was required by Europe's empires to improve communications with colonies in India and East Asia. The chief instigator was a French engineer, Ferdinand de Lesseps, who had obtained the concession for the construction of a canal from the Mediterranean to the Red Sea from Said Pasha, Egypt's ruler from 1854 to 1863. A deal was drawn up in the interests of the European builders and the users of the canal, so that the Egyptians themselves benefited little from its existence. The opening of the canal in 1869 – by the Empress Eugénie of France, with the Prince of Wales attending – was trumpeted as a great achievement of European technology, a fulfilment of Europe's role in bringing a new civilization to the land of civilization's origins.

The ruler of Egypt at the time of the opening was Khedive Ismael (r.1863–79), who was ready to welcome Europeans as a modernizing force in his country. He asked for an opera to celebrate the opening of another European import, the new

As Greek and Roman rule had done before, European imperialism brought increased tourism to Egypt. Like many areas under Ottoman rule, it had long been avoided by all but the most adventurous Europeans. Also, as Europe's middle class developed, more people outside the aristocracy had the wealth and leisure to undertake extended trips for pleasure. The oldest tour operator in the world, the English firm of Thomas Cook and Son, led the first guided tour to Egypt in 1869, with Cook personally escorting a group of 32. (This was some 600 years after the first known British tourist in Egypt, an Irish monk, had written an account of his own travels: *The Itinerary of Symon Semeonis from Hibernia to the Holy Land*.) Thomas Cook developed a fleet of tourist ships that specialized in providing the comforts of home to tourists who would otherwise have found the experience of travel intolerable: rodents and insects, unfamiliar food, uncomfortable beds, lack of modern Western-style plumbing and sanitation. The Victorian writer Amelia Edwards, who went to Egypt in 1873, wrote that she stayed long enough at Shepheard's Hotel in Cairo, much frequented by Europeans, to be able "to distinguish at first sight between a Cook's tourist and an independent traveler". The list of distinguished personages who toured in Cook's private boats or luxury liners included the archeologist Flinders Petrie, the American president Ulysses S. Grant, Lord Randolph Churchill (father of Winston) and the crown prince and princess of

Cairo Opera House. The work, he ordered, was to be "entirely antique and Egyptian in character". Europeans were in charge of the production. A libretto was composed by the director of Egypt's museum and antiquities service, the illustrious and versatile Auguste Mariette himself. His story line convinced the great Italian operatic composer Guiseppe Verdi, who had been initially reluctant to take on the commission, to provide the music.

So was born the opera *Aida*, the story of the love of an Egyptian general, Rademes, for Aida, an Ethiopian slave – the only "Egyptian" opera actually conceived in Egypt itself by an Egyptologist. Mariette even designed the sets, using the best research to provide authentic temples and costumes. The sets included a palace and a temple at Memphis, a hall in the palace, a princess' private apartments, the banks of the Nile, the city gate of Thebes and a dungeon. Unfortunately, sets and costumes were delayed in arriving due to the Franco-Prussian War of 1870–71, and *Aida* was not performed until December 1871. The first production in Cairo was an enormous success, and *Aida* has become one of the great operatic extravaganzas, always sumptuously produced. It fed the tradition of the grandeur of ancient Egypt which filmmakers were to exploit in the century to come.

ISRAEL IN EGYPT by the English artist Sir Edward Poynter (ABOVE), 1867. His approach was more realistic than that of the Romantics, but the themes were similar, and the portrayal of Egypt as a land teeming with half-naked slaves. The detail came from museum research, though research was no guarantee of authenticity: the temples in this painting are an amalgamation of four different sites and dynasties.

THE GOLDEN AGE of European empires was also a golden age of travel. Affluent Europeans – mostly British, French and German, but also Belgian and Dutch – and Americans went around the globe. Their luggage bore the evidence of their journeys; this is a hotel tag (RIGHT).

❖ SEX & DEATH
The Allure of the Naked Queen

Nineteenth-century Europe indulged wholeheartedly in projection: attributing to others what cannot be faced in oneself. The exotic Orient – above all, Egypt – was a convenient focal point for things that Europeans professed to deplore, such as sensuality. By focusing on particular aspects of one character, the queen Cleopatra, the European imagination produced a distorted image that has fascinated Western society ever since.

The French novelist and art critic Theophile Gautier enthused over Cleopatra as "the most complete woman ever to have existed, the most womanly woman and the most queenly queen, a person to be wondered at, to whom the poets have been able to add nothing, and whom dreamers always find at the end of their dreams." Her legend was known from classical authors such as Plutarch, but her story was manipulated – by Shakespeare, among others – to fit dramatic

DEATH OF CLEOPATRA from a miniature (BELOW) of 1505. An Oriental setting has not yet been introduced, but the painting is already overtly erotic.

needs. She was presented both as a tragic heroine and as a determined and independent woman able to hold her own against the world; as an evil seductress and as the personification of carefree sexuality.

Her death was even more fascinating. Historical accounts suggested that she had committed suicide by provoking the bite of a snake – the traditional protector of Egyptian monarchs, the *uraeus* on the crown. She was bitten on both arms and died wearing all her royal robes. Shakespeare and others preferred the the myth that she was bitten on the breasts, which gave artists an excuse to depict her naked, enhancing her reputation for unrestrained sexuality. To add yet more spice, she was portrayed not as a Greek (and thus essentially European), but as an Egyptian, surrounded by Egyptian furniture and architecture. This is the image that has dominated the dozens of films made about Cleopatra.

CLEOPATRA as drawn by Gustave Moreau (1826–1898) – the era's embodiment of the half-naked pagan queen (ABOVE).

CLAUDETTE COLBERT as "the wickedest woman in history" (RIGHT) in a 1934 Hollywood film.

Sweden. By cultivating a good relationship with Egyptian officials, the Cooks secured a virtual monopoly on Western tourism in Egypt. Their hotels and shipyards created many jobs for Egyptians. They also founded a hospital in Luxor and provided continuing financial support. Finally, they cooperated in the ongoing battle against vandalism and tomb-looting, and protected Nile wildlife by banning the shooting of game from the decks of their ships.

Other notables who visited Egypt included the American writer Mark Twain and the French novelist Gustave Flaubert. Twain wrote a satirical account of Egyptian railroad engineers fueling their engines with mummies. Flaubert consorted with prostitutes, suffered from flea bites, and took some of the earliest photographs of the ruins. Later writers used Egypt as a setting for their stories, among them Agatha Christie in *Death on the Nile*.

By the early 1900s Egypt was providing inspiration for the avant-garde in other arts. The world-famous Ballets Russes performed an opulently staged version of *Cleopatra* in 1909. Ancient Egyptian dances had been recreated by the American dancer and choreographer Martha Graham by 1920. In 1913 the Tiffany jewelry studio held a spectacular Egyptian theme party, complete with Egyptian costumes. Even the budding discipline of psychoanalysis was affected by Egyptomania. Sigmund Freud himself went through what has been described as "an intoxication" with Egypt in 1905, and the psychoanalyst Karl Abraham published a psychological assessment of the religious reformer Akhenaten. This was all testimony to the range of ideas inspired by ancient Egypt. The most attractive aspect of the "mystery" of Egypt may have been that it could be molded over and over to suit the imagination.

PAUL GAUGUIN absorbed Japanese, classical and Egyptian influences into his paintings and took photographs of these sources with him to Tahiti. "Ta Matete" (The Market) (BELOW) shows his typically flat, bright, symbolic colors and two-dimensional use of space. The pose of the women, with their faces in profile and their shoulders full-on, was directly influenced by an exhibition of Egyptian tomb painting in the British Museum.

An ALMANAC from 1924, imprinted with a fanciful image of Tutankhamun (RIGHT), whose discovery in 1922 took the world by storm. "In me each day you will find your fortune" reads the inscription on the front. Thus the almanac, a practical guide to meteorological conditions much consulted by farmers and fishermen, was linked to the occult wisdom of Egypt. The almanac, in fact, was invented by the Arabs and often included astronomical data and other miscellaneous information.

The Secrets of the Pyramids

As THE EXPLORATION of Egypt grew increasingly scientific, from the 1880s scholars and archeologists began to present Egypt as a land whose secrets were there to be revealed by patient decipherment and excavation. But this down-to-earth approach failed to inspire the sensation-seekers. Among them were the occultists and eccentric enthusiasts who were convinced that Egypt held special secrets for humankind.

One enduring focus of attention for such enthusiasts has been the Great Pyramid of Giza. From the archeological evidence, analysis of the structure of the pyramid, the buildings around it and its place within a long series of burial places for kings, scholars determined that it was no more than an extravagant tomb built by a totalitarian monarch. Others disagreed. In 1859 John Taylor

TUTANKAMEN

DANS MOI CHAQUE JOUR — TU TROUVERA TA FORTUNE

BEYOND THE GRAVE
The Pharaoh's Curse

In in the superstitious first millennium BC, no fear of curses stopped widespread graverobbing. Later, European tourists happily helped themselves to whatever they found. But when Lord Carnarvon died of an infected mosquito bite a few months after the tomb of Tutankhamun was opened, "curse" was on everybody's lips. Spiritualists immediately announced that they had warned Carnarvon. Stories circulated of tablets removed from the tomb so that the workmen would not read the frightening inscriptions and be warned off. (Never mind that the workmen could not have read the inscriptions.) It was said that at the moment of Carnarvon's death in Cairo, the city experienced a power failure; and that his favorite dog, left at home in England, howled once and keeled over, lifeless. The British Museum reported a sudden flood of anonymous gifts of Egyptian artifacts – carved figures and the body parts of mummies –

EVIL STALKS the unwary. From the 1959 film "The Mummy".

acquired by tourists who now wished to get rid of them, fast.

Howard Carter, who personally cleared the tomb, told the *New York Times*, "It is rather too much to ask me to believe that some spook is keeping watch over the dead Pharaoh." He lived on for 17 years, and the average lifespan of the members of his expedition was 76.3 years – well above average.

had published *The Great Pyramid – Why it was built and Who Built it?* Taylor argued that it would have been impossible for human beings to have constructed the pyramid in the millennium and a half since the creation of the world, and so it must have been built with divine guidance and for some divine purpose. Its very structure, its passageways and even its measurements must contain some message for humankind.

The challenge of decoding this message was taken up in 1864 by the gifted mathematician and Astronomer Royal for Scotland, Charles Piazzi Smythe. He took a large number of measurements of the pyramid and then rearranged them with dramatic effect. For instance, he measured the base of the pyramid (inaccurately, as it turned out) and divided it by 366, the number of days and parts of days in a year. He then claimed that the result represented exactly a length of one ten-millionth of the Earth's semi-axis of rotation. Other measurements could be rearranged to produce a figure for *pi*. According to Piazzi Smythe, the Egyptians could not have known *pi* themselves (in fact they did have an approximate knowledge of its value) – therefore, this was further evidence of divine inspiration. Piazzi Smythe also discovered the so-called "pyramid inch", which turned out to be almost exactly the same length as the British inch.

He even argued that the quarter measure used by British farmers for quantities of grain was exactly one quarter of the capacity of the sarcophagus found in the pyramid. These and other bizarre calculations earned Piazzi Smythe the nickname of "Pyramidiot". This did not deter his admirers, one of whom, Adam Rutherford, claimed in the 1930s that the "pyramid inch" provided evidence that the pyramids contained a specific message for the British Isles and that one diagonal of the pyramid was pointed at Britain. According to another admirer, Stonehenge was built by Egyptians. Other enthusiasts claimed that Egyptian civilization was founded by refugees from the lost land of Atlantis and actually existed in its original form some thousands of years before the unification of Egypt. The Sphinx, of course, is one of its monuments.

These claims persist despite a mass of evidence showing how Egyptian art and craftsmanship developed in the Nile Valley over centuries before unification. To archeologists there is no need to bring in a master-race from another time to explain the emergence of Egyptian civilization. Still more preposterous is the frequent suggestion that aliens were somehow involved, and that the Sphinx is paralleled by rock formations found on Mars. Others have claimed the pyramids as the recreation of a constellation of stars on earth, arguing that the Egyptians were the greatest astronomers of the ancient world, with memories of star patterns stretching back thousands of years. When Egypt-ologists ignore or refute these theories, they are accused of lacking common sense; of being too academic to see the truth; or of participating in a conspiracy to prevent the "real truth" about ancient Egypt being revealed.

Advocates of the far-fetched are the modern heirs of the treasure-seekers, who prefer mystery to knowledge and cannot be satisfied with history.

*S*TARGATE, *a film from the 1990s (poster,* ABOVE), *reflects contemporary preoccupations with the occult and extra-terrestrials. In the film, the correct alignment of hieroglyphs creates a gateway to a parallel Egypt ruled from space.*

*E*GYPT'S LEGACY *continues to be claimed by other cultures. This mural in Reading, England* (LEFT) *graphically demonstrates the application of this to Africa and the descendants of Africans.*

Egypt & the Cinema

The cinema has become the main home of things Egyptian in the popular imagination during the past hundred years: since the earliest silent era, more than 200 films have had Egyptian themes. The subjects, though, have been somewhat limited, and the most successful have been somewhat traditional, if visually spectacular, reworkings of encounters between Egypt and other civilizations: Moses rescuing the Israelites from the grasp of an all-powerful pharaoh, or Cleopatra's life and loves. Perhaps most in keeping with our own times is the mummy brought back to life to run amok in the modern world.

Vaudeville and other popular entertainment of the pre-movie era had borrowed freely from Egypt, and, inspired by the enthusiasm for things Egyptian of the late 1920s, the cinema architects of the 1930s remodeled the movie houses themselves as Egyptian palaces. Their exotic fittings and decor offered cut-price splendor to the movie-going public, and hinted at the romance of a culture less pompous than the classicism of mainstream architecture.

Some directors placed a higher priority than others on creating an authentic image of Egypt: Theda Bara's Cleopatra of 1917, like Claudette Colbert's of 1934, ruled over an Egypt that seemed to owe as much to the 20th-century designers as to Ptolemaic culture. Cecil B. deMille, who directed Colbert, had already visited Egypt in *The Ten Commandments* (1923): the main emphasis here was on spectacular production values and visually the film was little more than an animated version of the work of 19th-century painters such as Edward Poynter. DeMille's remake of the title in 1956 was more academically informed: but with set-piece scenes such as the erection of an obelisk using a cast of 20,000, he depicted Egypt as a nightmarish, totalitarian society from which Moses and the Israelites must escape. In 1963 Joseph Mankiewicz produced an epic of similarly extravagant proportions in his version of *Cleopatra* (1963), starring Elizabeth Taylor, but again, surface glitz utterly dominated the film: her status as queen of Egypt provided the excuse for an unparalleled descent into indulgence and glamor.

Since the earliest silent era, the notion of the mummy returning to life has haunted cinema audiences: most powerfully in Boris Karloff's

Above Released in 1963 by 20th Century Fox, *Cleopatra,* with Elizabeth Taylor in the title role, was one of the most expensive films ever made. Here the queen enters Rome with her son at her side, in front of a monumental head. The pragmatic Romans Caesar and Mark Antony were to show such pretensions to be shallow.

Below Egypt with its dangerous enigmas and booby-trapped tombs is one of several locations for the thrill-a-minute adventure *Raiders of the Lost Ark*, released by Paramount in 1981. The image of the hyperactive, whip-carrying archeologist Indiana Jones has bedeviled popular notions of Egyptologists ever since.

Far left Yul Brynner was the pharaoh in Cecil B. deMille's last spectacular costume epic, the hugely successful *The Ten Commandments,* also starring Charlton Heston. Ancient Egypt offered an opportunity for larger-than-life characters.

Above The Carlton Cinema in Islington, London, though no longer used for movie-going, still boasts an immaculate polychrome Art Deco facade in the Egyptian style.

Top The exotic Theda Bara – said to be the child of a French painter and his Egyptian mistress, and born in North Africa – was the obvious choice to star in Fox's 1917 version of the story of Cleopatra; Elizabeth Taylor *(above)* was more pertly seductive in the same role.

Right Mysterious deaths among the ruins, as Egyptian cruises provide the excuse for wealthy people to be closeted together.

The Mummy (1932: director Karl Freund), where the main character, Imhotep, is shown still alive while wrapped in his mummy's cloths. The theme of the revived mummy, cursed to dredge up ancient evils to stalk the present, has been reworked many times in moods that range from slapstick to sheer horror.

Only a few films have attempted to deal more seriously with life in Egypt beyond the level of palace intrigues and the casts of thousands; these include Ernst Lubitsch's *The Pharaoh's Wife* (1921), which boasted hieroglyphs in the credits and specially composed Egyptian music; Howard Hawks' macabre melodrama *The Land of the Pharaohs* (1955); and *The Pharaoh* (1965), a psychological drama by Polish director Jerzy Kawalerwicz. The science-fiction adventure *Stargate* (1994) also involved a serious attempt to recreate the language spoken on the ancient Nile.

Others have chosen Egypt and its ancient splendors as the backdrop for crime or thrillers: *Death on the Nile*, and *Raiders of the Lost Ark* were two such. A few comedy films have been set in Egypt, most of them caricaturing the more ambitious Egyptianizing films and relying on spoofs of Egyptian reliefs.

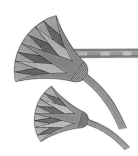
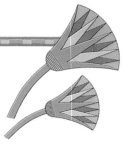

EGYPT & STYLE
Egyptomania & the Decorative Arts

L ong before the first European expeditions to the Nile began to uncover genuine Egyptian art, it enjoyed a revival as part of sixteenth-century Europe's rediscovery of classical Rome. As the ruler of Egypt for some 400 years, Rome was the repository of Europe's largest and most varied collection of Egyptiana; and although more than 1,000 years had elapsed since the fall of Rome, a host of obelisks, sphinxes, lions and pyramids had survived in the city. Now they excited new interest as Renaissance scholars revived the Hermetic tradition, linked by them to the ancient wisdom of Egypt.

What survived in Rome, however, was a strange collection, unrepresentative of true Egyptian art. There was no way of distinguishing between an original brought from Egypt and a fabrication made in Rome. It is hardly surprising that the first enthusiasts for Egyptian art uncritically inherited the tastes and prejudices of the Romans. Sphinxes, which had been placed by the Egyptians in lines along the great processional ways leading to and from the temples, were used purely decoratively by the Romans. They were now transplanted to the setting of formal gardens.

A WEALTHY LANDOWNER in England built this 9-meter (30-foot) steep-sided pyramid-monument (ABOVE) to his favorite horse in the 1730s. It was an example of a folly – a costly, purely ornamental building widely used in the eighteenth century to enhance landscapes. Follies were usually built to classical designs.

E TERNITY AND the awe of death inspired the pyramids of Etienne Boullée (1728–99), who planned several of them (BELOW), though none was ever built. Most European-built pyramids did not accurately reflect the originals.

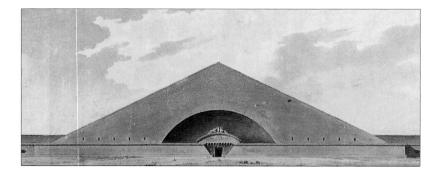

A TASTE FOR EGYPT was particularly common in the royal gardens of France. Sphinxes appeared in

Landscape with Sphinx

the parks at Fontaine-bleau and in the grounds of Louis XIV's magnificent palace at Versailles, and were soon copied elsewhere. Although Louis saw himself as the sun-king, he found his inspiration not in Ra but in the Greek god Apollo, and the sphinx was used not as a protector or even as a specific allusion to Egyptian mythology or its history, but purely to add a grand decorative feature to a terrace or flight of steps. Sphinxes appeared at many European country-houses and palaces in the eighteenth century – in the grounds of Chiswick House near London, for example, and in Austria at the Belvedere in Vienna. By this time the ordered artistic conventions of classicism were being challenged by more exotic fashions, and so sphinxes were found mingling with figures and buildings in the Chinese and Gothic styles.

The pyramid, too, was rediscovered. The only example yet known to the Europeans was from Rome, the tomb of the magistrate Cestius, which had been built with much more steeply angled sides than the original Egyptian design. Europeans came to think of all pyramids as having this shape; the enthusiastic Danish traveler Frederick Norden, whose *Travels in Egypt and Nubia* was published in 1757, mistakenly drew the Giza pyramids with the same slope as that of Cestius, although he was looking at the originals directly in front of him. The famous *Description de l'Égypte*, the published account of Napoleon's scientific expedition in 1798–1801, was valuable not only for its wealth of new information but also for correcting errors like this that dated back to the Roman empire.

Pyramids were attractive for their simplicity of form and their association with grandeur, death and eternity, although they also appeared in gardens; in one case, a pyramid in France was used as an ice house! The eighteenth century had a taste for the melancholic, and pyramids provided a perfect metaphor for death. The pyramid form, wrote the French architect Etienne-Louis Boullée (1728–99), presented "a mournful image of arid mountains and of immortality". He designed a series of funerary monuments which included pyramids that would have housed many hundreds of dead. The English Earl of Buckinghamshire built a pyramid-mausoleum for himself and his wife at their estate in Norfolk in the 1790s, and the Neoclassical sculptor Canova (1757–1822) used a pyramid form for his monument to Princess Maria Christina of Austria in the Augustinerkirche in Vienna. Canova's students built him a fine tomb in the shape of a pyramid in the Church of Santa Maria Frari in Venice.

WHILE THESE BASIC FORMS of Egyptian architecture were becoming recognized and adopted all over eighteenth-century Europe, Egyptian art itself was becoming more widely known through the publications of travelers up the Nile. At the same time, more finds showing the influence of Egypt were turning up elsewhere in Italy, notably in Herculaneum and Pompeii, where a first-century BC temple to Isis was uncovered.

Piranesi's Egyptian Psychedelic

However, up to this point there had been no synthesis of the known styles of Egyptian art; Egyptian elements were used in isolation from one another, with no accepted vocabulary of design in the Egyptian style. The first synthesis was provided by the Italian Giovanni Piranesi (1720–88). Piranesi was an enthusiast for the Egyptians, and he

GIOVANNI PIRANESI designed an extraordinary fireplace (BELOW) with many Egyptianizing elements. The two male figures at the sides of the fire are Antinous figures holding small "naos" shrines. On the mantelpiece are two large canopic jars with Apis bulls for heads. The hieroglyphs on the obelisks are nonsense, like those on the famous Roman tablet, the Mensa Isiaca.

was determined that his public should know that there was more to Egyptian architecture than sphinxes, obelisks and pyramids. His book *Diverse Maniere d'adornare i Cammini* ("Various ways of decorating rooms") came out in 1769. It was filled with designs of rooms loaded with Egyptian motifs, some of which Piranesi had invented, others of which he had copied from the huge range of sources he had consulted. It contained, as a later scholar commented, "a psychedelic extravaganza of sphinxes and statuettes, jackals and crocodiles, mummies, star-patterns and hieroglyphs".

Piranesi's next step was to create an actual Egyptian interior in the Caffe degl'Inglesi in the Piazza di Spagna in Rome. From the surviving illustrations of the walls, it must have been an extraordinary compilation of Egyptian and pseudo-Egyptian design. Its arrangement owed far more to the classical style of the eighteenth century than to any Egyptian building, and it includes elements such as monumental fireplaces completely un-known in Egypt. People laughed at the overblown

spectacle, but it was probably the first time since antiquity that someone had tried to create an Egyptian interior. Its influence on later designers was profound. With Piranesi – the first designer to give Egyptian art and architecture the same reverence as that bestowed on the art of Greece and Rome – Egyptian art became not merely fashionable but intellectually respectable. He insisted that Egyptian art was both beautiful in itself and a forerunner of the classical styles.

NAPOLEON took this Sèvres porcelain (RIGHT) with him into exile on the island of St Helena in 1815, where it excited the admiration of his dinner guests. Egyptian scenes inspired by the French expedition of 1798 graced the porcelain, along with portraits of various kings, pashas and other historical personages.

NAPOLEON'S EXPLOITS in Egypt were originally recorded – and greatly overstated – on this monumental vase (LEFT), made in 1806 by Blaise-Louis Deharme for the Tuileries palace in Paris. The vase itself stands 1.8 meters (6 feet) high and has a diameter of 95 centimeters (37 inches); its base is 1.32 meters (4.3 feet) high. Its form is classical rather than Egyptian, but many of the images on it were taken from Vivant-Denon's account of the French expedition. All references to Napoleon were removed in 1815 when he was finally deposed. They were replaced by standard images of Egypt: gods, pyramids, hieroglyphs, and so on.

THE EGYPTIAN HOUSE in Penzance, Cornwall (FAR RIGHT), in southwest England, built in about 1835, was closely modeled on the Egyptian Hall in London. It was originally a museum, but such Egyptianizing architecture was also found occasionally in private houses. The highly embellished elements of this building also owe something to the flamboyance of Piranesi's Egyptianizing designs.

of Egyptian monuments, including the temples of Philae and Edfu (complete with processional approach of ram-head sphinxes). Napoleon's first wife, the Empress Josephine, ordered a further set for herself as part of her divorce settlement.

The publication of the *Description de l'Égypte* between 1809 and 1828 meant that architects could see for the first time what Egyptian columns looked like. Soon the columns graced the facades of buildings in both France and England. The nineteenth century was the great age of public buildings, and the choice of an Egyptian exterior, even for a museum containing nothing historical, was deliberate. As a center of learning, ancient Egypt was considered an appropriate source of symbols with which to adorn places of learning. One example is London's Egyptian Hall, erected in 1812 to house a collection of natural curiosities. Its entrance columns, portals, statues and plinths were soon copied in smaller buildings throughout Britain. Zoological gardens, which at the time were seen as providing education as much as entertainment, followed in the tradition of presenting Egyptian structures in a garden setting. Fine surviving examples are found in the handsomely decorated buildings of the Antwerp Zoo (1855–56), built to resemble Egyptian structures. Above its entrance was an inscription in hieroglyphs in honor of King Leopold I, described as "the sun

WINGED SPHINXES support this Empire gueridon (BELOW)– a special table on which a candelabrum was placed. The winged sphinx and its feet which support the tabletop replaced the original French Empire design, which traditionally used an African figure with arms raised. The choice of the sphinx reflects contemporary Egyptomania rather than suggesting that such tables were used in Egypt.

The Rediscovery of Egypt

PIRANESI HAD PREPARED European artists and intellectuals for the flood of Egyptiana that appeared in the wake of Napoleon's expedition to Egypt in 1798. The expedition aroused enormous interest in Egyptian antiquities and provided, for the first time, accurate models which could be copied. Further inspiration came from Egyptian antiquities looted by the French from Italy, which included the kilted statue of Antinous which had originally graced Hadrian's villa at Tivoli. As Napoleon took control of France, admirers flattered his achievement in Egypt with a profusion of buildings, furniture and art objects in Egyptian styles. These were not limited to slavish imitation of originals, but were freely applied to furniture and smaller objects such as clocks, fire irons, inkwells, candelabra and porcelain dinner services. The English ceramics designer-manufacturer Thomas Wedgwood had already shown the way in the 1770s with jars and candlesticks in an Egyptian style, but the most extravagant pieces were produced in France by the Sèvres porcelain factory. The czar of Russia, Alexander I, who had been enthusiastic about the Egyptian campaign, was presented with a large service of some 72 plates and accessories, all in Egyptian style or decorated with Egyptian views. The centerpiece of the service was a reconstruction

type factory in northern England, complete with an appropriately decorated steam engine and a chimney disguised as an obelisk. He was cleverly exploiting the reputation of the Egyptians as the makers of the finest linen in the ancient world.

In many of these constructions there was only a marginal attempt to provide an exact model of what might have existed in Egypt itself. The structures drew complaint and ridicule for their outlandish appearance, their lack of authenticity and lack of proportion. Victorians believed that art reflected the moral state of a society; ugliness represented a moral failure. The English architect Augustus Pugin (1812–52), whose own obsession was the revival of Gothic styles, berated these buildings for their shoddy workmanship (many were built in cement, which did not look as good as granite or limestone), errors of scale and absurd attempts to mix ancient and modern. Pugin ridiculed bizarre juxtapositions such as "cast iron hieroglyphic gates and a huge winged Osiris bearing a gas lamp". His critique successfully blunted the revival of Egyptian architecture in Britain.

and life of Belgium, son of the sun". One British architect even designed an Egyptian-style courthouse and prison, perhaps more for the sake of using the imposing Egyptian architectural forms than for the sake of emphasizing the little-known Egyptian concept of ma'at – justice. Along with these public buildings, funerary monuments in the Egyptian style continued to be popular, with obelisks and pyramids widely used; and there were many nineteenth-century cemeteries, in the United States as well as Europe, which were fronted by pylons or gates carved with Egyptian motifs.

Egyptian symbols were appropriate not only for public buildings, but could also be adapted to meet the requirements of the new industrial age. Egyptian architecture was used to emphasize the exoticism of new structures introduced by the emerging technology. An Egyptian-style railway station, for instance, created an atmosphere of a journey to a different world. A suspension bridge used Egyptian-style pylons on which to rest its ropes. One such bridge, designed in the 1820s to span the river Neva in Russia, was to have the exploits of Czar Alexander I portrayed on the pylons, in the same manner as those of Ramesses II some 3,000 years before. The emblem of Russia was used in place of the Egyptian sun's rays.

Egypt also provided inspiration for those who wished to break up the monotony of massive new factories, office buildings and even water tanks. In 1842 a British linen merchant, John Marshall, created an Egyptian-

GIRAFFE HOUSE at the Antwerp Zoo in Belgium (ABOVE). Built in 1855–56, the zoo is one of the few examples of careful scholarship applied to an Egyptian-inspired European building. Its buildings were based on the temples of Philae and Dendara, and used hieroglyphs that actually meant something.

Educating Public Taste

As it became easier to travel to Egypt, artists were able to sketch and paint on the spot. Their images played an important role in educating the public taste and curbing the worst excesses of early nineteenth-century Egyptomania by showing the original art forms in their historical setting – not simply as isolated elements chosen for decoration. At the same time, however, a new obsession was developing. It probably had more effect than Pugin's essays on stemming the tide of undiscriminating use of Egyptian motifs.

The more scholarly Egypt enthusiasts had become obsessed with creating exact replicas. A German expedition to Egypt in the 1840s under the formidable scholar Karl Lepsius had

EGYPT INSPIRED much jewelry worn by affluent Europeans, such as this enamel and scarab pendant brooch and earrings (LEFT) by Émile Philippe. The design incorporates a winged goddess. A similar set by Philippe was shown at the World's Fair in Paris in 1878.

◤OWEN JONES
and the Grammar of Ornament

As the earliest industrial nation in the world, Britain not only had the first taste of the benefits of technology, it also had the first taste of its drawbacks. Alongside the social reformers who attacked the "satanic mills" of the industrial heartland were artists and writers who deplored the abundance of cheap factory-made goods. These critics argued that mass-produced goods were ugly and that they robbed workers of the pride associated with traditional handicrafts. This in turn lowered standards of production so that both quality and design suffered. The problem was considered important enough to merit a special Parliamentary Select Committee in 1836. By 1850, the

Arts and Crafts Movement had arisen in Britain to promote quality design and craftsmanship.

One of the first and most influential Arts and Crafts advocates was the designer, writer and architect Owen Jones (1809–74). He believed (along with many in the movement) that improving the standard of production was a matter of improving the general taste of the public – manufacturers, workers and consumers – by educating them in the basic principles of art. This was the theme of *The Grammar of Ornament*, published in 1856. In it Jones set out 37 "propositions" or

FLORAL MOTIFS from the Egypt section of Owen Jones' "The Grammar of Ornament" (ABOVE). Reeds and lotus flowers had been used on the earliest Egyptian buildings and had long been incorporated into European design through "Egyptianizing".

THE SPECTACULAR Egyptian Court (LEFT) for the Crystal Palace in London was one of Jones' projects. The splendor of the exhibition satisfied the public taste for sensation without sacrificing either historical accuracy or artistic merit.

principles which the public should be taught to recognize. He also illustrated the entire range of known historical styles from which artists drew on. Above all others, ancient Egypt was singled out for praise. Jones wrote that the development of other styles could be traced, but never that of the Egyptians, which appeared to have been directly inspired by nature. It was this, he believed, that made Egyptian art perfect above all other forms, and therefore most worthy of study. Egyptian art obeyed every one of his principles, effortlessly, in an age when everything was made by hand and crafts reached heights the rest of the world has been hard pressed to match ever since.

brought back a mass of antiquities which were then housed in a new museum in Berlin. The central room, modeled on an inner hall from the Ramesseum at Thebes, aimed to recreate the atmosphere of an Egyptian temple. Similarly, the Egyptian Court at the Crystal Palace exhibition hall outside London (built in 1851) reproduced two colossal statues from Abu Simbel. Though much of the Court was an artificial design, individual features such as columns, deities and hieroglyphs were copied from Egyptian originals.

The inspiration for the Egyptian Court came from Owen Jones (1809–74), who had traveled in Egypt and produced his own collection of views of the Nile in 1843. He collaborated with Joseph Bonomi, another draftsman who had worked in Egypt, to design the court. In 1856 Jones published a book on his theories of design with several plates of original Egyptian decorations from columns and temple facades. Jones argued that Egyptian art deserved special respect as art which relied directly on natural models – lotus leaves, for instance – and thus had never lost its original integrity and harmony.

Shortly after London's Great Exhibition came the Universal Exhibition in Paris in 1867. Auguste Mariette, the first Director of Antiquities in Egypt itself, had been asked by the Egyptian government to design a suitable pavilion for the occasion – one of two at the exhibition, indicating the popularity of the Egyptian theme. The other pavilion, designed by a French architect without reference to scholarly sources, was a typical jumble of incongruous objects and images. In sharp contrast, Mariette's pavilion – a temple modeled on the temple annexes of Dendara and Philae, with a processional route of sphinxes leading up to it – was brilliantly executed, and it caused a sensation. Inside were original objects from the Egyptian government collection and reconstructed models of tombs. The display of Middle Kingdom jewelry in the pavilion proved a particular inspiration for craftsmen. In the 1870s, the newly-founded French jewelry firm of Cartier created exquisite pieces with prominent motifs of pharaohs and lotus leaves. Cartier soon became world-famous.

Mariette, like so many other Egyptologists, believed in offering his knowledge to the widest possible audience to improve the world's general understanding of Egypt. He was always ready to advise artists on the correct style for any of their creations. So began an extremely fruitful collaboration between archeologist and artist in producing images of Egypt that were not only

COBRAS, falcons and vultures, the most widely used animal motifs in Egypt, are combined in this French Art Nouveau ceramic plant-holder by Émile Gallé (ABOVE), made in 1881. Making the wings meet in front was the designer's own invention.

artistically pleasing but also historically accurate. *An Egyptian Widow*, painted in 1872 by the British artist Lawrence Alma-Tadema (1836–1912), is a fine example of the genre. A woman weeps beside the mummy of her husband, which is about to be placed in a wooden sarcophagus. Against the wall of the temple shaven priests wail their ritual lament. Alma-Tadema had been inspired by the early British archeologist John Gardner Wilkinson's pioneering book on daily life in ancient Egypt, and he meticulously copied objects from the British Museum and the Louvre to ensure accuracy.

However accurate these paintings were in detail, they remained unmistakable products of the mid-nineteenth century and expressed the artists' own emotions, including their perception of the Orient, which almost always slanted their interpretation of Egypt's history and culture. The artists painted exotically beautiful women, often posed half-naked, languid as they lay in the heat being fanned by slaves. Some criticis argue that in such paintings the artist was sometimes using history as an excuse to explore a sensuality that, for the high-minded Victorian, was otherwise forbidden. Even the churches were prepared to condone such eroticism in art on the grounds that it exposed the shamelessness of pagan antiquity.

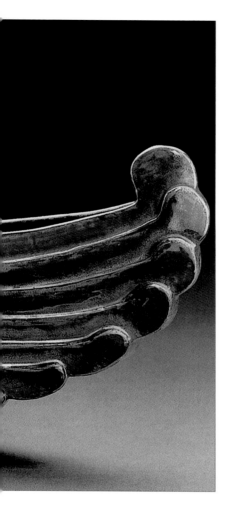

Into the Twentieth Century

EGYPT'S EXQUISITE craftsmanship had particular appeal as mass-produced factory goods flooded the markets of newly industrialized Europe. As early as 1857 the British artist William Holman Hunt (1827–1910), who had traveled in Egypt, designed an Egyptian chair from an 18th-Dynasty stool in the British Museum for his new home. He wanted "a permanent piece of beautiful furniture". Exact copies of the stool were being made for the mass market in 1884 by the London furnishers Liberty and Co, founded a year earlier. Once again Egypt was presented as a source of elegant objects that appealed to refined tastes. This style became permanently associated with Liberty.

By the turn of the century there were major Egyptian collections at museums in most of the principal fashion and design centers of Europe: London, Berlin, Paris and Turin, Italy. They

provided inspiration to a new generation of artists who sought to escape from the traditional bounds of European design. Their efforts produced a movement, Art Nouveau (known in German as *Jugendstil* and in Italian, curiously, as *Stile Liberty,* in association with the popular new British company). Art Nouveau was inspired by Egyptian art, with its distinctive grid-drawn proportions and its flat, perspective-free drawing style. Its elegance, superb craftsmanship and the quality of the materials used gained new respect for the Egyptian achievement. By now designers of objects for the affluent, including the jewelers Gallé and Tiffany, were incorporating Egypt as one of the many influences on their work. For the wealthy and sophisticated, Egypt-inspired objects – from furniture to perfume bottles, jewelry and china – offered the epitome of good taste allied to modernity, with overtones of exoticism and luxury.

Egypt was taken up enthusiastically by the twentieth century, blending into its thoroughly modern culture but still retaining its own unique stamp. On one hand, replicas of Egyptian furniture were popular because they echoed the sleek lines of contemporary art. On the other hand, Egyptian styles were still associated with history and tradition, so an Egyptian design was often proposed for grand public buildings and those associated with death, such as war memorials. The discovery of the tomb of Tutankhamun by Howard Carter in 1922 sent a new wave of "Egyptomania" through the Western world. The world of fashion and advertising, in particular, adopted

The sensual allure of the Orient is used in this card (TOP RIGHT) for a perfume company. The imagined luxurious lifestyle of ancient Egypt struck a chord with the hedonistic "Roaring Twenties". The woman shown looks like a flapper in spite of the Egyptian headgear.

The theme of plumage is used in this 1924 Art Deco costume for the character of the princess Amneris, Aida's rival in the opera "Aida" (RIGHT). The crossed flaps suggest wings, the train a feathered tail. She wears a headdress with the "uraeus".

Powdered glass was an ancient Egyptian technique revived in France at the turn of the century. This vase from the 1920s (LEFT) shows Egyptian inspiration in the figure of the harpist.

*A*RT DECO *was very influential in home furnishings of the 1920s. The theme of this French velvet and silk wallpaper of 1926* (LEFT) *was clearly inspired by images of Egypt. The sphinx's closed eyes accentuate the note of mystery. (It looks like the sphinx of Hatshepsut.) The "jungle" look, stylized flowers and vivid colors are quintessential Art Deco.*

*T*OTALLY DIFFERENT *in their appearance, but still pure Art Deco, are these elevator doors* (BELOW) *with a lotus motif from the Chrysler Building in New York. Their geometric, highly stylized patterns are executed in alternating wood and metal.*

Egyptian styles with new enthusiasm. In New York in the season of 1923 there were Egyptian sandals, pharaoh blouses and a Luxor frock "embroidered with striking vari-coloured Luxor motifs." "Paris Reads the Riddle of the Sphinx" proclaimed the leading fashion magazine *Vogue* in its introduction to the new fashions for the spring of 1923. That same year, Lady Elizabeth Bowes-Lyon, who later became queen of England (and then the Queen Mother), included an Egyptian-style dress in her trousseau. In 1925 Tiffany's designed an enamel and bronze dressing table set in the Egyptian style, complete with hairbrushes decorated with Tutankhamun's cartouche.

"TUTMANIA" PENETRATED popular consciousness in a way unknown in previous Egyptian revivals, just at the time that changes in popular taste were producing new contexts within which Egyptian influences could be expressed. One was Art Deco, named for the celebrated international exhibition of "Arts Decoratifs" in Paris in 1925 where the new style was dominant. The earlier Art Nouveau movement had drawn its inspiration from nature, using many flower and plant motifs and emphasizing their curving lines to produce an unmistakable look that was at once both modern (sleek) and romantic (floral and opulent). Art Deco emphasized straight or geometric lines that suggested manufacture by machine, even when the items were handcrafted or when the motifs echoed the shapes of nature. The simple lines of ancient Egyptian designs particularly appealed to Art Deco

The Brave New World of Art Deco

*T*HE GLAMOR *and novelty suggested by Egypt was used to market absolutely everything, even a product as unrelated to fashion as a soft drink* (LEFT). *The enigmatic sphinx and the world's favorite queen were still going strong in 1939 when this label for a brand of cola was printed.*

designers. "We have no jewelry," wrote the designer William B. M'Cormick in 1924, "excelling that of Egypt of the Twelfth Dynasty for decorative quality, beauty of design and suitability of the objects as things to be worn." But jewelry was not the only medium through which Art Deco was expressed. From toiletries to playing cards, from cars to haircuts, from plumbing fixtures and lamps to shoes – the new style was not so much a fashion as a complete lifestyle.

It was primarily a lifestyle for the rich. Like Egypt's luxury goods, most Art Deco objects were painstakingly crafted (in spite of their machined appearance) and made of the finest materials. Gold, silver, bronze, semi-precious and precious stones, ivory and exotic woods were favored, along with rediscovered Egyptian crafts such as faience (a type of glazed ceramic), glass, enamel and chased metalwork. The combinations of Art Deco echoed the ones found in ancient Egypt: gold inlaid with brilliantly colored glass; gilded wood. However, not all Art Deco was so exclusive. Some designers believed that modern art in a democratic age must be mass-produced so that it, too, was democratic – worlds away from the fabulous tomb treasures of Egypt's pharaohs. These designers reproduced Art Deco styles in cheaper materials – bakelite, plastic and chrome – and so made them available to a wider clientele in an age when the class barriers had been blurred by the impact of World War I.

But mostly Art Deco did not have any deliberate philosophy behind it. It was a style of the moment, emphasizing fun and "looks for looks' sake". It drew its inspiration from everywhere: from the Orient to tribal Africa, from the art of the ancient Aztecs to that of ancient Egypt. At the same time, it mingled with modern styles such as Cubism and Italian Futurism, led by artists such as the painters Pablo Picasso and Henri Matisse and Amedeo Modigliani – who themselves had been influenced by the exotic qualities of Egyptian art, its geometric lines and bold polychromatics. Modigliani proclaimed in 1911 that, apart from the Egyptian galleries, nothing in the Louvre Museum in Paris was worthy of his attention.

While the more exquisite productions of Egyptian craftsmanship continued to inspire designers, the monumental elements of Egyptian art also continued to have their impact. In New York the 1920s were the age of the skyscraper. Art Deco proved an ideal medium, both for the streamlined exteriors of these buildings with their stepped facades and for the details of opulent doorways, elevators and light fittings. Examples

THE HOOVER FACTORY in west London was built in 1931–32. It incorporates several distinct Egyptianizing themes in a typical Art Deco synthesis of styles. The brightly-colored central doorway (BELOW) is a Piranesian stepped motif, while the whole building is a streamlined interpretation of an Egyptian temple-front.

such as the Chrysler building of 1930 showed the confidence with which a variety of historical styles were merged into a coherent whole to suggest the glamor and power of the company's products. Egyptian motifs appear both on the grand scale on the outside of the building and in the lotus leaves that decorate the elevator doors in the interior. As in the nineteenth century, the addition of columns, often painted in polychrome colors, helped break up a heavy and often uninspired industrial facade. In London the Arcadia Works Building of Carreras

(1927–28) is pure Egyptian in concept, with its monumental central door surrounded by columns draped with lotus leaves as in the temples of Luxor and Karnak. Another celebrated example in Britain is the Hoover factory of 1931–32, on the western outskirts of London, whose front is clearly modeled on that of an Egyptian temple.

Yet it was in the cinema that the influence of Egypt had its greatest popular impact. As early as 1921, the Cinema Louxor in Paris had, as its name suggests, used Egyptian motifs to decorate its facade. The need to find a new architectural form within which to contain the large cinema audiences of the 1920s came just at the moment when the great temples of Egypt were in the popular mind.

The most celebrated of the new movie palaces was Grauman's Egyptian Theater in Hollywood, opened in 1922. Egyptianizing theaters spread throughout North America and to Britain. In the New Empress theater in Montreal, opened in 1928, movie-goers passed through columns, hieroglyphs, winged disks and Egyptian heads to reach the interior. There they were confronted by an auditorium in which panoramic scenes of ancient Egypt could be seen through fluted pillars topped with pharaonic masks. The entry into the darkened hall where a new life was revealed (this time on a screen) may have had its origins in Egyptian tombs and temples. Many of the films these palaces portrayed further evoked the atmosphere of ancient Egypt, with its clichéd "cast of thousands." Audiences could revel in a version of the Egyptian past that emphasized glamor, physical strength and phenomenal wealth.

Although Art Deco was out of fashion by the end of World War II and modern designers had turned away from historical allusions, ancient Egypt was not forgotten. It was cinema which above all sustained interest through the great epics such as Cecil B. deMille's new production of *The Ten Commandments* (1956), which went back to the Victorian obsession with Egypt as a backdrop of biblical history. The character of Cleopatra, too, attracted the leading beauties of the stage and screen, Vivien Leigh (in a film made in 1945) and Elizabeth Taylor (1963). For the public, Cleopatra's legend blended with the personal lives of these actresses as reported in gossip columns.

IN THE LATE 1960s there was an Art Deco revival, with jewelry designers such as Eric Russell

Egyptian Influences Today

reinterpreting the original shapes and sources of the movement so that Egyptian motifs reappeared in yet another context. High fashion designers such as Mary Quant revived the Egyptian look, with its heavy eye makeup and severe haircuts, and made it an essential component in Pop Art. With the return to historical styles in architecture in the 1980s and 1990s, Egyptian motifs returned to the fore again. Sometimes they were deeply integrated into an architect's style; James Stirling's Staatsgallerie in Stuttgart, Germany, merges a striking Egyptian cornice with Greek and Modernist elements to form a quite unique whole. Other motifs are reinterpreted more or less exactly, though with a sense of irony.

THE MAJESTIC GLASS PYRAMID (LEFT) built by the Chinese-born American architect Ieoh Ming Pei, opened in 1989, provides a highly dramatic entrance to the Louvre Gallery, Paris. The Louvre has one of the world's most important collections of ancient Egyptian art.

A MODERN DRESS by the designer Kenzo (BELOW), inspired by the subtle draping of Egyptian garments. The accessories also look Egyptian.

THE GLEAMING PLATINUM exterior of the Chrysler Building (ABOVE LEFT), completed in 1930 in New York and designed by William Van Alen, is said to have been inspired by costumes designed for Cecil B. deMille's Egyptian films.

EGYPTIAN MOTIFS cover this elegant evening bag (LEFT) of silk embroidered in silver and gold: stepped patterns, an inlaid frieze of lotus buds, the use of the solar disk motif, and the slim figure of the swimming girl, made in solid gold and patterned on ritual spoons found in Egyptian tombs. The bag, made in Paris in 1922, is an early example of Art Deco but incorporates favorite Egyptian themes.

In Wadsworth, Illinois, the American Jim Onan built himself a house in the form of a gilded pyramid complete with an avenue of sphinxes. In contrast, the Hotel Luxor at Las Vegas, also in the form of a pyramid, uses the associations of Egypt with untold wealth to create a playground where reality and proportion are abandoned at the door. The pyramid form has been revived in more distinguished fashion by the award-winning architect Ieoh Ming Pei, this time in metal and glass, freed from specific historical detail yet given powerful historical allusions by its location at the entry to the Louvre in Paris.

When the modern world meets the ancient, unexpected things can happen. The British painter David Hockney (1937–), known as a Pop artist with a preference for traditional subjects, did two pictures inspired by an Egyptian statue in the Pergamon Museum in Berlin. Hockney happened to see a man standing next to the statue, a life-sized wooden carving of an Egyptian woman, in a pose that reminded him of a formal wedding portrait. In his etching *The Marriage* and in his oil painting *The First Marriage*, the groom is a modern figure

wearing a suit, but the veiled bride is neither modern nor historical – a Pop art figure with features that are more Native American than Egyptian, and torpedo-shaped breasts.

Art Deco revivals; I. M. Pei's pyramid; Hockney's portrait – who knows what future artist might be inspired by these works inspired by Egypt? Ancient Egypt's continuing influence on the arts lies in the versatility of its motifs, whether in the pyramid shape, the temple facade, the drape of linen or the smallest piece of delicate jewelry. Its heritage appeals to those who appreciate graceful objects as well as to those who prefer austere monuments. By appealing both to the whim of an individual and to the collective taste of a sophisticated group, Egypt will continue to be a source of inspiration.

YESTERDAY & TODAY
Egypt in the Modern World

In Egypt today, the past is not merely found in the tombs and temples that draw several million tourists a year. Outside the cities of Alexandria and Cairo, in the small villages that make up the rest of the country, life goes on much as it did 4,000 years ago, in spite of modern trappings such as electricity. Farmers still strain their backs in the fields and walk behind plows pulled by oxen, in scenes familiar from tomb paintings. The pole-and-bucket rigging known as a *shaduf* is still used to draw water from the Nile, which still gives life to Egypt – navigation, irrigation, drinking water and bathing water.

Egypt's many holidays are living history. The annual flood of the Nile stopped with the building of the Aswan Dam in 1971, but it is remembered in a long summer festival beginning with the Night of the Drop on June 18. The name refers to the tears of Isis, which were once believed to begin the Nile's swelling. The festival continues into August, when more celebrations mark the former opening of canals throughout the country at the height of the inundation. Some of these canals were filled in 100 years ago, but the festival continues.

Another great festival of the past was Opet, when a statue of Amun was placed on a sacred bark and floated upstream from Karnak to Luxor to "visit" the god's southern temple. It has echoes in the Egyptian Muslim festival of the holy man

ONCE IT WAS NUBIA, now it is Lake Nasser (ABOVE). The construction of the Aswan High Dam in the 1960s created the lake and drowned a part of modern Sudan which was home to 100,000 people. Egypt and Sudan worked together to relocate the villagers, while a four-year project moved priceless archeological sites.

TIMETABLE

1517–1805	Ottomans rule Egypt
1798–1801	Napoleon's invasion
1869	Suez Canal opens; first commercial guided tour to Egypt
1882	Egypt under British occupation
1922	Discovery of Tutankhamun
1922	Egypt becomes independent
1954	Nasser becomes president
1956	Suez War
1960	Aswan High Dam is begun
1967	Six-Day War with Israel
1978	President Sadat signs peace agreement with Israel
1981	President Sadat assassinated
1990	Population reaches 55 million

Abu'l Haggag, in whose honor the Arabs built a mosque in one of the courtyards of Ramesses II at Luxor. To this day there is an annual celebration there. Its procession includes a holy boat, which is the object of reverence by the crowds. Remarkably, the festival seems to have been celebrated in this form long before the illustrations of the bark of Amun were unearthed from the sand.

Both Egyptian Christians and Muslims accept the tradition of the Holy Family fleeing to Egypt to escape the wrath of Herod. At El-Matariya, a village outside Cairo, is the Virgin's Tree, a sycamore where Mary is supposed to have rested with her baby. Alongside the tree is a spring whose waters, it is said, always run clear as a result of their presence. In 1967, when Egypt was disastrously defeated in the Six-Day War against Israel, crowds of both Muslims and Christians were drawn to a Coptic church near the Virgin's Tree where the priest claimed to have seen an apparition of the Virgin on the church roof.

Coptic Christianity itself is a living tradition of the past. The word Copt – derived from the Arabic word for Egyptian – is a reminder that virtually all Egyptians were Christians at the time of the Arab conquest in the seventh century AD. By that time Coptic Christianity had already broken from the Roman Church as a result of doctrinal disputes, particularly Rome's insistence that Christ was both

THE MONASTIC tradition of Coptic Christianity is undergoing a revival in modern Egypt as the church comes out of its 1,500-year-long isolation from Western Christianity. This young monk (BELOW) is a member of Deir es-Surian, "the monastery of the Syrians", one of the four surviving monasteries in Wadi Natrun, southwest of the Nile Delta. Behind him are enormous ancient waterwheels, abandoned in favor of electric pumps.

human and divine. The Copts believed that Jesus was wholly divine, and as a result they became isolated from mainstream Christianity.

Coptic Christianity was tolerated at first by the Arabs, but Islam and its culture eventually became the dominant force. The Coptic language was gradually supplanted by Arabic, and after 1250 the church went into steep decline. Monastic life, one of the great contributions of Egypt to Christianity, virtually disappeared after 1350. However, there has recently been some revival in the Copts' fortunes. Cairo boasts a new cathedral dedicated to St Mark the Evangelist – according to Coptic tradition, the founder of Egyptian Christianity.

A relic reputed to be the saint's bones, stolen from Alexandria by the Venetians in the ninth century, has been returned. And a more tolerant attitude among modern Christians has allowed Copts to build links with other Christian communities outside Egypt. Even the monastic tradition has been given new life after centuries in which the great monastic buildings of the Christian era were almost deserted. The largest and most prosperous of the Coptic monasteries is Deir el-Muharraq near Qusqam, where legend says the Holy Family lived in a cave for some three and a half years. The church there is claimed to be the oldest in Egypt, and a festival of the Virgin continues there today.

FRIDAY PRAYER at a Cairo mosque (ABOVE) usually draws a respectable crowd. Cairo began as an Islamic city, in contrast to Alexandria, which has always had large Jewish and Christian populations.

SULTAN QAIT BEY, one of the last of the Mamluk rulers of Egypt, built one of the most splendid tomb-mosques in the Islamic world (RIGHT) in 1472. Though not very large, it has especially magnificent stone carving and calligraphy. It is located in the City of the Dead, an area of Cairo devoted to tombs.

The Coming of Islam

THE MOST PERVASIVE influence on modern Egypt is its Islamic past. At first the Arab conquerors did little to upset the Egyptian way of life. They did not seize land or disrupt the taxation system left by the Byzantine empire. Rather than take over an existing city for their administrative seat, the Arabs founded a new one. Fustat was on the Nile not far from the site of Memphis, the most ancient Egyptian capital of all. Egypt was once again part of a larger empire, this time one whose capital lay first in Damascus and then in Baghdad. But there were periods when Egypt was virtually independent as Arab dynasties waned and rose again. In one such period, the late ninth century, the great mosque of Ibn Tulun was built just north of Fustat. One of Egypt's finest mosques, it still survives, its inner courtyard a haven of peace beyond the bustle of modern city life, although the fine gardens and waterways that surrounded it have long since vanished.

In 967, for the first time in history, Egypt was successfully invaded from the west by the Fatimids, who claimed descent from the prophet Muhammad through his daughter Fatima. For 200 years Egypt was the center of a powerful dynasty whose trading interests and sea power stretched into the Mediterranean. The Fatimids kept themselves aloof from the native population. They founded yet another administrative capital, Al Qahira. It was close to Fustat, which became Al Qahira's port.

Al Qahira – Cairo – became one of the world's great medieval cities. Its first mosque, al-Azhar, founded in 970, lays claim to being the oldest university in the world. The weakening of the Fatimids in the twelfth century coincided with the Crusades, when the Islamic world was drawn into the defense of the Holy Land. Egypt then came under the control of the greatest of the Islamic leaders of the period, Saladin (ruled 1171–93), who was originally Kurdish. Saladin brought new glories to Cairo with the building of a great citadel and a massive defensive wall which enclosed Fustat, the Citadel and Cairo.

The Citadel became the residence of Egypt's rulers, surrounded by high walls which concealed harems and gardens. In it there was an echo of the remoteness of the pharaohs, who were never even glimpsed by most of their subjects. One ruler, Al-Nasir (1313–38), brought granite columns from the ancient ruins of Upper Egypt for his palaces. Some Ptolemaic and Roman columns survive in a mosque of his which still stands in the center of the Citadel. Saladin's dynasty introduced to Egypt one of the most distinctive of Arabic buildings, the *madrasa*, a complex of four vaulted halls, each one dedicated to the teaching of one of the elements of traditional Islam. A fine surviving example in Cairo is the *madrasa* of Sultan Hasan (1356–63).

The Citadel was the training ground of the Mamluks – young men, mainly drawn from the Turkic peoples of central Asia, who were first soldiers and later administrators of the various Arab kingdoms. In Egypt they became especially skilled, and they defended Egypt successfully against both Europeans and the Mongols. By the thirteenth century the Mamluks had become the ruling class. They made Egypt once again a powerful and respected state, known throughout the Mediterranean for its prosperity and learning. It was in the following centuries that Arabic almost completely replaced Coptic and Greek as the national language of Egypt.

In 1517, after a period of dynastic squabbling among the Mamluks, Egypt fell victim to the Ottoman empire. The country was controlled from Constantinople (Istanbul), as it had been 1,200 years earlier when it was part of the Byzantine empire. Egypt was nominally ruled by the Ottomans until their empire's collapse in 1919 at the end of World War I. The Mamluk families remained powerful, however. From the late 1700s they in effect ran the country as an independent state within the empire. It was the Mamluk army which was defeated by Napoleon in 1798.

NAPOLEON'S CAMPAIGN had made Egypt the latest focus of the ongoing struggle between Europe and the Ottoman Turks. In doing so, it opened the door to a major new influence to Egyptian life. The Ottomans' viceroy, Mehmet Ali (ruled 1805–48), broke the power of the Mamluks forever by gathering 500 of them at a banquet in the Citadel and slaughtering them all. It was not merely an exercise in securing personal power but part of his determined efforts to modernize his country. To do so, he and his successors had to maintain strong links with Europe, drawing Egypt inexorably into the grip of European imperialism.

Egypt & Modern Europe

The Suez Canal, opened in 1869 by the Empress Eugénie, wife of Napoleon III, illustrates the paradox. It made Egypt an integral part of an expanding global trade network, an essential bridge between east (the Red Sea) and west (the Mediterranean). At the same time, because most of this trade was European, the security of the Suez became an obsession for the European powers. Britain went so far as to occupy the country in 1882 when Egypt failed to repay debts to the European powers. Even after Egyptian independence was restored in 1922 under a constitutional monarchy, British influence remained dominant, with Britain retaining responsibility for Egypt's defense. This continuing presence was resented by Egyptian nationalists, especially when Egypt was occupied during World War II, and when Britain supported the founding of Israel in 1948.

Like almost all Egypt's rulers since 300 BC, the new twentieth-century monarchs were not native Egyptians; they were Turkish-speaking descendants of Mehmet Ali. Neither Egypt's written constitution nor its independence was hardy. The British, the king and the Egyptians continued to contend for political control, in a period of frequent changes of government and political assassinations. Not until 1952 was an independent and populist Egyptian identity finally asserted, when the unpopular King Farouk was overthrown in a military coup. By 1954 the leader

NASSER TOWERS over his country (RIGHT) in this poster celebrating the opening of the Aswan High Dam. The style – "heroic socialist" – may have been copied from the Soviet Union, which was friendly to Nasser. Egypt's first great modern leader, he was mourned on his death in 1970 as the "last pharaoh".

RESCUED FROM the Nile, the ruins of Isis' temple at Philae are reassembled stone by stone (BELOW RIGHT). The temple was dismantled and moved to the higher-lying island of Agilkia 300 meters (984 feet) downstream. Agilkia's rocky surface was leveled to accommodate the temple.

▼THE SUEZ CANAL
Gift of the Pasha, Reclaimed by the President

The project was so ambitious, it was the nineteenth century's equivalent of building a Great Pyramid. For Europeans, whose empires extended into the Far East, the only way to send their great trading and military ships to the far side of the globe was to sail all the way around Africa and then up into the Indian Ocean. If a sea route could join the Mediterranean to the Indian Ocean via the Red Sea, it would improve matters greatly. The same idea had occurred to the Egyptians, who had long since dug canals from the Nile to the Red Sea.

This was Napoleon's reason for invading Egypt in 1798. The British had broken French contact with India in 1751, and Napoleon wanted a fast route to get back in. In 1798 the French government authorized him to build a canal through Suez, which meant he first

THE OPENING of the Suez canal on November 17, 1869

had to control Egypt. Although his army was defeated, the canal was not forgotten. Some 50 years later, a French diplomat in Cairo, Ferdinand de Lesseps, took up the preliminary survey made by Napoleon's chief engineer. De Lesseps was on good terms with Said Pasha, the viceroy, and in 1854 the pasha allowed digging to begin.

The 168-kilometer (105-mile) canal took 15 years to complete, and made use of three lakes along the route from Port Said on the Mediterranean coast to the Gulf of Suez in the south. Originally it was a scant 8 meters (26 feet) deep, its width ranging from 30 meters (100 feet) at the bottom to 58 meters (190 feet) at the surface. The canal has been widened and deepened many times over the past 100 years.

The canal has always been an intensely political issue. The British, suspicious of the French, tried to stop the project. However, the British Prime Minister Disraeli attended the opening ceremony in November 1869, which featured a song written by the Egyptologist Auguste Mariette – a good friend of de Lesseps'. The pasha's majority shares were later purchased by the British. When Egypt nationalized the canal in 1956, Britain, France and Israel invaded. They won, but strong political pressure from abroad forced them to withdraw, and the canal's profits reverted to Egypt.

Nasser was determined to improve the lot of Egypt's peasants, most of of whom were laborers

*Nasser &
the Aswan
Dam*

on large estates. His most ambitious project was to build a massive dam across the Nile at Aswan which would control the flow of water downriver. It was to finance this dam that he nationalized the Suez Canal, after a promise of funding was reneged on by the United States and Britain.

It was estimated that 40 percent of a normal flood disappeared into the Mediterranean – water that could have been used for irrigation. The new dam would allow two thirds of this water to be retained and released into the Nile valley at times of low floods. The surplus of an extra high flood could also be reserved to be released at the time of bad one. The Aswan Dam was to be nearly four kilometers (2.5 miles) long and nearly a kilometer (0.6 miles) broad at its base, a volume of building material 17 times that of the Great Pyramid. The dam would raise the height of the river behind the dam by 50 meters (164 feet), generating pressure to power a hydroelectric station. Some 4,200 square kilometers (1,620 square miles) of new land would become available for cultivation.

Unfortunately, the dam would also create a huge lake, 500 kilometers (310 miles) long, which would swamp much of what had been ancient Nubia (now part of the Sudan). This area was the traditional homeland of some 100,000 Nubians. There was also a major threat to the local archeological heritage, which included the great temple of Abu Simbel. At first the official response to this threat was hesitant. Some attempt was made to involve the United Nations Educational, Scientific and Cultural Organization (UNESCO) at a modest level. Funds were raised to record the sites in Nubia which would be covered, but there was no concerted effort to galvanize the international community.

In 1958, just two years before construction of the dam began, Egypt appointed a new Minister of Culture, Dr. Saroite Okacha. As soon as he was aware of the scale of destruction, Dr. Okacha determined to involve UNESCO on a major scale to coordinate a rescue operation on the main sites. In 1960 UNESCO became formally committed to the project. The flooded area was also subject to the most meticulous survey ever undertaken, by 40 different archeological teams, and a wealth of material on Nubian history stretching as far back as 10,000 BC was hastily accumulated as the flood

of Egypt was a former army officer, Gamal Abdul Nasser, who proclaimed a socialist state, one which would assume leadership of the Arab world.

It was inevitable that there would be conflict over the Suez Canal. Still guarded by British troops, it had remained as a symbol of Western imperialism. The Suez war of 1956, in which Britain, France and Israel launched an attack on the canal in an attempt to save it from nationalization by Egypt, was one of the last adventures of European imperialism. When the Israelis seized control of the Sinai in the Six-Day War of 1967, the canal was closed. It reopened in 1975, but many of the supertankers then in service were too large to use the canal without enlarging it.

waters rose. As the Director-General of UNESCO put it, "These monuments, the loss of which may be tragically near, do not belong solely to the countries who hold them on trust. The whole world has the right to see them endure."

So it came to pass that the great temple of Ramesses II at Abu Simbel was raised to a new position above the waterline, and the temple of Isis from the island of Philae was rebuilt on the new island of Agilkia. Another 20 small temples were rescued, and some of these were donated to the states which had contributed most to the rescue operation – a new angle on acquisitions of Egyptian antiquity by foreigners. The temple of Dendur went to the Metropolitan Museum in New York, attracting over a million visitors in its first year.

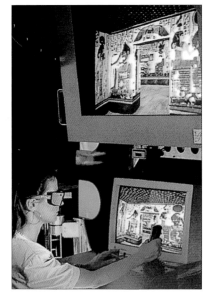

The Aswan Dam was completed in 1970, and the age-old ecology of the Nile valley with its regular annual flood was broken. For the farmers there was widespread disorientation as the natural rhythm of the floods was replaced by water released according to a state-controlled agenda. With the completion of the dam's power station in 1970, Egypt's output of electricity was doubled. This also affected the Egyptian way of life, as television found its way into the villages. There were even less welcome results. The fertility of the land had always depended on the flood to bring nourishing silt, which was now retained behind the dam. Artificial fertilizers are now needed to enrich the land, and the lack of silt has led to erosion of the river banks and to the creation of new islands in the Nile itself.

THE AVAILABILITY OF WATER continues to be a pressing issue in Egypt, particularly in its relations with its immediate southern neighbors Sudan and Ethiopia where the Nile, which has bestowed superior benefits on the Egyptians since the beginning of history, has its twin origins. In spite of the lavish gardens of modern hotels near Cairo, Egypt recalls the proximity of the desert and puts much emphasis on water conservation.

Egypt Today and Tomorrow

Dwarfing all other issues, however, is the problem of Egypt's expanding population. It has risen from 14 million in 1900 (just double the estimated figure of Ptolemaic times) to 55 million in 1990. Cairo is one of the largest, poorest cities in the world, with an estimated 15 million inhabitants. An astonishing 80 percent of its dwellings have been built illegally. Nearly a million people live in the "City of the Dead", the tenth-century cemetery district to the east of the city.

Quite apart from the human costs of such pressure on the land, there is the stress on the remains of Egypt's past. Many areas of unexcavated land, especially around Memphis, are now covered by dwellings. Growing pollution is having disastrous effects on monuments, particularly on

*"**K**HUFU IS ONE belonging to the horizon" is the official name of the Great Pyramid (LEFT). Buses disgorge tourists at its feet; local dealers offer camel rides. Both the pyramids and the nearby Great Sphinx are being damaged by pollution from Cairo.*

***V**IRTUAL TOURISM is one solution to the problem of too many people at fragile ancient monuments. This woman is using a virtual reality headset to explore the tomb of Nefertari (BELOW LEFT). As she "moves" through the tomb, she listens to a tape of someone reciting the ancient texts.*

***A** COLOSSAL STATUE of Ramesses II, taken from the ruins of his temple at Memphis, stands in front of Cairo's main railway station (BELOW). At his feet are his modern-day "subjects", who are by no means too much in awe of him to climb up and make themselves right at home.*

their paintings and reliefs. The Egyptian government is eager to encourage tourists and double or triple the numbers by the end of the century, but this means that temples and tombs suffer the relentless wear of endless visitors. The breath of tourists brings humidity into the closed, dry confines of the tombs. Salt forms on the walls, breaking up the wall-paintings. Restoration is slow and costly. In response to this problem, the Oriental Institute of the University of Chicago has set up a special survey to record reliefs and inscriptions threatened by pollution and decay. The work has now spanned 70 seasons and has preserved a mass of material for scholars to study. Recording is valuable, but the sites themselves are more valuable. Access to many sites will certainly have to be curtailed if they are to survive.

Modern Egypt prides itself on being an Arab nation, but it is also a part of Africa, whose history is becoming increasingly important in modern scholarship. Above all, in the words of Champollion, the French decoder of hieroglyphs: "Egypt is always herself, at all stages in her history, always great and powerful in art and enlightenment. Going back through the centuries, we see her always shining with the same brilliance, and all we lack to satisfy our curiosity is a knowledge of the origin and growth of civilization itself."

ABU SIMBEL Carved to Last for Eternity

Abu Simbel

GREAT TEMPLE
1   Terrace
2   Colossal statues
3   Great pillared hall
4   Second pillared hall
5   Sanctuary
6   Side chambers
7   Concrete dome
8   Rubble infill

SMALL TEMPLE
9   Colossal statues
10 Pillared hall
11 Sanctuary

The two temples carved into the living rock at Abu Simbel were the crowning achievement of Ramesses II's reign. They were placed deep into Nubia, some 250 kilometers (180 miles) south of the First Cataract, and were intended to awe the subjects of the king, ruling far away in the north.

The larger of the two temples honored Ramesses himself, deified in company with Amun-Ra, Ra-Horakhty and Ptah. The facade is guarded by four colossal statues of Ramesses, and inside is a great columned hall leading through to the inner sanctuary and decorated with records of the king's victories and enemies. The second temple is dedicated to Nefertari, the king's favorite queen. Here she is honored alongside Hathor, goddess of sexuality and motherhood. Again, the presence of Ramesses himself is felt, flanking the statues of the queen on the facade.

In the 24th year of his reign the temples were ready for dedication, and Ramesses, Nefertari and their daughter Merytamun sailed from the Delta up to Abu Simbel. The inauguration probably took place in February 1255 BC, but it is possible that the queen herself did not survive to enjoy the occasion: an inscription describing the inauguration does not mention her, and there are no later records of her alive. Seven years later an earthquake brought down one of the statues of Ramesses and cracked the columns and door of the great hall.

Over the centuries the temples became vulnerable to rising sands. When Greek mercenaries passed by in the 6th century BC, the sand already reached the knees of the statues: their names are visible, carved on the statues at this height. In AD 1813 the temples were rediscovered and Belzoni dug his way in four years later.

In the late 1950s, it became clear that the rising waters of Lake Nasser would engulf the temples completely. As the time for the completion of the Aswan Dam drew closer, frenzied attempts were made

Left This aerial view of the Abu Simbel site shows the relocated temple façades with the protective concrete domes. The temples have been rebuilt with the same orientation and relationship as before.

Right The temples were cut out piece by piece, and the statues stored while the interiors were moved. Here a 21-tonne head of Ramesses is put in storage. After rebuilding, the cut marks were systematically hidden.

Above Four statues of Ramesses II, each 21 meters (67 ft) high, flank the eastward-facing reassembled Great Temple. A row of falcons guard the base while, above, a frieze of baboons greet the rising sun.

Below Abu Simbel now forms one of the prime tourist destinations in Egypt, on a par with the pyramids themselves. Visitors marvel at the combination of modern and ancient technology represented by the site.

to find a way of saving the temples. It was considered important to preserve not just the monuments themselves, but their relationship with their immediate environment, so far as possible (a literally impossible task insofar as the environment was to be flooded). Many schemes were put forward, some more fanciful than others, including one idea of permitting them to be submerged but encasing them in a concrete bubble to keep the mud out, while allowing visitors access from above. Finally, it was agreed to cut the stone into blocks and to lift them some 65 meters (200 feet) up the hillside, where a protective concrete dome was erected to receive them. Much of the money for the project was raised by the United Nations Scientific and Cultural Organization (UNESCO).

A temporary dam had to be erected around the temples to protect them from the rising water. The project was completed in 1968, a feat as extraordinary in its way as the original construction. It was all rebuilt exactly as it had been, even the statue shattered by the earthquake of 1248 BC was left broken.

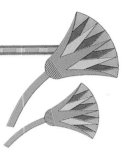

CONCLUSION

IN A RESTLESS AGE like the present, there is a strong need to believe that there are forgotten secrets of human existence that can be revealed to our generation by breaking through the restrictions of conventional thinking and making contact with the mystical knowledge of the past. For the last 1,000 years, while Egypt remained shrouded in mystery, the Sphinx, the pyramids and its other heirlooms provided plenty of opportunity for speculation about their significance. The mere fact that later, technologically superior modern cultures struggled to grasp the meaning of these structures suggested that the ancient Egyptians knew something that the observers did not. Although most of the story is known to us now, ancient Egypt continues to be a magnet for the desire to obtain ultimate wisdom.

Undoubtedly the Egyptians were exceptional people. But although they were wonderful builders, craftsmen, artists and organizers, theirs was essentially a conservative culture. They invented little, and were not even aware of the wheel until it was introduced from abroad around 1550 BC. They certainly observed the skies, had some understanding of the movements of clusters of stars, and used stellar observations to align their buildings with remarkable accuracy. They created their own calendar based on the stars, but when it fell out of line with the "real" year, they were unable to modify it. By contrast, Babylonian and Greek astronomers indulged in much more sophisticated speculation. Nor, despite centuries of careful observation of symptoms, is there any evidence of Egyptian medical breakthroughs. Their theory of how the body worked and their belief in the power that the gods exercised over health hindered successful treatment and independent thinking. Again, in this respect, the Greeks proved far superior to the Egyptians in the range and quality of their speculations.

THE FACE of a 5th-Dynasty scribe (ABOVE) still speaks to us after 4,400 years, while the timeless pastoral scene (RIGHT), near Memphis, would have been utterly familia. to him.

Where, if anywhere, is Egyptian wisdom to be found? It is hard to find in the Old Kingdom, where all the evidence suggests an authoritarian society in which the most important project was to provide a suitable tomb for the king – a megalomaniac venture requiring the hard labor of hundreds of thousands of peasants. It is hard to find in the New Kingdom, when the kingdom could only be sustained by imperialist expansion overseas. Perhaps the best balance between ruler and ruled can by found in the Middle Kingdom. The concept of *ma'at*, social harmony, the emphasis on the correct treatment of even the poor and the respect shown for natural resources are all relevant to the late twentieth century.

However, the belief that ancient Egypt provides a source of alternative wisdom is not likely to disappear. It satisfies too many needs by appealing both to the desire for mystery and to the hope of ultimate knowledge. The myth of mystical Egypt encourages further questions even after answers have been provided; how can the sober facts of history and archeology – wonderful though they are – compete with a tantalizing promise to reveal the very secrets of the gods? Facts are not enough. We remain superstitious and fanciful in spite of our science and technology. We want more. So the myths and the questions persist.

For most people, the mystery is much easier to grasp than the knowledge. A thorough understanding of the Egyptian past has become the preserve of academics, partly because the hieroglyphic texts are so difficult to master and partly because it takes years of an individual's life to assimilate the surviving evidence. The enthusiastic amateur cannot help but feel excluded, and so the tradition of Egypt's secret wisdom lives on. Like its most famous and misinterpreted ruler, Cleopatra, Egypt remains "the one whom dreamers always find at the end of their dreams."

administrative year A year of 365 days used by Egypt's bureaucracy. It fell a day behind the solar calendar every four years.

amulet A small ornament with protective powers, worn by the living and placed in the coffins of the dead.

ankh The *hieroglyph* for "life" and hence a symbol for eternal life.

Art Nouveau A design style of the 1890s (AD) characterized by free-flowing lines. Art Nouveau drew on some aspects of Egyptian art, such as its nature motifs.

Art Deco A design style of the 1920s and 1930s (AD) that was partly inspired by the precision crafting, polychromy and geometric shapes of Egyptian art.

Aten An aspect of the sun-god in the form of the solar disk, whose exclusive worship Akhenaten attempted to impose in the 18th Dynasty.

ba The soul of a dead person; the form he took in the *underworld*.

benben A sacred stone at Heliopolis that represented the original mound of creation (the *primeval mound*).

birth-house A small temple, found in Late Period or Greco-Roman Egypt, dedicated to the birth of a god.

Black Land *Kemet* – the fertile strip of land along the Nile valley; the ancient Egyptians' name for their country.

block statue A statue sculpted from a compact mass of stone in the form of a squatting man.

Book of the Dead The collective name for individual funerary texts with protective spells that were placed in tombs. Books of the Dead were used from about 1550 BC and replaced the earlier *Pyramid Texts* or *Coffin Texts*.

canopic jar One of four jars that stored the viscera removed from *mummies*.

cartonnage A material made by mixing plaster and linen and used to make coffins and masks of a deceased.

cartouche An oval-shaped *hieroglyph* (based on the sign *shen*, protection) enclosing the names of Egyptian kings.

cataract An outcrop of rocks that interrupts the flow of a river.

cella The Latin name for the Greek *naos*, the main room of a small temple where the image of the presiding deity was kept.

cenotaph A memorial tomb that holds no body.

classical world The civilizations of Greece and Rome.

clerestory A stone grill carved into the upper wall (below the roof) in the *hypostyle hall* of a temple to let in light.

cloisonné The art of mounting gems and stones within raised metal cells.

Coffin Texts A group of over 1,000 spells to protect the dead, inscribed on coffins in the Middle Kingdom. They were based on earlier *Pyramid Texts*, which were carved on the walls of pyramids and were thus reserved for royalty; the Coffin Texts could be used for commoners.

colossus A giant statue.

Coptic The Egyptian language written in Greek script; also used to describe the Egyptian Christian church, which conducted its services in that language.

crook A hook-shaped scepter symbolizing government and carried by kings along with the *flail*.

cubit A unit of measurement, about 45 centimeters (18 inches), which conventionally represented the length from a man's elbow to the tip of the thumb.

cult The practices associated with the worship of a particular god or goddess.

cuneiform A wedge-shaped script used to write Sumerian and, later, other languages of the ancient Middle East.

decan One of the 36 groups of stars into which the Egyptians divided the night sky.

demotic script A simplified Egyptian script derived from *hieratic script*, which it had replaced by the 26th Dynasty. It was originally used only for clerical and administrative purposes but was later adopted for religious, scientific and literary texts.

determinative A hieroglyph added at the end of a word to indicate the class of object it refers to.

djed A hieroglyphic sign of a pillar with three horizontal crossbars, a symbol of stability often used on decorative friezes (along with the *ankh* and the *was* scepter).

Egyptianizing design A design that selectively incorporates symbols or motifs from ancient Egyptian art into more contemporary designs.

Egyptology The study of ancient Egypt.

ennead A group of nine gods, led by Atum and divided into three groups of three generations of gods. The ennead was associated with the version of the creation myth that originated at Heliopolis.

faience A type of quartz-based ceramic, usually glazed in bright blue or green, used widely in Egypt to imitate the colors of gems such as turquoise and lapis lazuli.

false door In a tomb, a monumental closed door that symbolized the barrier between the living and the dead.

Field of Reeds The afterworld, normally portrayed on the walls of tombs as abundant and peaceful – the Egyptian version of heaven.

flail An object (possibly based on a fly-whisk) associated with the gods Osiris and Min and carried by kings along with the *crook* as part of their royal regalia.

God's Wife of Amun The office of human consort to the god Amun, a prominent position usually held by the chief queen or a princess. It apparently began in the early New Kingdom as a way to recognize the queen's role in conceiving a royal heir by Amun.

heka The generic Egyptian term for magic, whether it was worked by humans or by gods.

hermeticism The (European) belief that the Egyptians had a sacred wisdom normally hidden from human inquirers.

hieratic script From the Greek "sacred" – the cursive script used for administrative documents from the end of the Early Dynastic Period (c. 2600 BC) until it was replaced by *demotic* early in the Late Period (c. 650 BC).

hieroglyph A sign representing a word or syllable, used in carving formal inscriptions – the basis of Egypt's written language, invented about 3200 BC.

high priest The highest-ranking official in a *cult* temple, who was both the head of the priesthood and the chief administrator of the temple's often rich estates.

Horus name One of the names taken by a *pharaoh* to indicate his relationship to a particular aspect of the god; "Mighty bull, perfect of glorious appearances" was the Horus name of Tuthmosis IV. It was the first name written out with all his titles, and was normally enclosed inside a *serekh*.

hypostyle hall A large hall filled with columns, usually the most elaborate part of Egyptian temples; many temples had two.

ka The creative life-force of an individual which survived after death.

kha The appearance of the sun at dawn; also, the king's coronation ceremony.

king lists Lists of kings placed in temples for ceremonies honoring royal ancestors.

kiosk A small temple or shrine lining a processional route where the statues of gods were temporarily "rested".

kouros A sculpted male nude figure found in temple sites in Greece. It was probably inspired by Egyptian examples.

logogram An individual sign in *hieroglyphs* whose meaning is similar to its appearance.

Lower Egypt Egypt from Memphis northward, especially the Nile Delta. From the time of unification about 3100 BC it was traditionally divided into 20 *nomes*.

mastaba Traditionally, a bench outside an Egyptian house. The word is used to describe the shape of the monuments above early Egyptian tombs.

ma'at The qualities of truth, justice and harmony, often personified in the shape of a goddess with that name.

mortuary temple A temple where the final funerary ceremonies were carried before a high-ranking person was buried.

mummy A preserved Egyptian body which was prepared according to techniques developed early in the Old Kingdom (c. 2600 BC). The name comes from the Arabic "mummiya" (bitumen), which was erroneously believed to have been used as a preservative.

naos The central shrine in a temple where sacred statues were kept.

natron A mineral found in the Nile marshes, used to dry bodies as part of their preservation as *mummies*.

necropolis A "city of the dead", an area dedicated to tombs.

Nilometer A series of marks on a well or steps along the riverbank that measured the height of the Nile, particularly during the annual flood.

nomarch The governor of a *nome*.

nome The Greek word for each of Egypt's 42 provinces.

obelisk A tall needle-like stone monument, often erected in pairs outside temples. A derivative of the *benben* stone, it was connected with the cult of the sun; it had a *pyramid*-shaped tip, gilded to catch the sun's rays.

ogdoad Eight gods and goddess (four male frogs; four female snakes) who were associated with the first act of creation according to the *cult* of Thoth at Hermopolis.

Opening of the Mouth The final funeral ceremony, by which a deceased person was "brought to life" so that his *ka* could re-enter his dead body.

opet festival A major annual festival at Thebes in which images of the gods were paraded in public from Karnak to Luxor.

ostracon A broken piece of pottery on which informal text such as personal correspondence was written.

palette A flat stone, originally used to mix cosmetic powders, that acquired sacred significance as a votive object in predynastic Egypt.

papyrus A reed, native to Egypt, used for buildings, boats, ropes, etc. Writing material was made from the beaten pith.

pectoral A piece of jewelry, often *kiosk*-shaped, suspended upon the chest.

peristyle court An open court surrounded by columns under a roof.

pharaoh Literally, "great house"; used to refer to Egyptian kings after 1400 BC.

phonogram A *hieroglyphic* sign that represents a specific sound, normally of one or more consonants.

prenomen The name adopted by a king on his accession, also called the "throne name". It normally incorporated a reference to the sun-god Ra.

priest "A servant of God", an official responsible for the rituals surrounding the worship of a temple god.

primeval mound The mound that emerged from the primeval waters and symbolized the original act of creation.

pronaos The portico of a temple, in front of the *naos* or main shrine.

pylon A massive ceremonial gateway at the entrance to a temple.

pyramid A massive stone structure with four equal triangular sides meeting in a point, used as a tomb and monument by the kings of the Old Kingdom.

Pyramid Texts Early funerary texts found inscribed on the walls of late Old Kingdom *pyramids*.

pyramidion A pyramid-shaped top to a *pyramid* or *obelisk,* often gilded so that it caught the first rays of the rising sun.

Red Crown A tall chair-shaped crown with a coil; the crown of Lower Egypt.

Red Land *Deshret* – the color of the desert beyond the Nile Valley.

Rosetta Stone A *stela* inscribed with a decree of Ptolemy V in 196 BC, written in *hieroglyphs, demotic* and Greek, which was discovered in 1799. It allowed hieroglyphs to be deciphered.

sacred bark A ceremonial boat in which the god Ra passed through the *underworld*. The images of gods were also carried in procession on barks.

sarcophagus A stone container in which a coffin is placed.

scarab A sacred beetle, one of the most popular Egyptian *amulets*.

scribe Any literate official. Scribes made up the large Egyptian bureaucracy.

sed festival A jubilee held to celebrate 30 years of a king's rule.

Serapeum An underground complex of galleries at Saqqara where mummified sacred bulls were buried.

serekh A hieroglyphic symbol showing a paneled palace facade in which the king's *Horus name* was written.

shabti A miniature surrogate figure left in tombs to carry out manual labor for the deceased in the afterlife.

shaduf A water-lifting device consisting of a counterbalanced bucket on a pole.

sistrum A rattle used in religious ceremonies, especially in the *cult* of Isis.

solar year A year of 365 days 6 hours, measured from the annual first rising of the dog-star Sirius (July 19).

sphinx A mythical beast, normally portrayed as having a lion's body and a human face – typically that of a king. It represented protection, usually of royalty, and was widely adopted by ancient Middle Eastern neighbors of Egypt.

stela A slab of stone with an inscription recording a prayer, the deeds of a dead man or the victories of a king.

step pyramid The earliest form of *pyramid*, built as a series of stepped rectangles, one on top of each other.

syncretism The merging of one god with another to form a composite divine force, as with Amun-Ra, a synthesis of Amun and Ra.

triad A family of three gods – usually a father, mother and child, worshiped at a single shrine. The most famous Egyptian triad was that of Osiris, Isis and Horus.

Tutmania The wave of enthusiasm for Egypt after the discovery of Tutankhamun's tomb in 1922.

udjat eye The eye of Horus, a symbol of protection and strength.

underworld A shadowy and threatening region through which the sun-god Ra passed each night on his *sacred bark*.

Upper Egypt The 22 *nomes* of the Nile valley, south of Memphis.

uraeus An effigy of a rearing cobra, worn on the king's forehead to symbolize protection of the monarch and the destruction of his enemies.

Valley of the Kings The burial site of the New Kingdom rulers, below a cliff on the west bank of the Nile at Thebes, where it was hoped that their tombs would be safe from robbers. They were not, but it was there that Tutankhamun's tomb was discovered intact in 1922.

vizier The chief minister of the pharaoh, responsible for the administrative efficiency and stability of the state.

was scepter A straight shaft with a canine head and two prongs at the base, often shown being grasped by a god. The scepter was also buried with mummies until the Middle Kingdom, and was painted with figures on tomb walls to signify well-being in the afterlife.

White Crown A tall cone-shaped headdress with a knob on top, the crown of Upper Egypt.

winged disk The sun shown as a disk with the outstretched wings of a hawk. Originally a symbol for Horus, it came to stand for the king, and was often shown with the *uraeus* as a protective symbol.

wisdom literature Ancient Egyptian texts, traditionally said to date back to the 4th Dynasty, that gave advice on the correct way of living and/or meditations on the true meaning of life.

SOME GODS OF EGYPT

Ammut eater of the dead

Amun "the hidden one"; king of the gods; creator-god of Thebes

Amun-Ra creator-god and sun-god

Anubis jackal-god, protector of the dead

Aten the solar disk

Atum "the all"; creator-god and sun-god

Bastet cat-goddess; goddess of joy

Bes dwarf-god; god of the household

Geb earth-god; father of Osiris, Isis, Seth and Nephthys

Hathor cow-goddess; goddess of love, music and dancing

Horus falcon-god; sky-god; son of Osiris and Isis; royal protector

Isis goddess of healing; wife of Osiris and mother of Horus

Khnum ram-god; god of inundation and fertility; potter-god

Ma'at goddess of truth, justice and harmony

Min fertility-god

Montu war-god

Mut vulture-goddess; daughter of Ra

Nekhbet vulture-goddess of Upper Egypt

Nephthys wife of Seth, sister of Isis

Nut sky-goddess; daughter of Shu, wife of Geb; mother of Osiris, Isis, Seth and Nephthys

Osiris lord of the underworld; god of death, resurrection and fertility

Ptah creator-god; craftsman-god; god of words and learning

Ra sun-god; associated with the hawk and the ram

Ra-Horakhty "Horus of the Horizon"; an aspect of Ra combined with Horus

Renenutet cobra-goddess; protector of the king (in the form of the *uraeus*)

Sekhmet lioness-goddess; daughter of Ra

Serapis a fusion of Osiris and Apis (the bull) with several major Greek gods.

Seth god of chaos and confusion

Shu air-god, one of the first two creator-gods made by Atum

Sobek crocodile-god

Taweret hippopotamus-goddess; goddess of the household and of childbirth

Tefnut moisture-goddess, one of the first two creator-gods made by Atum

Thoth ibis-god; baboon-god; god of wisdom and writing; messenger-god

Wadjyt cobra-goddess; goddess of Lower Egypt; royal protector

From a combination of astronomical calculations and ancient documents, historians have pieced together the following chronology of Egypt's kings. In the Early Dynastic Period there is a margin of error of up to 150 years; in the New Kingdom, it is about a decade. For the 18th and 19th Dynasties, the dates used are a combination of the middle and latest possible figures. Most dates for the 12th Dynasty and all those after 664 BC are exact.

LATE PREDYNASTIC PERIOD c.3000
CAPITAL: ABYDOS
Zekhen
Narmer

EARLY DYNASTIC PERIOD 2920–2575

1st Dynasty   **2920–2770**
CAPITAL: MEMPHIS
Menes
Djer
Djet
Wadj
Den
Adjib
Semerkhet
Qa'a

2nd Dynasty   **2770–2649**
CAPITAL: MEMPHIS
Hotepsekhemwy
Reneb
Ninetjer
Peribsen
Khasekhemwy

3rd Dynasty   **2649–2575**
CAPITAL: MEMPHIS
Zanakht   2649–2630
Djoser   2630–2611
Sekhemkhet   2611–2603
Khaba   2603–2599
Huni   2599–2575

OLD KINGDOM 2575–2134

4th Dynasty   **2575–2465**
CAPITAL: MEMPHIS
Snefru   2575–2551
Khufu (Cheops)   2551–2528
Radjedef   2528–2520
Khephren   2520–2494
Menkaure (Mycerinus)   2490–2472
Shepseskaf   2472–2467

5th Dynasty   **2465–2323**
CAPITAL: MEMPHIS
Userkaf   2465–2458
Sahure   2458–2446
Kakai   2446–2426
Ini   2426–2419
Raneferef   2419–2416
Izi   2416–2392
Menkauhor   2396–2388
Izezi   2388–2356
Unas   2356–2323

6th Dynasty   **2323–2150**
CAPITAL: MEMPHIS
Teti 2323–2291
Pepi I 2289–2255
Nemtyemzaf 2255–2246
Pepi II 2246–2152

7th/8th Dynasty   **2150–2134**
CAPITAL: MEMPHIS
Numerous kings, including
Neferkare

1ST INTERMEDIATE PERIOD 2134–2040

9th/10th Dynasty   **2134–2040**
CAPITAL: HERAKLEOPOLIS
Several kings called
Khety
Merykare
Ity

11th Dynasty   **2134–2040**
CAPITAL: THEBES
Inyotef I (Sehertawy) 2134–2118
Inyotef II (Wahankh) 2118–2069
Inyotef III 2069–2061
(Nakhtnebtepnufer)
Mentuhotpe II 2061–2010

MIDDLE KINGDOM 2040–1640

11th Dynasty   **2040–1991**
CAPITAL: THEBES
Mentuhotpe II   2061–2010
(ruler of all Egypt from 2040)
Mentuhotpe III   2010–1998
Mentuhotpe IV   1998–1991

12th Dynasty   **1991–1783**
CAPITAL: THEBES
Amenemhet I   1991–1962
Senwosret I   1971–1926
Amenemhet II   1929–1982
Senwosret II   1987–1878
Senwosret III   1878–1841?
Amenemhet III   1844–1797
Amenemhet IV   1799–1787
Nefrusobk   1787–1783

13th Dynasty   **1783–after 1640**
CAPITAL: THEBES
About 70 kings, including
Wegaf 1   1783–1779
Amenemhet V
Harnedjheriotef
Amenyqemau
Sebekhotpe 1   c.1750
Hor
Amenemhet VII
Sebekhotpe II
Khendjer
Sebekhotpe III   c.1745
Neferhotep I   c.1741–1730
Sebekhotpe IV   c.1730–1720
Sebekhotpe V   c.1720–1715
Aya   c.1704–1690
Mentuemzaf
Dedumose II
Neferhotep III

14th Dynasty
CAPITAL: XOIS
A group of minor kings probably all contemporary with the 13th or 15th Dynasty

2ND INTERMEDIATE PERIOD 1640–1532

15th Dynasty (Hyksos)
CAPITAL: AVARIS
Salitis
Sheshi
Khian
Apophis   c.1585–1542
Khamudi   c.1542–1532

16th Dynasty
Minor Hyksos rulers, contemporary with the 15th Dynasty

17th Dynasty   **1640–1550**
CAPITAL: THEBES
Numerous kings, including
Inyotef V   c.1640–1635
Sebekemzaf I
Nebireyeraw
Sebekemzaf II
Ta'o (or Djehuti'o) I
Ta'o (or Djehuti'o) II
Kamose   c.1555–1550

NEW KINGDOM 1532–1070

18th Dynasty   **1550–1307**
CAPITAL: THEBES
Ahmose   1550–1525
(ruler of all Egypt from 1532)
Amenophis I   1525–1504
Tuthmosis I   1504–1492
Tuthmosis II   1492–1479
Tuthmosis III   1479–1425
Hatshepsut   1473–1458
Amenophis II   1427–1401
Tuthmosis IV   1401–1391
Amenophis III   1391–1353
Amenophis IV   1353–1335
(Akhenaten)
CAPITAL: EL-AMARNA
Smenkhkare   1335–1333
Tutankhamun   1333–1323
CAPITAL: MEMPHIS
Aya   1323–1319
Haremhab   1319–1307

19th Dynasty   **1307–1196**
CAPITAL: MEMPHIS
Ramesses I   1307–1306
Sethos I   1306–1290
Ramesses II   1290–1224
CAPITAL: PI-RAMESSES
Merneptah   1224–1214
Sethos II   1214–1204
Siptah   1204–1198
Twosre   1198–1196

20th Dynasty   **1196–1070**
CAPITAL: PI-RAMESSES
Sethnakhte   1196–1194
Ramesses III   1194–1163
Ramesses IV   1163–1156
Ramesses V   1156–1151
Ramesses VI   1151–1143
Ramesses VII   1143–1136
Ramesses VIII   1136–1131
Ramesses IX   1131–1112
Ramesses X   1112–1100
Ramesses XI   1100–1070

3RD INTERMEDIATE PERIOD 1070–712

21st Dynasty   **1070–945**
CAPITAL: TANIS
Smendes   1070–1044
Amenemnisu   1044–1040
Psusennes I   1040–992
Amenemope   993–984
Osorkon I   984–978
Siamun   978–959
Psusennes II   959–945

22nd Dynasty   **945–712**
CAPITALS: BUBASTIS & TANIS
Shoshenq I   945–924
Osorkon II   924–909
Takelot I   909–?
Shoshenq II   ?–883
Osorkon III   883–855
Takelot   860–835
Shoshenq III   835–783
Pami   783–773
Shoshenq V   773–735
Osorkon V   735–712

23rd Dynasty
Various contemporary lines of kings recognized in Thebes, Hermopolis, Herakleopolis and other cities; precise order is disputed
Pedubaste I   828–803
Osorkon IV   777–749
Peftjau'awybast   740–725

24th Dynasty   **724–712**
CAPITAL: SAIS
Tefnakhte   724–717
Bocchoris   717–712

25th Dynasty   **770–712**
CAPITAL: THEBES
Kashta   770–750
Piye   750–712

LATE PERIOD 712–332

25th Dynasty   **712–657**
CAPITAL: THEBES
Shabaqo   712–698
Shebitku   698–690
Taharqa   690–664
Tantamani   664–657

26th Dynasty   **664–525**
CAPITAL: SAIS
(Necho I   672–664)
Psamtek I   664–610
Necho II   610–595
Psamtek II   595–589
Apries   589–570
Amasis   570–526
Psamtek III   526–525

27th Dynasty   **525–404**
(Persian)
Cambyses   525–522
Darius I   521–486
Xerxes I   486–466
Artaxerxes   465–424
Darius II   424–404

28th Dynasty   **404–399**
CAPITAL: SAIS
Amyrtaios   404–399

29th Dynasty   **399–380**
CAPITAL: MENDES
Nepherites I   399–393
Psammuthis   393
Hakoris   393–380
Nephrites II   380

30th Dynasty   **380–343**
CAPITAL: SEBENNYTOS
Nectanebo I   380–362
Teos   365–360
Nectanebo II   360–343

2nd Persian Period   **343–332**
Artaxerxes III Ochus   343–338
Arses   338–336
Darius III Codoman   335–332

GRECO-ROMAN PERIOD 332 BC–AD 395

Macedonian Dynasty   **332–304**
CAPITAL: ALEXANDRIA
Alexander III the Great   332–323
Philip Arrhidaeus   323–316
Alexander IV   316–304

Ptolemaic Dynasty   **304–30**
CAPITAL: ALEXANDRIA
The order and number of the kings is disputed
Ptolemy I Soter I   304–284
Ptolemy II Philadelphus   285–246
Ptolemy III Euergetes I   246–221
Ptolemy IV Philopator   221–205
Ptolemy V Epiphanes   205–180
Ptolemy VI Philometor   180–145
Ptolemy VII Neos Philopator   145
Ptolemy VIII Euergetes II (Physkon)   170–163, 145–116
Cleopatra III & Ptolemy IX Soter II (Lathyros)   116–107
Cleopatra III & Ptolemy X Alexander I   107–88
Ptolemy IX Soter II   88–81
Cleopatra Berenice   81–80
Ptolemy XI Alexander II   80
Ptolemy XII Neos Dionysos (Auletes)   80–85, 55–51
Berenice IV   58–55
Cleopatra VII   51–30
Ptolemy XIII   51–47
Ptolemy XIV   47–44
Ptolemy XV Caesarion   44–30

Roman Emperors 30BC–AD395
From 30 BC, the Roman emperors ruled Egypt as a province under their personal control. In AD 395, Egypt passed to the control of the emperors in Constantinople.

ACKNOWLEDGMENTS

1 Background BPK/Jürgen Liepe/ SMzB-PK, Ägypt. Mus. **1l** ET Archive **1r** Hulton Getty **2–3 Background** BPK/Jürgen Liepe/SMzB-PK, Ägypt. Mus. **2–3t** BAL/Bradford Art Galleries & Museum **2b** Martin Breese/ Retrograph Archive **3r** AKG/Erich Lessing **4 Background** BPK/Jürgen Liepe/SMzB-PK, Ägypt. Mus. **4t** Stephane Couturier/Arcaid **4b** Per Eide/IB **6** ET Archive **7** The Illustrated London News Picture Library **8–9** John G. Ross/Robert Harding Picture Library **9c** H. Gruyaert/Magnum Photos **10t** WFA/Dr. E. Strouhal **10b** WFA/Schimmel Collection, New York **11l** & **11r** K. Nomachi/RF **12b** MIC **12–13** K. Nomachi/RF **14t** Dr. Stephen Coyne/Bruce Coleman Collection **14b** Guido Alberto Rossi/ IB **15** Graham Harrison **16** Hjalte Tin/Still Pictures **17t** Copyright BM **17b** WFA/Egyptian Museum, Cairo **18t, 18cl** & **18b** PA Jürgen Liepe **19** WFA/ Egyptian Museum, Turin **20–21** WFA/BM **21tl** AKG/Erich Lessing **21tr** & **21tt** K. Nomachi/RF **21tb** John G. Ross **22** PA Jürgen Liepe **23t** Musées Royaux d'Art et d'Histoire/Photo:Heini Schneebeli **23b** WFA/ Ashmolean Museum, Oxford **24t** PA Jürgen Liepe **24b** WFA/Ashmolean Museum, Oxford **25** The Visitors of the Ashmolean Museum, Oxford. 1892.1171 and the Trustees of the British Museum, London. EA 20791/Photo:Heini Schneebeli **26** & **28t** WFA/Egyptian Museum, Cairo **28b** Copyright BM **29t** PA Jürgen Liepe **29b** WFA/ Egyptian Museum, Cairo **30t** WFA/ Musées Royaux du Cinquantenaire, Brussels **30b** PA Jürgen Liepe **31** P. & G. Bowater/IB **32tr** John G. Ross **32cl** & **32b** Axiom/James Morris **33tr** WFA **33b** Guido Alberto Rossi/IB **34t** PA Jürgen Liepe **35br** WFA/St. Louis Art Museum **36t** & **36b** PA Jürgen Liepe **38–39** Copyright BM **38b** C M Dixon **39tr** & **39cr** BAL/ Louvre, Paris **40** PA Jürgen Liepe **41t** Peter Clayton **41b** PA Jürgen Liepe **42t** Copyright BM **42b** AKG/Erich Lessing **43** BAL/Fitzwilliam Museum, University of Cambridge **44l, 44r** & **45t** PA Jürgen Liepe **45cr** Museum of Egyptian Antiquities, Cairo/Photo: Barry Iverson **45bl** & **45br** Copyright BM **46–47** PA Jürgen Liepe **47** ET Archive/Egyptian Museum, Cairo **48** & **49tl** Axiom/James Morris **49tr** PA Jürgen Liepe **49b** Copyright BM **50t** BPK/M. Büsing/SMzB-PK, Ägypt. Mus. **50b** Axiom/James Morris **50–51** Peter Clayton **52t** AKG/Erich Lessing **52b** BPK/M. Büsing/SMzB-PK, Ägypt. Mus. **53** AKG/Erich Lessing **54t** Guido Alberto Rossi/IB **54b** PA Jürgen Liepe **55** Sylvain Grandadam/ Colorific **56–57** MIC **57** PA Jürgen Liepe **58t** WFA/Schimmel Collection, New York **59b** Ashmolean Museum, Oxford **59c** BPK/Jürgen Liepe/SMzB-PK, Ägypt. Mus. **60t** AKG/Erich Lessing **61bl** Musée du Louvre, Paris/ Rollin-Feuardent Collection/Photo: Heini Schneebeli **62t** K. Nomachi/RF **62b** BPK/Jürgen Liepe/SMzB-PK, Ägypt. Mus. **63cl** SMzB-PK, Ägypt. Mus. 24300. Permanent loan from Humboldt. Universität zu Berlin/ Photo:Jürgen Liepe **63cr** PA Jürgen Liepe **64** AKG/Erich Lessing **65t** BAL/Oriental Museum, Durham University **65b** Sonia Halliday Photographs **66** AKG/Erich Lessing **67t** BPK/Jürgen Liepe/SMzB-PK, Ägypt. Mus. **67b** C. M. Dixon **68–69** K. Nomachi/RF **69c** MIC **70t** PA Jürgen Liepe **70b** & **71** AKG/Erich Lessing **72** Copyright BM **72–73** PA Jürgen Liepe **73** WFA **74bl** PA Jürgen Liepe **74b** WFA/Egyptian Museum, Cairo **75** BAL/Francesco Turio Bohm **76t** AKG/Erich Lessing **76b** PA Jürgen Liepe **76–77** WFA **78** & **78–79** PA Jürgen Liepe **79** AKG/ Erich Lessing **80–81** PA Jürgen Liepe **80t** WFA/Egyptian Museum, Cairo **80cl** PA Jürgen Liepe **80cr** WFA/ Schimmel Collection, New York **80b** AKG/Erich Lessing **81t** WFA/Dr. E. Strouhal **81b** Copyright BM **82–83** Axiom/James Morris **82t** WFA/BM **82bl** PA Jürgen Liepe **82–83** Copyright BM **83t** F L Kenett/Robert Harding Picture Library **83cr** AKG/Erich Lessing **84t** MIC **84b** AKG/Jürgen Sorges **85b** BAL/ Giraudon **86t** ET Archive/Devizes Museum **87t** Copyright BM **88t** PA Jürgen Liepe **88b** Copyright BM **89t** BPK/Jürgen Liepe/SMzB-PK, Ägypt. Mus. **89br** PA Jürgen Liepe **90t** & **90cl** Copyright BM **91** & **92l** PA Jürgen Liepe **92–93** AKG **93b** PA Jürgen Liepe **94tl** Copyright BM **94tr** WFA **95t** Axiom/James Morris **95br** WFA **96tl** & **96r** Copyright BM **96–97** PA Jürgen Liepe **97tl** MIC **97c** AKG/Erich Lessing **97cr** Copyright BM **97bl, 98t** & **98b** MIC **99** SMzB-PK, Ägypt. Mus. 23731/Photo:Jürgen Liepe **100** Copyright BM **101** BAL/ Stapleton Collection **102t** AKG/Erich Lessing **102b** PA Jürgen Liepe **103t** Musée du Louvre, Paris/Photo:Heini Schneebeli **103b** PA Jürgen Liepe **104b** ET Archive/Egyptian Museum, Cairo **105** PA Jürgen Liepe **106bl** Copyright BM **107** Axiom/James Morris **108t** John Launois/Colorific **109tl** WFA/Egyptian Museum, Cairo **109tr** John G. Ross **110t** John Mead/ Science Photo Library **110b** PA Jürgen Liepe **111** WFA/Louvre Museum, Paris **112tl** Axiom/James Morris **112b** AKG/Erich Lessing **113** MIC **114t** BPK/Jürgen Liepe/SMzB-PK, Ägypt. Mus. **114b** K. Nomachi/ RF **115** ET Archive/BM **116t** WFA/ Ny Carlsberg Glyptotek, Copenhagen **116b** WFA/BM **117t** Copyright BM **117b** Photo RMN **118t** WFA/ Egyptian Museum, Cairo **118–119** BPK/Jürgen Liepe/SMzB-PK, Ägypt. Mus. **119t** SMzB-PK, Ägypt. Mus./ Photo:Jürgen Liepe **120–121** BPK/ Jürgen Liepe/SMzB-PK, Ägypt. Mus. **120t** Photo RMN-Chuzeville **122–123** Walter Rawlings/Robert Harding Picture Library **123c** BAL/ Stapleton Collection **124** AKG/Erich Lessing **125t** Peter Clayton **125b** PA Jürgen Liepe **126l** AKG/Erich Lessing **126b** Photo RMN **126–127** B. Regent/Hutchison Library **128t** PA Jürgen Liepe **128–129** AKG/Erich Lessing **129t** Sonia Halliday & Laura Lushington **130** Konrad Helbig/Zefa Pictures **131** BPK/Jürgen Liepe/ SMzB-PK, Ägypt. Mus. **132** Photo RMN **133l** Peter Clayton **133b** C M Dixon **134t** WFA/Courtesy Christie's London **134b** Graham Harrison **135** Gerard Champlong/IB **136l** BAL/BM **136r** Scala **137** ET Archive **138** BAL/Private Collection **139** BAL/ Louvre, Paris **140t** AKG/Erich Lessing **140b** BAL/ BM **141** K. Nomachi/RF **142** BAL/ Christie's London **143** Axiom/James Morris **143l** WFA **143r** Ch. Larrieu/Photo RMN **144t** Hutchison Library **144b** AKG/Erich Lessing **145t** Axiom/ James Morris **145b** AKG/Erich Lessing **146, 147t, 147b** & **148t** Scala **148b** BAL/Freudmuseum, London **149** Pl. 138 from *L'Antiquité Expliquée et Représentee en Figures,* 1722–24, Vol. II, by Bernard de Montfaucon/Fotomas Index **150** Staatliche Sammlung Ägyptischer Kunst, Munich **150–151** C M Dixon **152t** & **152c** AKG/Erich Lessing **152–153** John G. Ross **153t** Scala **153r** AKG/Erich Lessing **153b** Axiom/James Morris **154t** Mansell Collection **154b** ET Archive/Egyptian Museum, Cairo **155** AKG **156** C M Dixon **156–157** PA Jürgen Liepe **157t** Scala **158–159** BAL/Russell-Cotes Art Gallery & Museum, Bournemouth **159t** Photo RMN **159b** Musée du Louvre, Dépt. Grecques et Romaines Antiquités **160t** C M Dixon **161t** Robert Harding Picture Library **161r** BAL/by courtesy of the Board of Trustees of the Victoria & Albert Museum **162t** BAL/British Library **162–163** BAL/O'Shea Gallery **163t** Scala **164–165** BAL/Giraudon **165c** By courtesy of the Board of Trustees of the Victoria & Albert Museum **166** & **167t** Peter Clayton **167b** BAL/ Lauros-Giraudon **168t** Griffith Institute/Ashmolean Museum, Oxford **168b** from *Description de l'Egypte* Pl. 7. HN Vol. I–Zoologie. Oiseaux, by Jules-César Savigny/Fotomas Index **169t** BAL/Lauros-Giraudon **169c** Page 109 from Champollion's *Grammaire/* Bibliothèque Nationale, Paris **170–171** ET Archive **170c** MEPL **171b** MEPL/Institute of Civil Engineers **172t** BAL/British Library **172b** Mansell Collection **173** BAL/ Kunsthistorisches Museum **174** ET Archive/Louvre, Paris **175t** MEPL **175b** Mansell Collection **176** Griffith Institute/Ashmolean, Oxford **177t** & **177b** Alexander Tsiaras/Science Photo Library **178–179** Hulton Getty **178tl** BPK/M. Busing/Egyptian Museum, Cairo **178tr** Griffith Institute/ Ashmolean Museum, Oxford **178b** PA Jürgen Liepe **179t** & **179r** Griffith Institute/Ashmolean Museum, Oxford **179b** Derek Berwin/IB **180t** Scala **180b** SR Kaplan, US Games Systems Inc./Images Colour Libray **181** MEPL **182t** BAL/German Theatre Museum **182–183** BAL/Christie's London **183t** ET Archive **184l** ET Archive/Mander & Mitcheson Theatre Collection **184b** Département de la Musique: Bibliothèque-Musée de l'Opéra/Bibliothèque Nationale, Paris **185–185** BAL/Guildhall Art Gallery, Corporation of London **185b** Martin Breese/Retrograph Archive **186t** JG Berizzi/Photo RMN **186bl** AKG **186br** Ronald Grant Archive **187** Oeffentliche Kunstsammlung Basel, Kunstmuseum/Gift Dr. h.c. Robert von Hirsch 1941/Photo:Martin Bühler **188c** Hammer (Courtesy Kobal) **188t** Martin Breese/ Retrograph Archive **189t** Ronald Grant Archive **189b** Martin Anderson **190tl** & **190tr** Ronald Grant Archive **190b** Lucasfilm Ltd/Paramount (Courtesy Kobal) **191tl** Ronald Grant Archive **191tr** Angelo Hornak Library **191bl** & **191br** Ronald Grant Archive **192t** Joe Low/Arcaid **192b** Scala **193** Giovanni Battista Piranesi, *Diverse Maniere d'Adornare i Cammini* (Rome:Salomoni, 1769) **194** & **195t** Photo RMN **195bl** BAL/Partridge Fine Arts, London **195br** Richard Bryant/Arcaid **196t** Mark Fiennes/ Arcaid **196b** E. Philippe/Christie's Images **197t** BAL **197b** Mansell Collection **198–199** Photo RMN **198b** A. Stewart Court/Galerie Moderne **199t** Martin Breese/ Retrograph Archive **199b** Bibliothèque Nationale, Dépt. de la Musique:Bibliothèque-Musée de l'Opéra **200t** Musée de l'Impression sur Étoffe, Mulhouse **200r** Angelo Hornak Library **200b** Martin Breese/ Retrograph Archive **201** Richard Bryant/Arcaid **202t** Marc Romanelli/ IB **202b** Badisches Landesmuseum, Karlsruhe **203t** Malcolm Dixon/ Arcaid **203r** Peter Lindberg **204** MIC **205** Graham Harrison **206** Susanna Burton/Horizon/Images Colour Library **207** Graham Harrison **208** AKG **209t** Bruno Barbey/Magnum Photos **209b** Erich Lessing/Magnum Photos **210t** Magnum Photos **210b** PH Plailly/Eurelios/Science Photo Library **211** K. Nomachi/RF **212bl** Guido Alberto Rossi/IB **212br** Terence Spencer/Colorific **213t** Brian J. Coates/Bruce Coleman Collection **213b** David W. Hamilton/IB **214** ET Archive **215** Penny Tweedie/Colorific.

ABBREVIATIONS

t = top, **b** = bottom, **c** = centre, **l** = left, **r** = right

AKG Archiv für Kunst und Geschichte, London
BAL Bridgeman Art Library
BM British Museum, London
BPK Bildarchiv Preussischer Kulturbesitz
IB Image Bank
MEPL Mary Evans Picture Library
MIC Macquitty International Collection
PA Photo Archive
RF Rex Features
SMzB-PK, Ägypt. Mus. Staatliche Museen zu Berlin, Preussischer Kulturbesitz, Ägyptisches Museum und Papyrussammlung
WFA Werner Forman Archive

Every effort has been made to trace copyright holders of the pictures used in this book. Anyone having claims to ownership not identified above is invited to contact Andromeda Oxford Limited.

FURTHER READING

C. Aldred, *Akhenaten, King of Egypt* (London, 1988; New York, 1991)

C. Andrews, *Ancient Egyptian Jewelry*, (London ,1990; New York, 1991)

J. Baines and J. Malek, *Atlas of Ancient Egypt* (London 1984; New York 1984)

The British Museum Dictionary of Ancient Egypt (London, 1995)

W.V. Davies, *Egyptian Hieroglyphs* (London, 1987; Berkeley, CA, 1988)

E. Doxiadis, *The Mysterious Fayum Portraits: Faces from Ancient Egypt* (London, 1995)

I. Edwards, *The Pyramids of Egypt*, (revised edition, London, 1991; New York, 1986)

Egyptomania: Egypt in Western Art, 1730–1930 (Ottawa and Paris, 1994)

B.M. Fagan, *The Rape of the Nile: Tomb Robbers, Tourists and Archaeologists in Egypt* (London, 1977; Wakefield, RI, 1992)

C. Frayling, *The Face of Tutankhamun* (London and Winchester, MA, 1992)

N. Grimal (tr. Ian Shaw), *A History of Ancient Egypt* (Oxford and Cambridge, MA, 1992)

L. Habachi, *The Obelisks of Egypt* (London , 1978; New York, 1985)

L. Hughes Hallett, *Cleopatra: History, Dreams and Distortions* (London, 1990)

E. Iversen, *The Myth of Egypt and its Hieroglyphs in European Tradition* , (Princeton, NJ, 1993)

T.G.H. James, *Howard Carter: The Path to Tutankhamum* (London , 1992; New York, 1992)

A. Kuhrt, *The Ancient Near East, c. 3000–330 BC* (London and New York, 1995)

M.Lichtheim, *Ancient Egyptian Literature: A Book of Readings* (Berkeley, CA, 1973-8)

J. Nunn, *Ancient Egyptian Medicine* (London, 1995)

S. Quirke and J. Spencer (eds.), *The British Museum Book of Ancient Egypt* (London, 1992)

S. Quirke, *Ancient Egyptian Religion* (London, 1992; New York, 1993)

N. Reeves, *The Complete Tutankh-amun* (London, 1990; New York, 1995)

A.J. Spencer, *Death in Ancient Egypt*, (Harmondsworth, 1982)

W. Stevenson Smith, *The Art and Architecture of Ancient Egypt* (New Haven and London, second revised edition, 1981)

E. Strouhal, *Life in Ancient Egypt* (Cambridge, 1992; Norman, OK, 1992)

J. Tyldesley, *Daughters of Isis: Women of Ancient Egypt* (London, 1994; New York, 1995)

J. Tyldesley, *Hatshepsut* (London, 1996)

R.H. Wilkinson, *Reading Egyptian Art* (London, 1992; New York, 1994)

R.E. Witt, *Isis in the Greco-Roman World* (London and Ithaca, NY, 1971)

INDEX